Univers

Mixtec Transnational Identity

Mixtec Transnational Identity

Laura Velasco Ortiz

The University of Arizona Press   Tucson

The University of Arizona Press
© 2005 The Arizona Board of Regents
An earlier version of this book was published as *El regreso de la comunidad: Migración indígena y agentes étnicos; Los mixtecos en la frontera México–Estados Unidos* (México. El Colegio de México; El Colegio de la Frontera Norte, 2002).
⊗ This book is printed on acid-free, archival-quality paper.
Manufactured in the United States of America
10   09   08   07   06   05   6   5   4   3   2   1

Library of Congress Cataloging-in-Publication Data

Velasco Ortiz, M. Laura.
Mixtec transnational identity / Laura Velasco Ortiz.
p. cm.
Includes bibliographical references and index.
ISBN-13: 978-0-8165-2327-6 (hardcover : alk. paper)
ISBN-10: 0-8165-2327-4 (hardcover : alk. paper)
1. Mixtec Indians—Ethnic identity. 2. Mixtec Indians—
Migrations. 3. Mixtec Indians—Social conditions. 4. Migration,
Internal—Mexico—Oaxaca (State). 5. Oaxaca (Mexico : State)—
Emigration and immigration. 6. United States—Emigration
and immigration. I. Title.
F1221.M7V43 2005
305.897'6307274—dc22   2005017469

Publication of this book is made possible in part by the proceeds of a permanent endowment created with the assistance of a Challenge Grant from the National Endowment for the Humanities, a federal agency.

Contents

Figures

Tables

Preface

After several years of research into ethnic identity among Mixtec communities in Tijuana, I discovered, in the early 1990s, that an active questioning was taking place among these communities about their situation as indigenous people beyond the confines of their original lands. This led me to focus my attention on their practices and discourse concerning their past, present, and future as an ethnic group in the Mexico–U.S. border region and their relations with the villages and towns of the Mixteca region of Oaxaca.

In the following pages the reader will find a reconstruction of the Mixtec experience of migration, following three lines of analysis: the formation of organizations beyond the confines of the migrants' hometowns; the emergence of indigenous migrant leaders; and the shaping of an ethnic consciousness assimilating the experiences of a dispersed community straddling the border. The appearance of indigenous organizations formed by Mixtecos in alliance with Zapotecos and Triquis signals the revitalization of ancestral community life in their new situation as farmworkers, urban employees, residents, or undocumented migrants on the U.S. side of the border. The research brought to light the way in which the geographic dispersion of members of different communities was offset by the formation of networks of migrants with family and community ties, and how the politicization of these networks facilitated the formation of both hometown associations and transnational pan-ethnic organizations in the late twentieth century.

Collective and individual agents play an important role in re-creating ethnicity as a sense of belonging to a big family located in the hometown. This belonging helps migrants face the vulnerability they experience outside their communities of origin. Under migration, those agents meet new ethnic interlocutors, negotiate the relationship of migrant communities with the Mexican state, and promote the insertion of Mexican indigenous communities into the social, political, and cultural fabric of the United States. Ethnic agents emerge from within an ethnic political space that transcends national frameworks, reviewing and redefining Mexican indigenous identity from a position of geographic mobility and residence in a foreign country.

The Mixtecos are not the only indigenous people to have become geographically dispersed as a result of domestic and international migration in the twentieth century; Zapotecos, Triquis, Otomíes, Purépechas, and Nahuas as well have migrated beyond the borders of Mexico. Thus the present work is a contribution to the incipient field of Mexican indigenous migration to the northern border and the United States and, more specifically, an attempt to identify the effects of future migrations on ethnic identity.

Acknowledgments

The English-language edition of this book would not have been possible without the generous support of Michael Kearney. His intellectual insights have been a source of inspiration for my research. I am also grateful to the leaders of migrant organizations on the Mexico–U.S. border for entrusting me with accounts of their experiences of migration and social participation.

I am particularly grateful to Sergio Méndez, Rufino Domínguez, Juan Lita, Rogelio Méndez, Algimiro Morales, Ofelia Santos, Tiburcio Pérez, José Rojas, Arturo Pimentel, Gregorio Santiago, Gonzalo Montiel, Antonio López, Bernardino Julián Santiago, Rafaela Hernández, César Sánchez Liévano, Olga Quiroz, Centolia Maldonado, Rosalba López, Maura Salazar, Santiago Ventura, Antonio Reyes, José Onofre, Pedro Camacho, Daniel Niño López, Rodolfo Martínez, José Palma Niño, Avelino Ortiz Vázquez, Florencio Hernández Galindo, Rafael López, Juliana Sánchez, Salvador Caballero, and Isaías Vásquez.

I am profoundly grateful to Rodolfo Stavenhagen. He was an important guide and interlocutor in the research process. I also wish to thank Orlandina de Oliveira and Manuel Angel Castillo for their observations about the Spanish-language edition. John Rex's teaching on immigrant organizations in Great Britain was of considerable value during the revision of the book. I am especially grateful to the anonymous referees of the University of Arizona Press for their penetrating comments. They helped me to rethink some of the data and ideas in light of other viewpoints and research findings.

Thank you to Christopher Follett, who translated the book, and to Susan Lulic Enholm who edited the translation with a professional interest and dedication to the text. I thank Patricia Rosas for her expertise in translating material critical to the book's completion. Thanks, too, to Miriam Gabriela García for her impeccable computer and word-processing skills.

I am also grateful to El Colegio de la Frontera Norte, where I found support for my research work during the last twelve years; to the Ford and Rockefeller Foundations, both of which gave me research grants at the fieldwork stage; to the Mexican National Science and Technology Council (CONACYT), for having honored me with the Cátedras Patrimoniales de Excelencia grant, which enabled me to conclude the fieldwork and give it its final written form; to the Women in the Coalition Research Center—particularly the Rural Women's Empowerment Project (RWEP)—at the University of California–Riverside; and to the Fondo Nacional para la Cultura y las Artes (FONCA) for its financial support. FONCA enabled me to update the research information. Without its support, the English version of the book would not have reached publication.

In the journey to finish the book, I had the unfailing support of two special people. I am grateful to Oscar Contreras for the friendship he proffered and for his unreserved constructive criticism. To him and my son, Oscar, thanks for their constant patience and loving affection.

Abbreviations

ACBJ	Asociación Cívica Benito Juárez
ACCR	Agricultural Commissioners' Crop Report
AIM	Alianza Indígena Migrante
AMBJ	Asociación Mixteca Benito Juárez
ASMIRT	Asociación de Mixtecos Residentes en Tijuana
CAADES	Confederación de Asociaciones de Agricultores del Estado de Sinaloa
CASS	California Agricultural Statistics Service
CCB	Consejo Central Binacional
CCPM	Comité Cívico Popular Mixteco
CCPT	Comité Cívico Popular Tlacotepense
CEAMO	Coordinación Estatal de Atención al Migrante Oaxaqueño
CEDRI	Centro de Desarrollo Regional Indígena
CEHAM	Centro de Estudios Históricos del Agrarismo en México
CEIM-BC	Coordinadora Estatal de Indígenas Migrantes y Asentados en Baja California
CEMOS	Centro de Estudios del Movimiento Obrero y Socialista
CIESAS	Centro de Investigaciones y Estudios Superiores en Antropología Social
CIOAC	Central Independiente de Obreros Agrícolas y Campesinos
COCIO	Coalición de Comunidades Indígenas de Oaxaca
COCOPLA	Comité Comunitario de Planeación
COESPO	Consejo Estatal de Población de Oaxaca
COLEF	El Colegio de la Frontera Norte
COLMEX	El Colegio de México
COLMICH	El Colegio de Michoacán
CONACULTA	Consejo Nacional para la Cultura y las Artes
CONACYT	Consejo Nacional de Ciencia y Tecnología
CONAPO	Consejo Nacional de Población
CRLA	California Rural Legal Assistance
CROC	Conferación Revolucionaria de Obreros y Campesinos
CTM	Central de Trabajadores de México
DIF	Desarrollo Integral de la Familia

EAP	economically active population
EZLN	Ejército Zapatista de Liberación Nacional
FCE	Fondo de Cultura Económica
FILT	Frente Indígena de Lucha Triqui
FIOAS	Federación Independiente de Obreros Agrícolas y Campesinos de Sinoloa
FIOB	Frente Indígena Oaxaqueño Binacional
FM-ZB	Frente Mixteco-Zapoteco Binacional
FNIC	Frente Nacional Indígena y Campesino
FOCOICA	Federación Oaxaqueña de Comunidades y Organizaciones Indígenas de California
FONCA	Fondo Nacional para la Cultura y las Artes
IBAI	Investigación Básica para la Acción Indígena
III	Instituto Indigenista Interamericano
IIS	Instituto de Investigaciones Sociales
INAH	Instituto Nacional de Antropología e Historia
INEGI	Instituto Nacional de Estadística, Geografía e Informática
INI	Instituto Nacional Indigenista
INS	Immigration and Naturalization Service
IRCA	Immigration Reform and Control Act
MIULI	Movimiento Indígena de Unificación y Lucha Independiente
MUJI	Movimiento de Unificación de Jornaleros Independientes
MVT	Movimiento Vamos por la Tierra
NAFTA	North American Free Trade Agreement
NAO	Nueva Alianza Oaxaqueña
NAWS	National Agricultural Workers Survey
OPEO	Organización del Pueblo Explotado y Oprimido
OPT	Organización del Pueblo Triqui
ORO	Organización Regional de Oaxaca
PAN	Partido de Acción Nacional
PCME	Programa para las Comunidades Mexicanas en el Extranjero
PNUD	Programa de las Naciones Unidas para el Desarrollo
PRD	Partido de la Revolución Democrática
PRI	Partido Revolucionario Institucional
PRONASOL	Programa Nacional de Solidaridad
PRONJAG	Programa Nacional de Jornaleros Agrícolas

PSUM	Partido Socialista Unificado de México
RIIO	Red Internacional Indígena Oaxaqueña
RWEP	Rural Women's Empowerment Project
SAGARPA	Secretaría de Agricultura, Ganadería, Desarrollo Rural, Pesca y Alimentación
SAW	Special Agricultural Worker program
SCIRP	(U.S. Congress) Select Commission on Immigration and Refugee Policy
SEDESOL	Secretaría de Desarrollo Social
SEP	Secretaría de Educación Pública
SINGOA	Sindicato Independiente Gremial de Obreros Agrícolas
SRA	Secretaría de la Reforma Agraria
SRE	Secretaría de Relaciones Exteriores
STPS	Secretaría del Trabajo y Previsión Social
UABC	Universidad Autónoma de Baja California
UABJO	Universidad Autónoma Benito Juárez de Oaxaca
UAH	Unión de Alianzas Huitepec
UAM	Universidad Autónoma Metropolitana
UCBJ	Unión de Comerciantes Benito Juárez
UCSD	University of California, San Diego
UCSO	Unión de Comunidades Serranas de Oaxaca
UFFVA	United Fresh Fruit and Vegetable Association
UNAM	Universidad Nacional Autónoma de México
UNICEF	United Nations Children's Fund
UPN	Universidad Pedagógica Nacional
UVAM CS	Unión de Vendedores Ambulantes y Anexos Carlos Salinas de Gortari

Mixtec Transnational Identity

Introduction
New Ethnic Agents on the Mexico–U.S. Border

In September 1994 the city of Tijuana witnessed the birth of a new organization, the Frente Indígena Oaxaqueño Binacional (FIOB). The participants in this meeting came from cities and towns along the Mexico–U.S. border. They represented diverse organizations of indigenous migrants from the state of Oaxaca. Many arrived in groups of three or four, carrying their personal possessions in small totes or plastic bags. Some of them had departed the night before from the San Quintín Valley; others had left from Los Angeles in the early hours of the same day. Participants from Tijuana, Nogales, and the San Joaquin Valley (California), and those coming from Oaxaca, met the night before the meeting to finalize their plans.

Welcomes were exchanged, spoken in Spanish mixed with Triqui, Zapotec, Mixe, and Mixtec. The assembly proceeded with formalities and followed an agenda that included a report by the outgoing coordinator of the Frente Mixteco-Zapoteco Binacional (FM-ZB, now defunct) as a preliminary to creating the new Frente. The new organization would incorporate more organizations representing indigenous migrants while broadening the Mixtec-Zapotec alliance to include Triquis and Mixes. Although the auditorium was crowded, not all of those present were activists or leaders of indigenous migrant organizations. The audience included state government officials from Baja California and Oaxaca, representatives of the Mexican consulate in San Diego, and delegates from nongovernmental organizations in Baja California and Oaxaca, as well as academics and activists from both sides of the border. Voting followed discussions, and at the end of the meeting there was entertainment from the Yatzachi El Bajo band and the Maneadero violin and guitar musicians. Traditional dances known as Los Rubios and El Torito Serrano were performed by troupes from the San Joaquin Valley and Los Angeles, and then, led by local indigenous teachers, everyone joined and sang the traditional "Mixtec Song" in the Mixtec language. A meal followed this highly emotional closing ceremony, which took place amid lively conversations and the sounds of exuberant children. Afterward, the members of the new Frente marched through the main streets of the city to the U.S. border to protest the anti-immigration policy of California's then governor, Pete Wilson.

As far as the local press was concerned, talk about the Mixtecos was nothing new. Nor was it new for academics, activists, and government officials to be present at a Tijuana event organized by indigenous migrants from Oaxaca—particularly Mixtecos—or for government officials from the state of Oaxaca to come so far to attend a meeting of Oaxaqueños. Ever since the 1980s, the political[1] and cultural presence of migrants of Mixtec origin in Tijuana and San Diego was as noticeable as that of Zapotecos in Los Angeles. However, for the organizations of Oaxacan indigenous migrants along the border, this particular event did represent a substantial breakthrough in their political and social history.

The organizational process started at the beginning of the eighties with organizations of indigenous migrants in Mexico City and the fields of Sonora, Sinaloa, and the San Quintin Valley, extended to Tijuana, and finally reached several communities in California. During those formative years, the first "hometown associations" were formed, including the Comité Cívico Popular Tlacotepense (CCPT), the Organización del Pueblo Explotado y Oprimido (OPEO), representing the village of San Miguel Cuevas, and the Asociación Cívica Benito Juárez (ACBJ). After a two-year relationship of ethnic alliance between Mixtecos and Zapotecos in the United States, the FIOB set to work to extend the alliance to Triquis and Mixes. The FIOB wanted to increase its geographic influence on the Mexican side of the border, which was the reason for selecting Tijuana as the meeting site.

The presence of government officials, activists, and academics at events held by organizations of Oaxacan indigenous migrants was not unprecedented. This time, however, the political arena claimed by the new organization was clearly marked; in particular, relations with the Oaxacan state government and the Mexican consulate in San Diego were explicitly defined. As its name made clear, the Frente constituted a binational convergence of Oaxacan indigenous organizations. Adoption of the newly formulated "Oaxacan indigenous" category enabled the former Frente Mixteco-Zapoteco Binacional to be incorporated with Triqui and Mixe organizations on both sides of the border. These events should be seen, moreover, in the context of the Zapatista proclamation (January 1994) and the revival of the indigenous resistance movement throughout Latin America. After years of association as migrants of Mixtec or Zapotec origin, or in separate groups representing other indigenous peoples, they now achieved unity as Oaxacan indigenous people straddling two nation-states.

The number and diversity of organizations in the Frente required a change of direction in a process that organized collective action on an ethnic basis. The process had evolved over the previous twenty years among the migrant populations of this region. Michael Kearney and Carol Nangengast (1988) were the first to point out this change in the identity of Mixtec migrants in California. Nevertheless, until the late 1990s there was no systematic research into the relationship between collective agency and the process of reconstituting migrant ethnic identity. This book takes a multimethodological approach to that issue, combining survey, ethnography, and biography.

The Indigenous Migration and Organization Process on the Mexico–U.S. Border

In the mid-1990s, fourteen Oaxacan indigenous migrant organizations, mainly of Mixtec origin, were registered. The organizations covered a binational region, taking in various localities in California (primarily Madera and San Diego Counties) and Baja California (the San Quintin Valley, Maneadero, and the city of Tijuana). There were also connections to several towns and villages in the Mixteca region of Oaxaca. A second period of field research in 2000–2001 allowed me to document twenty-two organizations in the same region.

The number and diversity of the organizations pointed to a significant presence of Oaxacan indigenous peoples and their participation in the labor markets on both sides of the border. In the early 1990s, some 50,000 indigenous Oaxaqueños were estimated to be living in California (Runsten and Kearney 1994); around 40,000 in Baja California, most of them in the San Quintin Valley (PRONASOL 1991); and in smaller numbers in Tijuana (Velasco 2000). Depending on the agricultural season, numbers might rise to 100,000. For the most part, Mixtecos were already established on Mexico's northwestern border. By the end of the decade, 60,000 farmworkers were registered in San Quintin, most of them Mixtecos. Meanwhile, in Tijuana new colonies of the same ethnic group had appeared. It is quite likely that the Mixtec population (and that of Oaxaqueños in general) had increased and multiplied along the border in the last decade.

Since the 1960s, many people have left their homes in the Oaxacan Mixteca in search of work in the labor markets of northwestern Mexico and the southwestern United States. Over the years, this articulation of Mixtec migration and seasonal agricultural labor has acquired new characteristics, largely because of changes in U.S. migratory policies during the 1980s. The 1986 Immigration Reform and Control Act (IRCA) altered the legal situation, affecting the mobility of these migrants in the fields of California, Oregon, and Washington, while permitting incipient colonies of Mixtecos in urban zones of California. Simultaneously, and in close relation to what was happening on the U.S. side of the border, neighborhoods of indigenous migrants began to settle around the fields of the San Quintin Valley and in

Tijuana. The new inhabitants were no longer the single men who had characterized the agricultural camps of Culiacán and San Quintin; women and children—who had already made a tenuous appearance in the camps—were an important factor in the growth of the new urban and semiurban settlements. In Tijuana and Nogales, the urban labor of Mixtec women brought palpable changes to these frontier cities and diversified the home survival strategies of the migrants. According to the census of 2000, the Mixtecos were the largest indigenous migrant group in the Mexico–U.S. border area.

The organizational activities of these migrants were defined by the specific needs of new residents and agricultural workers, by their status as undocumented migrants, and by their condition as indigenous Mexicans in the United States. However, after almost two decades of mass migration to this region, it had become evident that their hometown roots, and their sense of ethnic identity as Zapotecos, Mixtecos, and so on, still exercised a powerful influence on their patterns of association. Similarly, when faced with finding employment, finding a place to live, and resolving problems with neighbors or legal residence (in the case of the United States), their sense of ethnic belonging—as Mixtecos, Zapotecos, Triquis, or simply as indigenous Oaxaqueños—continued to be a source of solidarity.

While it can safely be stated that important changes took place in the family and everyday life of the communities of migrants, such transformations did not follow the patterns laid out by the assimilationist or integrationist thesis. Theorists had predicted an increasing adoption of the lifestyles of the host society, or alternatively a process of social disintegration resulting from the gradual loss of contact with the basic point of reference—the hometown and ancestral territory along with its cultural traditions.

The constitutive assembly of the FIOB, of which we caught a glimpse at the beginning of this introduction, suggests how much had changed in less than thirty years; a discourse and an organizational practice had come into being, articulating a transnational ethnic identity. How did this transformation come about? Who were the promoters of such a process? What was the new reality that enabled a group of organizations to refer to themselves—in terms far from naive—as binational indigenous Oaxaqueños?

The present work answers these questions by examining the process by which ethnic identity changes under the conditions of international migration. The emergence of organizations and their leaders as collective and individual ethnic agents of change is given special attention. Narratives of the ethnic communities arise from practices and discourses at the center of the transnational political arena.

An important focus of analysis in this book is gender differentiation within the narratives of the ethnic community. Political and cultural representations of community seem to reproduce gender subordination, lacking emphasis on female concerns such as domestic issues.

My general research hypothesis is that ethnic identity is a social construction with an important political dimension. It can be differentiated from other types of identity in the international migration context by the role of historical and geographic origin in the discourses and by the practices of the community agents.

Ethnicity and Migration

To appreciate the concept of ethnicity, it is important to consider previous studies on migration. The earliest of these addressed the colonial situation and can be divided into studies of internal migration within colonial countries and studies of migration toward metropolitan centers. In both cases, migration leads to an encounter with a different culture—the "other"—and the experience of a new and different life in the emerging colonial cities or in the developed countries. It was during the 1970s that the concept of ethnicity appeared. The subjects of study were rural migrants to the cities of developing countries of Africa, Asia, and Latin America, and arrivals from the now decolonizing Third World to the United States and Great Britain. In this historical context, scholars predicted that adaptation and assimilation would gradually weaken the practical and symbolic links of migrants with their places of origin. Versions of this assimilationist thesis varied little between studies of internal rural–urban migration and those of international migration.

The notion of ethnicity seen in these studies rests on a culturalist view of ethnic identity and shows a solid theoretical affinity with the functionalist concept of modernization (which takes for granted a lineal course of transformation of society). According to this paradigm, migrants represent the traditional sector, which would accelerate that sector's transition toward modernity through the experience of migration; migration was analyzed as a process responding to the two polar forces of attraction and expulsion, or "push and pull," causing the links in the chain connecting place of origin and destination to disappear. Seen from the point of view of the places of arrival, migration, especially international migration, was a problem to be resolved by means of assimilation or integration—the celebrated melting pot.

The United States was a cradle of sociological theories that associated ethnicity with the polemics of the melting pot and the phenomenon of migration.[2] In this scenario, migrants soon found themselves transformed into ethnic minorities, being differentiated from both "Negroes"—later "blacks" (who were characterized as a "race" rather than an ethnic group)—and whites (who possessed neither race nor ethnicity, since they were the majority). At the dawn of the 1960s, the thesis of the melting pot came into crisis because of a substantial change in the national origin of immigrants, the struggle of the black population (Martin Luther King Jr. and "civil rights," Malcolm X, the Black Panthers, and "black power"), the recategorizing of blacks as Afro-Americans, and the emergence of the Chicano movement. Thus, a new set of ethno-political identities became evident.

Nathan Glazer and Patrick Moynihan (1963) pointed out that the melting pot simply did not exist, nor was it a likely future scenario in the United States. According to these authors, Afro-Americans were an ethnic group like the Puerto Ricans or the Irish. Under the influence of Abner Cohen's (1969) instrumentalist concept, these authors regarded ethnicity as a product of modernity—a group manifestation motivated by political and economic interests. The novelty of this thesis, and of Glazer and Moynihan's later one (1975), was that the category of ethnicity was intersected by other categories, such as race, nationality, and the concept of minority, and at the same time defined in terms of its relationship with the state rather than cultural heritage.

Articulation was another important concept in international migration studies. This implied a shift away from the neoclassical and functionalist paradigm and toward a historical-structural vision. In this concept, both expulsion and attraction answer the same logic of accumulation in the world capitalist system, which links different modes of production with workforces. This point of view brought to light structures such as social networks and migratory chains, with their accompanying traditional practices, rituals, and customs. Such social networks articulate work experience in distant California, for example, with family life in Oaxaca. Thus, the linkage between two different areas of the migrants' social life also involves or integrates two different modes of production, and the process as a whole has consequences for the reconstruction of ethnic identity (Kearney 1986).

In the 1990s a new approach to the study of international migration—also of relevance to the study of migrant identities—appeared. This is the "transnational" approach (Glick-Schiller, Basch, and Blanc-Szanton 1992a), which stresses migrants' capacity to construct a social field crossing national boundaries. This has three conceptual implications for ethnicity: first, the approach posits that ethnicity is constructed by social agents as part of the prevailing social order; second, the approach places the capacity to act—ethnic agency—within the structural framework of capital and the national state; and third, the approach brings us closer to understanding the ethnic consciousness of a new transnational community. In the political arena, ethnic consciousness expresses itself through the leadership's discourse and by organizational practices both in places of origin and in places of arrival, discourses and practices that often cross the national border.

The Emergence of Ethnic Agents

Analyzing the relationship between ethnicity and social agency brings us closer to the subject of ethnic agents and their roles. The conceptual systematization of social agency requires two axiomatic assumptions: (1) that men and women are defined as active beings capable of transforming the course of their lives; and (2) that the social order is in some sense ethnic—that is, built up through the social action of human beings in a system of ethnic relations.

The first axiom refers to the creative capacity of human beings and enters into a polemic with the idea of human beings as socially determined subjects that we find in Marxist structuralism or Parsonian functionalism. The point of view in this book is that social action is a means of production of society and that men and women are agents in this process of construction (Bourdieu 1990; Bourdieu and Wacquant 1995; Giddens 1979, 1995; Touraine 1995). The concept of agent differs from that of subject in presupposing the capacity of individuals to modify objective structures or to create new ones (Bourdieu and Wacquant 1995) and to opt between varieties of possible actions (Giddens 1995, 51). Thus, the social structure cannot determine—in the sense of necessitating—the concrete action of the individual; it can only limit the range of options.

The capacity of human beings to choose among different courses of action depends on their position in a field of relations and on the volume and composition of their capital (Bourdieu 1995, 73). The agent's capital, according to Giddens (1995, 51), may take the form of the variety of his/her structures of knowledge. In this constructivist approach to the social order, social action is not opposed to social structure; it is the duality of the structure that confers its dual status as constituted by, and constitutive of, the social action of individuals. Thus, in constituting himself or herself, the individual is simultaneously producing society.[3] Accompanying the concept of agent is that of agency. Agency refers to a transforming relation, whereas agent refers to an identity arising from this relation.

The second axiom refers to the social order considered in its ethnic dimension and rests on two assumptions: on the one hand, individuals are members of a collective with its common historic origin in the framework of a specific national state; on the other, each member of a given national community occupies a position within a hierarchy peculiar to that community. Such hierarchies not only entail differentiated social practices but also regulate access to resources, giving rise to asymmetric relations of power.

The ethnic social order, with its hierarchy and consequent forms of domination, rests in part, therefore, on a historical dimension; but this—and its constant updating—in no way prevents the emergence of forms of resistance.

The possibility of resistance allows us to insist on the viability of an ethnic agent involved in a constant struggle to influence the course of action of others and at the same time mold his/her identity. It is not surprising that theories change in our effort to conceptualize collective action as a process of identity. Action vis-à-vis others is seen to be fundamental for defining cultural differences as frontiers distinguishing "ourselves" from "the others," that is, defining the ethnic community in the context of a particular nation-state. For the Mixteco, the migration experience created a transnational context in which identity is defined through a dual-state condition. The mestizo-indigenous dichotomy becomes a central point of differentiation in the Mexican context, but beyond the frontier other categories appear to be relevant, such as Mexicano, "gringo," or Chicano.

One can observe the influence of reflexive sociology on both these major conceptual axes (ethnicity and the constitution of social agents).[4] Thus, it seems reasonable to attempt a synthesis of the constructivist contributions to ethnicity[5] with Giddens's (1995) theory of structuration as a way to study the emergence of ethnic agents and their role in the reproduction and dissemination of ethnicities. In line with Giddens's concept of social agency (1995, 51),[6] an ethnic agent can be defined as an individual or collective with the capacity to transform its environment through strategically concerted action. In this process, there is a deployment of causal powers, including the power to influence actions set in motion by other human beings mutually defined in a field of ethnic relations (Baumann and Sunier 1995; Govers and Vermeulen 1997; Stavenhagen 1996).

From this theoretical perspective, ethnicity is a product of political agency that constructs the limits of affiliation between "us" and the "others." Here, agency works to construct the ethnic community in the form of a narrative, as discourse and day-to-day practice. In this context, cultural contents become relevant in defining ethnic boundaries only if they are interpreted as marks or emblems of ethnic identity or ethnicity. Through translation to emblems, there is a constant updating of the traditions that define a community even if that expresses a reified image of the traditions.

Ethnic agents play a strategic role in the narrative construction of the ethnic consciousness by updating the meanings of marks or emblems as the situation and the system of ethnic relations evolve, nourishing the ethnic consciousness. This implies not only a subjective state but also differentiating practices that make possible the day-to-day renovation of ethnic boundaries.

The institutional framework of the national state defines the last horizon of possibilities for the ethnic groups' action.

To summarize, the construction of an ethnic community is not only subjective but interactive. Both dimensions may characterize the community's ethnic consciousness and bring it into a relationship with other systems of social differentiation such as social class, gender, and generation. This theoretical approach is further developed in chapters analyzing migrant organizations as ethnic agents.

A Note on Methodology

This book is the result of a multi-methodological approach to research into Mixtec migrant organizations and their leaders. The groups studied were located on both sides of the border between Baja California and California, and they maintained strong links with towns and villages in the Mixteca region of Oaxaca. In identifying the organizations of indigenous migrants from the Mixteca on this frontier, it became clear that it would be important to include Zapotec and Triqui organizations, since these are also part of the political sphere of Oaxacan migrants. Despite the effort to include as many organizations as possible in the sample, a number were left out. Time constraints precluded extensive coverage. When organizations had little or no recognition among their peers or when—during the two periods of field research from 1994 to 2001—they appeared briefly and then disappeared, they were omitted. The method used to detect these organizations was the same as that used in the individual interviews—"snowballing." One organization led to another, and so on in succession. The work of discovering leaders or representatives occurred in two stages. The first involved the same "snowball" technique: the leader of one organization gave me the name of someone known to him or her in another organization, and so on. When an organization and an activist were identified, the second stage began, which consisted of verifying with other members or activists the legitimacy of a particular person as a leader or representative.

The geographic dispersion of the organizations challenged my analytic and empirical capacity to trace the boundaries of the social and political field. The work of Marcus (1995, 106–111) on multisited ethnography helped me maintain confidence in the sound analytic sense of this strategy despite the obvious empirical difficulties. My final research sample consisted of fourteen organizations and twenty-four representatives or leaders of these organizations.

Identifying the organizations took place between 1994 and 1996, with periods of intense fieldwork from January to September of the first year and April to September of the second year. During 1997 and 1998, I made sporadic visits to some of the leaders in order to detect possible changes in the organizations. Final fieldwork was carried out in 2000–2001, particularly in Oaxaca. My time was also spent clarifying certain issues that arose during preliminary analysis of the empirical data accumulated during fieldwork and in reviewing the interview transcripts with most of the respondents, requesting their authorization to quote them, and receiving comments on the texts. Only on a few occasions did I receive comments on the texts; most of the male leaders accepted my quoting them; some female leaders asked me to alter their names, while others asked me to eliminate certain passages about their political participation.

I followed three principal strategies to gather the empirical information on which this study is based.[7] The first was to participate in meetings, assemblies, and other events sponsored by the organizations, as well as in community festivities. The second was to construct life narratives through in-depth interviews with leaders or representatives of the organizations. The third was to analyze the contents of journalistic materials, internal documents of the organizations, and some surveys conducted during the 1990s and at the beginning of 2000. Only the leaders' life stories were submitted to qualitative analysis using The Ethnograph and ATLAS.ti computer programs even though most of these materials ultimately took the form of texts. The instruments were useful in systematizing the biographical trajectories of migration, employment, and political participation, and also in creating simultaneous cohorts for relating individual biographical events to those at community, national, or international levels. I constructed the biographies of each organization by connecting individual life histories. Through joint analysis of biographical accounts it was possible to discover the political networks and, behind them, the migrant networks that formed a variety of associations, including the original hometown associations and the more recent fronts, coalitions, coordinating groups, and federations.

To sum up, the organizational practices and the discourses of the leaders built a transnational ethnic consciousness of community and ethnic boundaries, but that consciousness was, to some extent, a collective memory of international migration. Furthermore, the narrative that emerged from joint analysis of the different accounts was a valuable tool for studying the transnational ethnic consciousness.

Organization of the Text

Chapter 1 presents the theoretical and empirical assumptions of the transnational approach to the study of international migration and seeks to use these as a framework for viewing the emergence of migrant organizations and conceptualizing them as ethnic agents.

Chapter 2 examines transnationalization as a result, on the one hand, of the articulation between the regional labor markets and a workforce provided by Mixtec migration and, on the other, of government policies on controlling national frontiers. Both of these factors encourage the transnationalization of the inhabitants of certain municipalities of the Mixteca region as a workforce and as subjects of state control. The interplay of these factors constrains migrants' options for action and impels the structuring of their social agency.

Chapter 3 deals with the process of transnationalization as viewed through the social agency of migrants. A chronological account of the emergence of indigenous organizations in the context of migration to the Mexico–U.S. border sets the scene for an analysis of the experience of migration, collective agency, and the construction of ethnic boundaries. Throughout the chapter, the ethnic configurations at chronological stages of the collective agency are reconstructed. The development during the last two decades from hometown associations to pan-ethnic organizations involving Mixtecos, Zapotecos, and Triquis along the Mexico–U.S. border has not always been a straight line. The transnational process of grassroots organizations is analyzed in the frame of regional markets and the effects of government controls on migration.

Chapter 4 adopts a transversal perspective for analyzing migrant associations in order to study their field of collective action. The migrant networks are analyzed as an empirical prior condition. Before associations arise, networks may already exist as social structures that lead to revitalization of community links. Within this framework, migrant associations are collective ethnic agents distinguished by their degree of institutionalization and transnationalism and their specific interests.

Chapter 5 analyzes the construction of ethnic consciousness through the discourse provided by the voices of indigenous intellectuals. These individual ethnic agents mobilize interests and resources and guide the migrant indigenous community's political or cultural projects.

By analyzing the social agency of women, chapter 6 shows how female concerns arise in the space of the organizations. The introduction of gender subordination adds complexity to the account of ethnic consciousness presented in the previous chapters while revealing new areas of interest and struggle broached by these organizations.

Finally, chapter 7 sets out to systematize the main empirical findings in an overall framework of the relationship between international migration, social agency, and ethnicity. At the conclusion, I describe a viable indigenous community dispersed along the Mexico–U.S. border.

1

Migrant Organizations
The Ethnic and National Frontiers

The fact that Mexican migrants organized is hardly unusual. Manuel Gamio (1975, 20) has noted the activism of clubs and associations founded by Mexican immigrants in the United States at the beginning of the twentieth century. At that time, labor agreements between the two countries opened the way for encounters between migrants from similar localities outside of Mexico. At the end of the twentieth century, it was possible to observe a change in the dynamics of migrant organizations with the spread of electronic communications. This ingredient has had a profound effect on the way migrants experience space and time, increasing the ability to maintain close links with their places of origin and to create a transnational community.

Chapter 1 presents a conceptual discussion of migrant organizations in the context of transnational processes resulting from migration between Mexico and the United States. These organizations are conceptualized as ethnic agents, and current thinking on these transnational processes is explored.

Crossing the Border: Migration and Transnational Processes between Mexico and the United States

During the 1980s, the term *transnational* made its appearance in the literature on immigrants in the United States. Since then, references to transnationalism have become ever more frequent in articles on international migration, many of which deal with Latin American countries that have a tradition of migration to the United States. Almost twenty years after the first appearance of the term, there is less controversy about its viability as an analytic tool. As an approach, it addresses, in general terms, the framework of the world system, with particular attention to the role of the nation-states.

Several scholars from different disciplines have pointed out that a new pattern of migration has come into view,[1] with a new type of migrant population, characterized by networks, activities, and lifestyles mixing elements of both original and host societies. Transnationalism refers to a process through which migrants cross national boundaries and synthesize two societies in a single social field, linking their country of origin with their country of immigration. For the second generation, place of origin may increase in symbolic meaning as a place of ancestors.

In recent years, this transnational perspective has acquired an important place in the literature on Latin American migration to the United States.[2] To understand how transnational migration evolved, one must understand the causes and persistence of migration itself. The migration experience brings about new interests and new resources, transforming the individual capacity to face life. Transnationalism is grounded in the daily lives, activities, and social relationships of migrants. Although migrants' principal status is that of workers, they live a complex existence that leads them to confront and re-make cultural boundaries based on differences in nationality, ethnicity, race, and gender.

A dualistic vision of international migration (in terms of origin-destination, expulsion-attraction, and permanent-temporary migration) interferes with understanding the different patterns of individual and collective migration. New concepts such as networks, circuits, institutions, and migrant agents help us understand the complexities of the structuring processes of a local community that extends beyond its original territory.

From this perspective, national frontiers become zones of fragmentation and continuity. They mark the territorial limits of the state and also indicate the transit areas between two nation-states. In view of these two facets of frontiers, it is urgent to revise migration policies that affect the living conditions of the migrants, in particular policies related to citizenship status.

Transnational Communities and Space

The transnational approach first became associated with the study of migratory networks and circuits in the 1970s. Perhaps the most eloquent example in this literature is Roger Rouse's work on transnational circuits (1989, 1992). Rouse (1989) reviews notions such as "spatially extended communities" (Whiteford 1979)—or "multilocal" communities, as they are known to students of internal migration in the Latin American context (Roberts 1974; Lomnitz 1976)—and similar concepts such as "binational networks" of peoples (Mines 1981) or "binational communities" (Baca and Bryan 1981). Out of these, Rouse distills the image of a community that has overflowed its original territory and at the same time reconstructed it via migratory circuits based on kinship or local community relations.

These new terms and images were the basis of the analytic entity known as the "transterritorial," or transnational community. There is agreement in the literature that the transnational community is a result of international migration and implies the construction of a social space that preserves the existence of a collectivity in more than one national territory (Besserer 1996; Georges 1992; Goldring 1992; Kearney 1994; Kearney and Nangengast 1989; Smith

1995). The ability to span national frontiers is a central element that distinguishes this phenomenon from others, such as diaspora (R. Cohen 1997, 190), and helps to clarify the type of practical and symbolic links established with the original territories.

Some authors have expressed reservations about the concept of "transnational community" (Pries 1998) because it tends to present a reified image of the community, often failing to distinguish between the analytic use of the concept and its empirical existence as a phenomenon. In other words, in the eyes of the critics, such communities do not exist other than as a series of practices involving transnational interchange, or in instances of political or economic exchange; and such acts do not necessarily imply that such communities exist subjectively.

Several types of evidence support the transnational approach. First, there is the diversity of exchanges between community members across national frontiers. The practices accompanying such exchanges demonstrate a family or community commitment by migrants to their places of origin. According to Goldring (1992, 323), exchanges between migrants and their communities of origin (especially remittances) help maintain the feeling of home-community membership. A second type of evidence consists of social practices in which communication technologies are used to maintain and strengthen links between the territories of origin and the places of new settlement. Such technologies, along with videos and modern means of transportation, facilitate the "simultaneous" existence of the community in the towns and villages of Mexico and in the places of settlement in the United States (Boruchoff 1997; R. Smith 1995, 15). A third type of evidence is the migrant organizations' help in articulating the territorial experience, "reterritorialization," providing a local base for contingents of dispersed and mobile populations (Besserer 1996, 6; Kearney 1994, 1995a; Rivera-Salgado 1999;). Such social and political organizations constitute political agents that work to resist state policies of control.

With the exception of Kearney (1994), the literature is indefinite about how the transnational community achieves substance and explicit expression. The ambiguity may arise because the community is understood in terms of mechanisms of cohesion at the practical or interactive level, not necessarily in terms of discourse. Thus we lose sight of the community as a construction imagined in symbolic terms, one that requires constant reshaping and that is an open and incomplete construct.

How, then, are we to analyze this subjective construction of the transnational? In the literature on transnational communities,[3] a number of methodological strategies have been developed with one important point in common: the transnational community is seen as a social space constructed by the actions of migrants and sensitive to technology, capital, and government policies of control. It is neither a homogeneous nor an autonomous space but one in which different spheres of construction of the transnational can be observed. In addition, various agents participate in the construction of this space. In the above-mentioned literature, the spheres and agents involved in constructing the community are differentiated based on the perspective adopted by each study and the spheres of activity observed. For example, according to Kearney (1995a, 237), the transnational community exists because its reproduction—demographic, social, and cultural—takes place basically outside the original national space as a two-faceted process. It operates, on the one hand, through an articulation of modes of production linking members of the same community in different places, and on the other, by blurring the frontiers between nation-states (Kearney, 1986, 1994). For Besserer (1997, 22), the transnational community is the historical result of the incorporation of its members into the global system of production through the migration. For Robert Smith (1995, 14), it is a local construction, resulting from a transnational social and political process facilitated by the use of communication technologies and the periodic return of migrants to their community of origin. This takes place within the national framework but apart from the state and society in which it is situated.

Based on this set of theoretical-methodological assumptions, five primary hypotheses guide the present work:

1. International migration is a historical process experienced by individuals in so far as they belong to a collectivity: the community. The premise states that men and women, while possessing their particular characteristics as unique beings, are also social beings defined by their belonging to multiple social collectivities that may differ in their bases and in the mechanisms of cohesion and conflict. For Mexican migrants in the United States, the community of origin is a fundamental source of identity. However, once migration has occurred, the mechanisms of community reconstitution are transformed. New conventions of recognition, communication, cohesion, and conflict are incorporated into a transnational space.

2. Two macrostructural processes delimit construction of the transnational community: the international labor markets and the migratory policies of national governments. On the one hand, because Mexican migration to the United States is labor based, the migrant communities are especially sensitive to fluctuations in market and labor conditions that affect wages, work processes, and the relocation of production processes. On the other hand, government control of national frontiers affects the degree and

conditions of migrant mobility and the migrants' links with other migrants and with non-migrants. This also affects the integration of the transnational community.

3. Migration has a dual impact on the collective sense of the community. First, this experience affects not only migrants but non-migrants in Mexican localities through family ties and regional dynamics. Second, the status of immigrants, in terms of time of arrival and ethnic or national origin, has a strong influence on daily life in U.S. immigrant communities. For instance, the ways of remaking the sense of belonging to the local community would be different in an ethnically mixed and new community than in an ethnically homogeneous and old settlement. In addition, a new tension arises between the definition of "belonging" held by a local community and that held by a transnational community. In each community, dispersion and territory arise as two primary concerns.

4. The sense of community is reconstituted thanks to the social action of its members. One advantage of the transnational approach lies in its view of migration as a process in which migrants promote their own interests. From the decision to leave their places of origin to settlement at a specific migratory destination, and throughout their personal and labor history, migrants may opt for different courses of action. This enables us to imagine transnational agents that influence the production of a transnational field, not only in practical terms but also in terms of social consciousness.

5. With local bases in different national territories, the transnational community experiences a "simultaneous existence." This is the result of particular mechanisms and agents that rearticulate the fragmented experience of the territory. In my opinion, this less developed aspect in the literature juxtaposes the concept of social space with that of social time. The idea of simultaneous existence poses a challenge—already pointed out by Anderson (1993, 63)—regarding the mechanisms by which the community is imagined, whether local, ethnic, or national. For the Mixtec migrants, communication plays a pivotal role in rearticulating a sense of belonging, as chapter 4 shows with an analysis of migrant networks. In addition, discourses by association leaders about the individual's simultaneous existence lend cohesion as they elaborate and interpret the collective myths and symbols as new memory of the dispersed local or ethnic community (see chapter 5).

In addition to the preceding hypotheses, it is important to consider how the scale of the territory influences state policies. In the local community, there is a shared sense of place derived from personal interactions (Sack 1988, 228) in ceremonial or festival rites. Meanwhile, the national community relies on communication through newspapers, magazines, radio, and television or on national myths promulgated by political rule. Local, regional, or national scales create different challenges for government policies promoting attachment to a particular territory.

With this frame, the principal contribution of the present work is in analyzing the role of organizations and their leaders as ethnic agents in re-creating the community in a transnational context. Migrant networks are critical to the emergence of ethnic agents. Agents and network contribute—with the support of modern communication technologies—to promoting the experience of ethnic belonging in multiple places.

Migrant Organizations as Ethnic Agents

The preceding argument rests on two axiomatic assumptions stated in the introduction. The first axiom concerns the creative nature of human beings, the second the ethnic dimension of the social order. The present section develops and expands a set of concepts associated with these two postulates, in order to relate them to the idea of indigenous migrant organizations as ethnic agents.

Between Options and Social Restrictions: The Nature of the Social Agent

The first postulate holds that human beings are capable of transforming the course of their own and others' actions, thus enabling them to transform the social order in which they act. This does not deny that such actions take place within a fabric of power relations organized around the resources that individuals mobilize during their social interactions. The framework of interaction is defined by the ownership of resources, which bestow power, and the hierarchical position of individuals in a given social sphere. The nature of resources is a complex issue, not only because the resources can be human or nonhuman[4] but also because any element can become a resource in a specific frame of interaction. That is, a wide range of elements can become resources depending on the individual or collective creativity. The creative capacity of human beings lies in their ability to transfer resources successfully from one interaction context to another. A context of interaction has a historical and cultural horizon, which can illuminate or obscure certain resources and possibilities of action.[5]

For the purpose of analyzing the continuity of identity, it may be said that agency[6] is the capacity to transfer and extend the cultural schemes that all the competent members of a society share in new social contexts (Sewell 1992, 18). There is a dialectical relationship between schemes and resources: each implies the other. In other words, schemes and resources constitute the social structures that define a social system. Each of the resources is viable within a set of mental schemes or rules that make them culturally possible in a particular social context. In the case of international migration, for example, leaving the home village is only a possibility when both the necessary resources and an associated cultural scheme exist.

According to Sewell (1992, 20), despite the fact that the capacity for agency—wishing, forming intentions, and acting creatively—is inherent in all human beings, this capacity exists as a potentiality. Like the ability to use language, it has to be developed and thus may take on a variety of historical and cultural forms. It also differs among the individuals of a social system. This lack of uniformity in the exercise of agency within a society allows us to speak of different degrees of agency. Such differences are largely related to the social position of each individual according to how cultural differences are organized (gender, ethnic group, social class, sexual orientation, and generation) in a given social system. The last point is important, since this study is based on the assumption of a social order differentiated by systems of relations subject to an ethnic and gender hierarchy. To show the specific way in which gender relations influence the social agency of individuals, we need to incorporate into the analysis the axis of the sexual division of labor. With this in mind, we can identify the different possibilities for action available to men and women in specific cultural scenarios. The reader will find in chapter 6 an analysis of female participation in the Oaxacan migrant organizations of the northern border region and the dynamics of gender subordination in women's everyday lives as mothers, wives, and workers that limits their leadership.

There are many theoretical positions on the nature of the agent. While some authors give pride of place to the individual agent (Bourdieu 1990; Giddens 1979), others stress the collective or class nature of the agent (Touraine 1995). According to Sewell (1992, 21), agency is both an individual and a collective process; the transference of schemes and mobilization of resources that characterize agency always presuppose processes of communication with others. Agency entails an ability to coordinate actions with and against others, to form collective projects, to persuade, and to coerce. Thus, the agency exercised by persons is collective, both in its sources and the ways it is exercised; personal agency is charged with differences produced through power and exercised collectively. Therefore, it is implicated in collective struggles and resistances and can even be seen as historical, as Thompson (1994) points out. This comes close to the view of Ritzer and Gindoff (1994), who consider one of the great contributions of agency theory to be that it stresses the role played by each person in the social change, no matter how small his or her contribution. In the last instance, social change is the consequence of what people do together. While it is true that, in distributive terms, each person's capacity for agency is different, the process of social change is the joint result of such capacities for action.

I recognize both individual and collective agents, assuming that each one expresses a different kind of agency in the same social space. To talk about collective agents in transnational space, it is necessary to define "social space." I will consider Bourdieu's and Giddens's contributions to this issue, because each one stresses different aspects of this concept. Bourdieu and Wacquant (1995) define the social space as similar to a social field, as both an objective structure of relations and a symbolic structure representing such relations; the agents are distributed according to the volume and composition of their capital. For Giddens (1995) the social space has a central geographic dimension. In his view, social space is a structure of social relations localized in a specific territory where local and global processes overlap. Both Giddens and Bourdieu define social space as a structure of relations that is not limited to face-to-face interactions but includes all those interactions responding to processes of systemic integration on the broader geographic scale. To close this section, I want to point out that the present work defines the social space as a historical configuration of social relations, resulting from the action of specific agents with a specific territorial reference. Such spaces function as structures of options and restrictions for the agents.

Ethnicity and Social Order

This subsection outlines the second postulate presented at the beginning of this section: the existence of an ethnic dimension in the social order. In Mexico, studies of ethnicity can be traced back to the encounter of Mexican indigenist thought with the North American culturalist approach of the late 1940s to the end of the 1960s (Aguirre Beltrán 1957b; Caso 1948; Gamio 1948).[7] During the 1970s in Mexico—unlike in the United States or Great Britain—instrumentalism was not well received; instead, a Marxist structural approach was developed that linked ethnic category with social class (Bonfil 1981; Pozas 1971; Warman et al. 1970). Along the same lines, and in combination with Latin American dependency theory, a specific theory of internal colonialism was developed that characterized the Latin American states as colonial with respect to their internal territories (Stavenhagen 1968). Taken as a whole, these studies were elaborated on by scholars of former colonies as part of the intellectual movement against Spanish colonial and Mexican nation-state domination. The new theory of internal colonialism focused on the role of the nation-state in defining the position of the indigenous within the system of ethnic relations (Stavenhagen 1996).

At the end of the twentieth century, this Mexican thought encountered the "constructivist" approach to ethnicity (Barth 1994; Vermeulen and Govers 1994a, 1997). Such an approach stresses the social construction of cultural differences as ethnic boundaries (Banks 1996; Bartolomé 1997; Govers and Vermeulen 1997) in the frame of relations between the ethnic groups with the nation-state (Stavenhagen 1996).[8] From this point of view there is an ethnic order that implies different opportunities for people depending on their position in the ethnic relation system.

For instance, throughout the centuries the identity of the Mexican indigenous has been defined as the product of subordination to the colonial regime and the nation-state. Cultural differences in language, religion, territory, and history became a sign of ethnic belonging. Under the "constructivist" approach, those cultural elements are marks of identity that differentiate ethnic groups. The meaning of those cultural differences is important for determining the position of a person in the ethnic order. For this reason, according to Vermeulen and Govers (1997, 5), cultural differences take on full meaning only subjectively, and so the boundaries are, likewise, subjective. This subjectivity takes objective expression in the system of political and economic opportunities, not just horizontally, but vertically, too.

Following Williams (1989), in political terms, ethnic groups compete among themselves not only for resources (as instrumentalist theorists maintain)[9] but for becoming political brokers to negotiate state-making and to change their position in that system.

In this book the ethnic agent is conceived as an individual or collective subject who acts in order to modify his or her position in the field of ethnic relations and vis-à-vis the national state.

The New Ethnic Agents:
The Indigenous Migrant Organizations

Migrant associations are a good example of the human capacity for agency and the strength of territorial communities, whether local, regional, or national. Hometown associations worldwide have been identified by different scholars (Goss and Lindquist 1995; Jenkins 1988; Rex 1991; Rex and Mason 1986; Roosens 1994). No matter how far from home an individual emigrates, if two people from the same place of origin meet, it is possible for them to act jointly to achieve a common goal. A convergence of conditions is needed to transform those encounters into a migrant organization, as will be shown in subsequent chapters.

As already mentioned, Manuel Gamio noted the existence of associations of Mexican migrants in the United States as early as the second decade of the twentieth century. Similarly, Weber (1994) observed that contemporary hometown associations have their roots in mutual-benefit associations that were active in the first decade of the twentieth century in the agricultural areas of California. Such associations were rooted in common origins and provided a base of solidarity when newcomers faced the difficulties of social integration.

More recently, literature on Mexican migration has presented abundant evidence of migrant associations organized on the basis of shared local belonging from Michoacán, Zacatecas, Oaxaca, Guerrero, Guanajuato, and Puebla (Besserer 1988; Espinosa 1999; Hirabayashi 1985; Kearney 1996; Krissman 1994a; Lowell and De la Garza 1999; Massey et al. 1987; Orellana 1973; M. Sánchez 1995; R. Smith 1995; Zabin and Escala 2002). Espinosa (1999, v) mentions the existence in 1998 of approximately 500 Mexican hometown associations in the United States that were linked to villages in Mexico.

However, only in recent decades have such associations become the subject of research.[10] In the late 1990s, the first studies of pan-ethnic associations, clubs, federations, and organizations of Mexican migrants in the United States focused on the traditional emigrant states such as Zacatecas (Goldring 1997) and Michoacán (Espinosa 1999) and on others not so traditional such as Oaxaca (Kearney 1991; Rivera-Salgado 1999). Among the issues that researchers studied was the role of such organizations as protagonists of the social and economic development of the towns and villages of origin (Alarcón 2000; Lowell and De la Garza 2000). In addition, organizations assume the role of transnational agents, questioning the mechanisms by which local and national citizenship is constructed (Goldring 1997; Rivera-Salgado 1999). Very close to this view and the concerns of this book, other scholars see migrant organizations as cultural agents who develop transnational political strategies and new forms of ethnic consciousness (Kearney and Nangengast 1988; Krissman 1995).

Beyond these case studies, migrant organizations have not usually been a topic for study or a subject for general reflection. Coincidentally, the studies of the late 1990s, which stress the new forms of citizenship and the emergence of identity-creating agents, have dealt with populations of Mexican migrants of indigenous origin. Although Durand (1999, 90) points out that in the 1990s Mexican migrants ceased to be predominantly mestizo, investigations of the ethnic diversity of the Mexican international migration phenomenon are lacking. Thus, the research on these migrant organizations is affected by the scholars' capacity to clarify the ethnic dimension of their migratory behavior.

The dominant conception of these organizations under Giddens's definition is as social institutions.[11] From this theoretical perspective, institutions are social structures constituted through everyday practices, implying a set of rules and social resources. Thus, a migrant organization is just one of many social institutions in their societies of origin and destination (Goss and Lindquist 1995; Krissman 1994a; Rex and Mason 1986) that owe their existence to the processes of international migration and the presence of migrant communities.

The present work considers such studies as theoretical and empirical antecedents to the conceptualizing of organizations as ethnic agents in the cultural-political field. Such agents are defined not only by the constraint of long-term social structures of domination and subordination, but also by their capacity to influence that long-term social structure through their own ethnic project or agenda. To a large degree, this approach comes close to the vision of collective action theory, particularly the "orientation of identities" paradigm offered by Pizzorno (1989) and Melucci (1992). For these authors, the process of collective action brings a sense of history into the cultural sphere. The concept is similar to Thompson's (1994) idea of the historical agent. They emphasize the capacity of individuals to give meaning to action within a specific cultural context. This is not to say that history is the result of an intentional project, but that it is a contingent product of the individual actions of human beings.[12]

At this point, a question arises: What were the minimum conditions that permitted a migrant Mixtec organization to emerge as an ethnic agent so far from the homeland? To answer this question, it is necessary to review the conditions that, according to other studies, have been associated with the appearance of the hometown associations.

There are at least three hypotheses about the conditions necessary for the emergence of a hometown association (Hirabayashi 1985, 580–581; Hirabayashi 1993; Orellana 1973; Roosens 1994, 94–95). The first assumes that the migrants in question have previously experienced a strong tradition of community. For instance, they have participated in civic-religious cooperative systems based in a common identity and ethnic heritage. The second stresses that family and friendship networks must be politicized before immigrants are ready to join forces in a formally organized hometown association. The third says that the associations set up in the places of residence must maintain a link with the social and political system of the place of origin.

These three conditions have implications at different levels of analysis. The first is that migrants as a collectivity possess a history that goes beyond the migratory experience. Participation is part of community life in the places of origin. A strengthened network of migrants also implies a maturity in the migration flow, which requires time. Finally, the links with the hometown's social and political system imply a certain degree of permanence in the place of destination.

While these conditions do facilitate, in theory, the emergence of the associations, they do not explain why migrants choose to associate. In other words, they do not clarify the meaning or purpose of the collective actions that serve to sustain an association or organization of migrants. According to Jenkins (1988), such associations perpetuate interest in hometown politics while helping members to adjust to their new societies. At the same time, they represent a special interest of an ethnic group that may agree or conflict with the interests of the receiving society. Jenkins maintains that associations help migrants deal with the challenges related to migration and give a sense of continuity to their life and identity. In this functional vision of the associations, little attention is paid to individuals' need to reconstitute a social order that gives them continuity as members of a collectivity with a history; the process of reconstituting that social order is something to which individuals commit their own identity. From this perspective, the associations may be understood as collective agents with the capacity to organize a strategic action that promotes their own identity in a transnational context (Melucci 1992; Pizzorno 1989; Touraine 1995). To be considered agents, organizations must explicitly define their objectives.

Migrant Networks and the Reconstitution of the Community

How, then, do migrants articulate collective action under conditions of mobility and geographic dispersion? According to Giménez (1997, 18), one of the social conditions facilitating formation of a social group is the proximity of individual agents in a social space, which—in this case—is supplied through modern communications media and the migrant networks. The social space, which creates the migrant networks, embraces the many places to which people migrate and their hometowns.

From a sociological point of view, such networks are a necessary condition for the emergence of a migrant organization. According to the dualistic approach that dominated studies of international migration in the 1970s, the *migrant network* made it possible to observe the processes set in motion by migration, and to understand migration as more than the result of poverty and the attraction of labor markets (Massey et al. 1987). Like any field of social relations, the migrant networks depend on the existence of social ties. These bring to life a set of relations that define a network; the dynamics of the network are not limited to the movement of people, but include the movement of objects, information, and meanings. The nature of social links has been one of the preoccupations of the theory of social networks and of sociology in general. This set of links, while obviously connected with the mechanisms of social cohesion, is also connected with the mechanisms of differentiation and social conflict.

The role of differentiation and conflict within the networks is underdeveloped in the literature, and some authors regard this as one of the most significant weaknesses of migration theories. According to Kearney (1996, 124), the theory of networks presents obstacles for understanding multiple identities and the salience of social class. In view of these difficulties, Kearney (1996, 126) offers his own concept of the globalized reticulum, which operates within nations, communities, and many other social bodies and spaces. Kearney's definition incorporates both the potentialities of the network concept in the study of the transnational community and the unlimited extension of social relations with a geographically localized origin and the morphological complexity of the network. At the same time, he adds an image of the networks as a complex of communication channels. The network, as a means of communication, facilitates identity construction. Networks are based on the use of information generated and channeled through extensive social relations. Communication is one of the factors that, according to Kearney (1996, 124), differentiates the transnational community from the corporate community. At the same time, the concept of the reticulum[13] as a communication network is to be distinguished from that of *migratory circuit*, since it introduces the positions of power that the members of the network occupy in the broad system of social relations. Differences of class, gender, age, and ethnic group—which organize cultural differences in a given social system—are present in the universe of relations within the network, rendering it more complex and heterogeneous.

It is worth adding a reflection on the reticulum metaphor, which suggests that the basic function of the network of migrants is to channel information. While it is important to imagine a configuration of social relations by means of which information is exchanged, it is fundamental to understand this configuration as a set of social practices; in doing so we achieve a better and broader understanding of the diverse functions of social networks. When visualizing migrant networks, it is also useful to distinguish two functions: that of adaptation-selection and that of connection. The former facilitates international movement and contributes to reducing the costs and risks of migratory movement, thus increasing the possibility of access to an income. The connection function, on the other hand, constitutes a social support system that re-creates the community links of migrants. It can function both as social capital that migrants can draw on individually to find employment in foreign countries (Gurak and Caces 1992; Hugo 1981; Massey 1990) and also as cultural capital for collective action (Melucci 1991).

To sum up, the concept of the migrant network involves a configuration of social interrelations originating in migration. The network thrives on the constant exodus and return of members of a territorial community. The network enables us to grasp the dynamics of a phenomenon that has been constantly increasing in complexity, in part because of the diversity and the rhythms of the geographic mobility. Adding to that complexity are the consequences of the social links established between those living away from their communities and those remaining within them. Communication technologies are a central instrument for the dynamics of these networks, or the reticulum: they increase the speed and the content of the information flow and also influence behavior within the network. In addition, migrant networks can be conceived as a mechanism for structuring community links within a set of practices that—on becoming routine—give birth to institutions. Another way of seeing networks is as structures of rules and resources that make possible and constrain the actions of individuals. Given that the migrant networks are a product of the social action of both migrants and nonmigrants, they can also be regarded as the unplanned effect of such action. The set of practices that maintain and produce such social networks is pervaded by a practical consciousness, made up of accumulated knowledge about "us" as different from "them." Networks in turn enable further configurations of social relations to come into being, projected as forms of collective action with explicit purposes. This occurs in migrant organizations, within which—unlike in the networks—a discursive consciousness is produced with explicit meanings.

Without the social networks, the migrant organizations could not exist. In line with Giménez's observations (1997, 18), one may perceive—as far as the conditions facilitating the emergence of collective action—that such networks enable the proximity of individual agents in the social space. How else could a migrant activist in the San Joaquin Valley of California be close in social space to activists in San Miguel Tlacotepec, Oaxaca? In terms of geographic extension, the migrant network transcends the multiplicity of places of migration and the hometown; the migrant organizations politicize the social links that sustain the network and hence also its social space.

Migrant organizations are relational entities, which as totalities must be distinguished from the individuals that compose them (Lipiansky 1992, 8, cited by Giménez 1997, 17). As Pizzorno remarks (1989, 381), often a man or a woman's personal project can be appreciated only when we situate him or her as a member of a collectivity; and conversely, the collectivity finds its expression only through individual actions. By keeping this in mind, we can avoid reifying collectivities or groups and at the same time distinguish the individual level of social agency and the role of particular individuals in the mobilization of collective interests.

The different degrees of social agency—measured by the capacity to trans-form the course of action of others—can be partly explained by the differ-ing types and degrees of individual knowledge, capacities, and skills (Sewell 1992). It also reflects the fact that not all the participants of a collective action share the same sets of social representations that define them subjectively as part of a collective identity (Giménez 1997, 18). This vision goes beyond the idea of brokers and stresses the role of individuals in collective identity, constituting themselves as spokespersons of the group.

Those individual agents may be labeled as organic intellectuals, following Gramsci's definition (1998, 10). They are not professional or artist figures, but activists of the everyday struggles of a specific social class. I will use the concept of organic intellectuals in a close examination of Mallon's view of local intellectuals in Mexico and Peru to distinguish those who "labored to reproduce and rearticulate local history and memory, to connect community discourses about local identity with constantly shifting patterns of power, solidarity, and consensus" (Mallon 1995, 12).

Mallon considers as intellectuals in the peasant context those who have knowledge of community matters, such as political officials, teachers, elders, and healers.[14] I would add to this list the grassroots leaders in the migration organizations. Migration experiences have brought new knowledge to inter-national migrants, with new issues shaped by the urban life, modern agricul-tural jobs, and human rights. In this view, activism in the new places appears to be an important element defining an intellectual in the everyday life of the Oaxacan migrants.[15]

Those intellectuals who act as voices reproduce hegemonic order in a complex power relationship of domination and resistance in a dual national and state system.[16] Transnational migration brings a new demand to act as intellectuals in the field of politico-cultural representation beyond the ethnic and national border. This issue will be developed in the chapter 5; meanwhile I would like to distinguish the meaning of *representation*. According to Agnes Heller (1998, 341), *representation* has two meanings, not necessarily mutually exclusive. A first meaning is associated with the process through which the artist or individual portrays desires, sentiments, needs, interests, and behavior of the members of a social group. A second meaning refers to a group delegat-ing to a particular person the right to act in the place of the group. While the first meaning carries a cultural connotation, the second possesses a quasi-legal or political meaning. However, in both cultural and political representation, intellectuals speak and act for the communities to which they belong or claim to belong (see chapter 5). The gender and generational composition of these intellectuals is a fundamental aspect to have in mind if we want to understand the mechanisms through which ethnic consciousness is constructed and certain social categories are included or excluded in the process of politico-cultural representation.[17] Analyzing group spokespersons, in terms of gender, what type of ethnicity they promote, and their practice and discourse, may help clarify the gender relations underlying the constitution of these agents on both the individual and the collective level.

Summarizing, we can say that migrant organizations require the prior existence of social networks, which allow geographically dispersed interests and resources to be linked. Understanding the historical dimension of the ethnic subjects who make up these networks is fundamental if we are to account for the constitution of the organizations and the emergence of intellectuals. Equally important is understanding their institutional field of political action, which goes beyond the national frontier. Finally, the present work stresses how the concept of ethnic agent helps us study the community in a situation of geographic dispersion. This concept allows us to trace the new paths taken by the ethnic community and clarifies the mechanisms that make continuity possible.

2
Mixtec Migration and
National Frontiers
Labor Markets and Policies of Migration

In 2001, Maura Salazar provided a glimpse of the Mixtec migration history to northern Mexico and the southwestern United States when she said,

> In 1986, I left my seven children with my mama [in San Juan Mixtepec], and we came up here—my husband and I—to Oregon. I don't know where we crossed [the border] because I didn't know anything in those days. My husband was the one who led me on foot across the mountains. When we arrived in Arizona, we slept in the orange groves for two nights, and afterward we went on to Oregon. There, for some months, we were working, planting and picking strawberries. We lived in a little house that the labor contractor gave us. After a few months, we went to Washington to work in the bean harvest. When the work ran out, we went back to Oaxaca.

The inhabitants of the Oaxacan Mixteca region have settled in a wide area along the border. Prompted by the Bracero Program in the mid-twentieth century, labor migration has resulted in an interdependence between the communities where migrants have settled and their places of origin. The present study focuses primarily on a part of the Mixteca region known as the Mixteca Baja (Lower Mixteca)—a region consisting of the districts of Huajuapan de León, Teposcolula, Silacayoapan, and Juxtlahuaca. The migrants who founded the organizations being studied came from these regions. The study of migrant organizations cannot be restricted to the Mexico–U.S. border owing to the exceptionally strong social, cultural, and economic ties between the inhabitants of the final destinations of migrants from this region and the villages of origin in Oaxaca. These strong ties allow us to refer to the "transnationalism" of the Mixtec towns and villages. Transnationalism between Mixtec regions and the United States is in part the result of two factors. First, the articulation of different modes of production links the Mixtec labor force with transnational capital on the northwestern Mexican frontier and within the southwestern United States. Second, the Mexican government agreed to furnish *laborers* to its northern neighbor in response to the U.S. labor crisis during the first half of the twentieth century. As background for understanding the migrant organizations as ethnic agents, this chapter describes the evolution of migration from the Oaxacan Mixteca to northern Mexico and the southern United States in relation to regional labor markets and migratory policies. Before describing Mixtec migration, an overview of the Mixtecos as one of the indigenous peoples of Mexico would be beneficial.

The Mixtecos: Their Cultural Background

Today the Mixteca region straddles the states of Puebla, Guerrero, and Oaxaca. The Oaxacan Mixteca is in turn divided into the upper, lower, and coastal zones, corresponding with the altitude of the terrain.[1] The origin of this division goes back to the ancient Mixtecos, who divided their domain into three parts: the upland, or Mixteca Alta (its Mixtec name, Ñudzahui nuhu, means "a divine and highly esteemed thing"); the lower or intermediate zone, Mixteca Baja, which they call Ñuine, referring to the higher temperatures; and the southern coastal zone, which bears the name Ñundaa because of its relative flatness (Romero-Frizzi 1996, 47).

The purpose of this section is to place four cultural elements into historical context: the Mixtec language, kinship ties, territory, and the civic-religious system. These elements are important to understand the Mixtec migrant organizations at present.

According to the 2000 census, Mixtec is the second-most used pre-Hispanic language at the state level and fourth-most used at the national level. There are 444,498 speakers of Mixtec. In general, speakers of indigenous Mexican languages were 7 percent of the total population in the same year. This percentage should be seen in a post-Conquest context. At the time of the Spanish Conquest, in the sixteenth century, the population of the Mixteca was estimated at 700,000 inhabitants (Borah 1968, cited by Romero-Frizzi 1996, 144; Hassig 1994, 84); by 1620 it had shrunk to a mere 25,000 people. The Spanish invasion and other factors contributed to the erosion of the indigenous population and its languages. After two centuries of colonial rule, the newly independent nation promoted the mestizo as the model citizen. In this vision, indigenous languages did not have a future within the Mexican nation. In the early twentieth century, educational policies along with policies concerning indigenous peoples were central to suppressing native speech. Still, many of the indigenous languages have survived. They were used for private, secretive communication within the native population; they worked as mechanisms of resistance. Domestic life was an important niche for the reproduction of indigenous languages. Many Mixtec indigenous migrants from Oaxaca recall receiving severe punishment when they spoke their language in school. At home, however, they could talk freely in

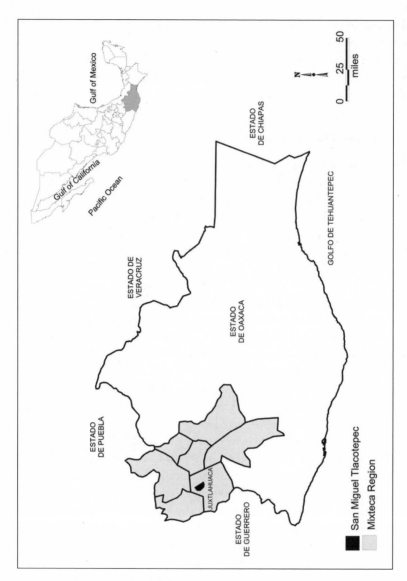

Figure 2.1 Location of the Juxtlahuaca district and the San Miguel Tlacotepec municipality. (Map by Luis Francisco Lares Serrano and Laura Velasco.)

Table 2.1   Indigenous Languages Most Widely Spoken in Mexico:
1930, 1990, 2000

Language	Number of Speakers		
	1930 Census	1990 Census	2000 Census
Nahuatl	670,595	1,197,328	1,448,936
Maya	279,093	713,624	796,314
Zapotec	216,825	403,527	452,887
Mixtec	172,114	386,874	444,498
Tzotzil	34,253	292,203	297,561
Otomí	218,811	280,238	291,722
Tzetzal	40,342	261,084	284,826
Totonac	90,607	207,876	240,034

Sources: 1930: Basauri 1990; 1990: Manrique 1994; 2000: INEGI 2000.

the Mixtec language with their parents and other relatives. Those language deprivation experiences began in the mid-twentieth century, when they were children and their parents began to leave home. Because of schooling, many Mixtec speakers were becoming bilingual. Between 1930 and 2000 (table 2.1), Mixtec speakers tripled, many bilingual in the indigenous and the Spanish language. However, the 2000 population census showed that 23 percent were still monolinguals (INEGI 2000).

The Oaxacan Mixteca was linguistically heterogeneous. In 1940, Aguirre Beltrán (1957a, 14) documented that indigenous speakers were concentrated in the Mixteca Baja, mainly in Juxtlahuaca district (83 percent). Most of the subjects of this study were born in the district of Juxtlahuaca. In their life stories, they express concerns about the discrimination shown indigenous speakers in their towns or villages. They note the existence of different degrees of *indianism*, depending on the number of Mixtec speakers in their villages. This concentration may coincide with the size or the degree of isolation of those villages. For example, some people living in the largest population centers do not recognize themselves as indigenous or Mixtecos. They apply the term to people who live in small, distant, or isolated villages. The 2000 census (INEGI 2000) registered seven municipalities in the Juxtlahuaca district that fluctuated between 21 and 99 percent Mixtec speakers. The linguistic vitality of the Mixtec language seems to derive from its preservation in family and community life, isolation and lack of communication technology, and the absence of governmental institutions since colonial times.

Some of the interviewees thought that the Catholic Church, schools, and government activities had a negative impact on indigenous languages. Policy makers imposed an official language of communication, thus eliminating the Mixtec language from the public sphere.

The rates of indigenous language usage were affected by demographic changes. For instance, during the last three decades of the twentieth century, the population of speakers of indigenous Mexican languages increased at a higher rate than the overall national population. Increased fertility and improved health conditions contributed to the increase (Valdez 2000, 222). Migration is another factor that affects the use of indigenous languages. There are continual references in migrant accounts to the linguistic problems they encountered on the road to the northern border. Many of them learned to speak some Spanish during the migration experience in order to find a job or deal with risks during the journey.

In addition to language, kinship ties to cultural reproduction have been an essential element of the Mixtec people. The social organization of Mixtecos (Pastor 1987, 41) has been based on the extended family since pre-Hispanic times. The family included not only cousins and more distant relatives but also ancestors—a concept designated in Spanish by the term *parentela*, the big family. This social unit was also associated with a specific territorial unit: the *calpulli*, *siqui* (Pastor 1987, 34), or barrio (Zeitlin, 1994, 291). Mixtec people represent the interconnection of different parentelas, which are a collection of lineages with different hierarchy but sharing a common mythic origin.[2]

According to Carmagnani (1993, 14), colonialism in Oaxaca undermined some indigenous institutions; others, however, such as the parentela and territorial belonging were reconstituted around the community. Just as the family kept the indigenous language alive, the community was where the sense of parentela and territorial belonging was reproduced throughout the years. The civic-religious system played a significant role in the cultural reproduction of the Mixtec communities as cultural, social, and territorial units. This system organizes community members under moral principles of service and mutual aid, always in support of the collective wealth. There are significant scholarly findings (see Butterworth 1975; Diskin 1990; A. Flores 2000; Monaghan 1995; Ravicz 1965) about the continuity of that system in the Mixteca Alta and Baja regions and its role in cultural reproduction through the centuries. At the end of twentieth century, it is possible to observe that system in collective work, or *tequio* and *cargo* systems.

Collective work has been the basis of the indigenous economy—for instance, the growing of corn (maize) involves all members of the family or all members of the parentela. The annual calendar follows the cultivation of maize, integrating all the members of each family into collective labor. According to Pastor (1987), in the sixteenth century the only way to express the concept "I work" in Mixtec language was by saying "I do the tequio," using a

Native American word that refers specifically to tributary common labor. At that time, the concept of individual work did not exist. Actually, tequio was considered part of community service and followed the moral principle of common wealth, as in the cargo system. It can be traced to pre-Hispanic times and is defined as a mutual-aid institution of exchange. Service and obligation are the basis of the tequio, and exchange implies that all members of the community are considered equivalent parts of the whole—the ethnic group. Although the tequio is an institution of mutual aid, its organization reproduces the status divisions of the community. The tequio can be organized by the privileged members of the community or the local authorities. Those who provide the labor for an individual or collective project are the poor Indians. Scholars (Monaghan 1995; Pastor 1987, 344) confirm that for these less privileged people the tequio is an obligation that, owing to their subsistence economy, is based on a solidarity that is more than an abstract ideal; it is one of several conditions necessary for survival.

On the other hand, the cargo system included the *mayordomías, cofradías,* and civic cargos for the *cabildo,* or town council. The mayordomía is an individual responsibility, while the cofradía is a collective responsibility. According to Florescano (1998, 212) the cofradía, or fraternity, is Spanish in origin and flourished in the colony of New Spain among a variety of social groups from the sixteenth century onward.[3] At that time there were cofradías of Indians, Negroes, and free mulattoes and other cofradías of rich white traders or poor craftsmen. According to Pastor (1987, 247), in the late seventeenth century, hundreds of cofradías appeared in the Mixteca region; through these organizations communities were able to transfer all their wealth to those fraternities under ecclesiastical patronage.[4] Like other institutions of the colonial indigenous world, the cofradías were a hybrid, a product of cultural syncretism. The idea of a corporation of persons grouped according to common interests and needs under the protection of a patron saint was of European origin, but it coincided with the concept of the ancient Mixtec parentela protected by the group's particular god.[5]

A cargo is a position that implies both a public responsibility and a commitment to the community. Routinely, authorities elect a community member to occupy a cargo, which can be civil or religious. According to Diskin (1990, 269), in some localities in Oaxaca the two cargos are interrelated. These public responsibilities are compulsory and until the early twentieth century were occasionally remunerated; they are organized hierarchically in such a way that once a young man occupies the *topil* post, he must continue until reaching the position of *principal,* which is a position of honor, not of public office. The same is true of the religious positions, whose highest rank is that of mayordomo. Because both civil and religious responsibilities are mechanisms for citizenship, they are ways of earning the community's recognition and acceptance. At the same time, those responsibilities are part of the system of authority that coexists alongside the official forms of the municipal authority in modern Mexico.

The intense participation of community members derives from the collective ethic that underlies the collective work and cargo system. The system depends on the number of religious and civic cargos and the number of families in each local community. Monaghan (1995, 170) gives the example of Santiago Nuñoó in the Mixteca Alta in the 1980s, where there were four hundred families and eighty cargos. This implies that one family in five had to take one cargo annually. In the same research, Monaghan (1995) found that each person of that town worked sixty-three days a year as part of the tequio commitment. The time adds up to more than two months each year.

Further observation suggests that this civic-religious system has contradictory effects on community survival. On the one hand, it is a mechanism of individual socialization within community life. On the other, it can work like a push factor in the choice to migrate. For many migrants, the cargo commitment is strong proof of belonging to the community; at the same time, some people gave it as the one reason for abandoning their towns. A woman related that she decided leave her town for the first time when her father was elected to take the mayordomía of San Miguel Tlacotepec. This meant that he had to organize and finance the San Miguel patron saint festival. Until 1996, that village had twelve mayordomías, each responsible for a particular festival. Family members went to Sinaloa and picked tomatoes for six months. At the end of the season, they had saved enough money to pay for the festival of San Miguel. According to the testimony of migrants, many people have left their hometowns because of cargo responsibilities and the burden of financing patron saint festivals. A group of moneylenders, charging high rates of interest, has arisen around the service system.

Migration has challenged all of the cultural institutions. Because of migration to the United States, indigenous languages are blended with Spanish as well as English. Migrant conditions have led to changing the rules for electing representatives in some cargos, taking into account those who live in other places. In addition, migrants have organized in order to continue having a presence in the life of their communities of origin.

The next section traces the origin and development of migration from the Mixtec region to the northern border.

The Route of Mixtec Migration from Oaxaca to the Mexico–U.S. Border

Oaxacan Mixtecos have been migrating for several centuries. From the eighteenth century onward the common lands of the Oaxacan Mixteca went through a process of privatization that left many people without land to grow subsistence crops. This initiated a fragmentation of the communities and an acculturation (Pastor 1987, 262),[6] in which the relationship between indigenous identity and territory was undermined. According to indigenous tradition, a person without land is no longer, properly speaking, a person and must therefore either emigrate or put himself up for hire as a "peon serf" on a ranch or hacienda.[7]

In the eighteenth century, the *haciendas volantes*[8] in the Mixteca introduced a progressive privatization of communal property through renting of the land of caciques and common indigenous people (Romero-Frizzi 1988, 156). Nevertheless, not until the mid-nineteenth century was the communal regime abolished under the Leyes de Reforma (Reform Laws). The objective of these laws was to end the corporate ownership of land by the communities and the church. In Oaxaca, many communities divided the land among residents, who paid an amount of money to the *ayuntamiento*, or town council, to avoid being landless (Esparza 1988, 287–288). By the early twentieth century the territorial fragmentation was irreversible. In the period following the Mexican Revolution, it was no longer possible to reconstruct indigenous territories in the region. In the second half of the twentieth century, the age-old problem of fragmentation was scarcely offset by the meager land grants. Between 1962 and 1986, the Mixteca was one of the regions that least benefited from the process of land grants in the state of Oaxaca. It received only 8.7 percent of the total land redistribution carried out in the state.[9] Precise figures on the number of people who benefited from such actions during this period are unavailable; we know only that beneficiaries received on average 0.58 hectares,[10] one of the lowest allocations for the entire state during this period. Although land in *ejidos* and communal property together accounted for 64.5 percent in 1970, the proportion of private estates for the same year (33.5 percent) was above the average for the state of Oaxaca (23 percent).

This long process of territorial privatization and fragmentation was joined by industrialization and urbanization, which reoriented and intensified migration from rural zones like the Oaxacan Mixteca.[11] The literature agrees that Mixtec migration formed part of the general process of migration from the countryside to the cities that occurred throughout Latin America during the mid-twentieth century. Such migrations commenced after World War II and at the start of the region's industrialization period.

In Mexico, industrialization overlaid an economic structure based on agriculture. Urbanization took place along parallel lines, with industry concentrated in certain regions that attracted people from the rural areas. Most of the interviewees in this research were born in Juxtlahuaca, some in the Silacayoapan and Huajuapan de Leon districts of the Mixteca region. By systematizing the life stories of this study and combining them with statistical information and the results of other case studies,[12] three different periods of Mixtec migration to the Mexico–U.S. border can be identified.

The first stage began in 1940 and ended in 1960, with Veracruz, Mexico City, and the United States as primary destinations. The interviewees remember when they and their parents went to Veracruz to pick pineapples and cut sugarcane. In the memories of interviewees, there were no bus roads from their towns to Veracruz. They had to walk or ride a donkey over the mountain to Huajuapan de León. From there, they took a bus to Veracruz. Some recalled that many contractors arrived in the towns looking for workers. Those who were recruited often did not go to the new jobs alone; it was common for the entire family to migrate to Veracruz. That explains why there were Mixtec colonias in that state in the 1950s. Some of the migrants living in Tijuana and San Quintin in Baja California and California were born in Veracruz.

> I was born in Omealca, Veracruz, in 1956. The Mixtecos went there, and I am of Mixtec origin. In that time there were many Mixtec workers in the sugarcane harvest. There my parents lived as immigrants picking sugarcane, as my grandparents did. Although I was born in Omealca, a few years later we came back to the town [San Miguel Tlacotepec] where I went to primary school. I have only four years of basic school. . . . I belong to San Miguel Tlacotepec, even though I was born in Omealca, Veracruz. (Algimiro Morales 1996)

The life stories show that migration created a triangle between a town in the Mixteca region, Veracruz, and Mexico City. The journeys to cities of Oaxaca and Puebla and to Mexico City were very important since they incorporated women into migration; typically, they were employed as domestic workers in urban middle-class homes. Girls of fourteen or fifteen were sent to live far from their towns and would return to visit their families for holidays or a family crisis. Sometimes the girl's contract was made with a parent or brother without sufficient information about her duties, salary, and labor conditions. Family migration to Mexico City brought the same type of employment for women. In the 1950s there was a building boom and an increase in the middle-class population. Men were hired in the construction and service industries. Some of the interviewees grew up in Mexico City and received a basic academic education.

Mexican workers had been in demand in the United States since the first Bracero Program agreement.[13] Workers were needed to replace men sent to fight in World War I. In 1917, the United States launched the first recruitment program (Durand 1994, 89), to which thousands of Mexicans workers responded. During the second Bracero Program (1942–64), 7,000 agricultural workers left the Mixteca Alta and Baja as braceros (L. Sánchez 1994, cited in A. Flores 2000, 50).

The Bracero Program turned some Mixtecos into pioneers in long-distance migration. This followed two patterns: the first was via collective recruitment by contractors in the region; the second consisted of the independent flow of Mixtec braceros. In the first, migration was both highly selective—with direct contact with employers at the place of employment—and risky. Migrants traveled in small groups but in large numbers to California.

In 2000, the mayor of San Miguel Tlacotepec spoke of his adventure crossing the border several times with groups of men under the Bracero Program. In 1947, he crossed legally under the program guidelines; at other times, he crossed without permission. He remembers being sent to jail several times, along with his fellow workers, before being deported to Tijuana or Mexicali.

When the program ended in 1964, a significant number of migrants continued to live in the border towns—waiting to return to work in the United States. The connection between the migration flow to Veracruz and that to the United States is not clear. It seems likely the two migration flows were independent of each other. On the other hand, migration to Sinaloa was connected with the Bracero Program in the 1960s and will be discussed later.

The second stage of migration covers the years from 1961 to 1980. These years were marked by the consolidation of the northwestern agricultural economy. The increase in economic development was aided by U.S. investors, the proliferation of labor-intensive agriculture, and the rapid growth of Mexico City and, even more so, the border towns. Sinaloa and Sonora are places of memory for Mixtecos. Sinaloa appears in all of the life stories recorded by the author of this book. Even a person who has never left his hometown knows about Sinaloa. In the second phase of migration, women had their first encounters with northern agriculture through the departure of male family members, and eventually they began migrating as part of the family group.

> Once we got married, we went to Veracruz. We stayed there for two years cutting sugarcane. We didn't feel very good because this job was so hard. Then, we came back to our hometown to grow corn, beans, green beans, and little squash. It was 1963. I remember in that year my first child was born; she was a girl. From there, we went to Tapachula, Chiapas, bringing our child with us; she got sick. . . . We stayed a short time there and then came back to our hometown. After a little while we went to Sinaloa to pick tomatoes. We stayed there for several months, maybe three months.

Again we came back to our hometown to grow corn. In this way, we were six months in Sinaloa and six months in Oaxaca repeatedly. During that time, my children were born. (Rafaela Hernández 1994)

Migrants in both Veracruz and Sinaloa, and later San Quintin, did agricultural work and were recruited in the same way. Contractors or labor brokers recruited workers in the villages and transported them to agricultural fields. In the mid-1940s, a group of northern farmers made an agreement with the Mexican federal government to move thousands of workers from the Mixteca region. Under the Bracero Program, they would pick cotton in the Hermosillo (Sonora) coastal region (L. Sánchez 1994, cited in A. Flores 2000, 50).

Urban and rural routes of migration were interrelated in a migration strategy that resulted in secure employment, reaching even to the "other side"—the United States. In the 1960s, an agricultural crisis in southern California coincided with a boom in mechanized agricultural workers' trade unions in northwest Mexico. The routes of migration extended to other states—Washington, Oregon, Alaska, and even Canada. Women were now integrated into the agricultural journey as part of family groups; important settlements appeared in Mexico City, Tijuana, the San Quintin Valley (Baja California), and Guadalajara (Jalisco).

By the 1980s, migration had become a path to survival for the inhabitants of the Mixteca. According to projections made by Nolasco (1979), in 1980 the region would have two-thirds of the population it had in 1970. In the 1980s, the most frequent destinations continued to be Mexico City, the city of Oaxaca, the states of Veracruz and Sinaloa, and, to a lesser degree, Morelos, Puebla, and Baja California.

The third stage comprises the years 1981 to 2000. It is defined by the settlement of Mixtec immigrants on both sides of the border. San Quintin (Baja California) flourished during the 1980s as the most important modern agricultural region of northern Mexico. As was mentioned, this valley used the same methods of recruitment, contract, and production as in Sinaloa. Many Mixtecos arrived in San Quintin by following the route from Sinaloa. They traveled with groups of relatives, leaving the tomato fields of Sinaloa with the money they had saved.

I grew up with migration. I left Oaxaca on May 13, 1974, to go to Sinaloa with my father and my big brother. . . . We worked one month there, just to save the money to go to Baja California. This was our aim. . . . When we arrived here, we found that this land is good to live in because of its weather. It is not quite hot and not so cold. It was very enjoyable. We decided to stay without a clear vision of getting a piece of land or building a house. We thought simply about being daily workers. (José Rojas 1996)

The urban settlements on the Mexican side of the border created demands for services and land. New jobs opened up in the informal sector—men became construction workers and gardeners, women worked as street vendors. On the U.S. side of the border, the Immigration Reform and Control Act (IRCA) of 1986 launched a process of legalization that enabled migrants to move freely across the border. Under the family reunification program of the IRCA, many Mixtecos brought their wives and children to the United States. The new legal status raised concerns about family rights and residency. At the same time, the program created inequalities among family members, particularly for women and children (Stephen 1999, 122).

In the 1990s indigenous migrant settlement along the Mexico–U.S. border was a fact. The first consequences of settlement were that a generation of indigenous Mexicans was being raised on California soil and had access to the U.S. welfare system. During this period, there were already political and economic links with the places of origin. The migrants had vigorous networks and organizations at local, regional, and transnational levels.

As already stated, the protagonists in this book came from towns in the Juxtlahuaca district and are part of the mainstream of Mixtec migration to the United States. According to statistical sources, in 1990 a significant part of the population of the districts of Centro (Zapotec) and Juxtlahuaca and Huajuapan (mainly Mixtec) left Oaxaca for the United States (CONAPO 1990, 95). The life stories suggest that Mixtec migration has traced a northern route that links places like the San Quintin Valley, Tijuana, and areas in California—Madera and San Diego (Runsten and Kearney 1994). This is consistent with statistical data showing that during the 1990s most of the Oaxacan migrants went primarily to California. At that time, the crossing points available to the migrants were Tijuana and Mexicali (70.6 percent) and, less frequently, Nuevo Laredo and Matamoros (29.4 percent) (COLEF and COESPO 1995).

The Mixtecos beyond the Nation's Border: Transnational and Border Labor Markets

Since the 1970s, there has been a significant population of Mixtecos on the northwestern frontier of Mexico. In fact, many personal histories of migration that took place even before that decade contain references to Tijuana, San Quintin, and California.

According to different sources, there were approximately 200,000 indigenous Oaxaqueños in California and Baja California in 2000. A significant number came from the districts of Huajuapan de León, Silacayoapan, and

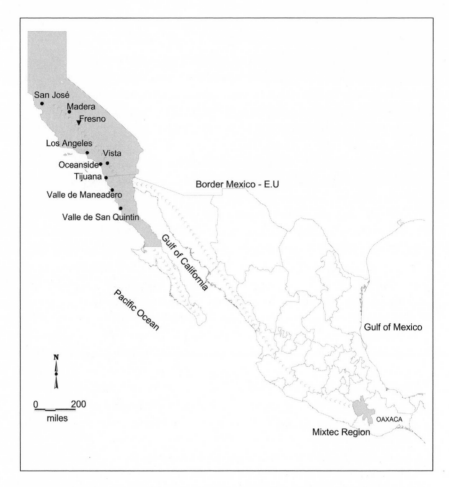

Figure 2.2   Location of the Mixtecos in the northwestern region of Mexico and in California. (Map by Luis Francisco Lares Serrano and Laura Velasco.)

Juxtlahuaca—Oaxaca's Mixteca Baja. This population is one of the most important sources of labor for the agricultural economy and street trading. Many people are commuters—that is, they live in Mexico and work in California—and must deal with the structural relations between Mexico and the United States every day. Fluid binational trade contrasts with rigid political and administrative border barriers. The strong demand for Mexican workers is counterbalanced by legal and military control of that border.[14]

What follows is a brief account of the Mixtec presence in the regional labor markets on both sides of the Baja California–California border.

Tijuana: Urban-Border and Cross-Border Employment

Tijuana is a strategic point on the route of Mixtec migration to the Mexican northwest and the southwestern United States. The first Mixtec settlements appeared in the 1970s, although the arrival of Mixtec pioneers can be traced back to the 1960s. As the migrants' own accounts relate, the Bracero Program seems to have been an unprecedented event in Mixtec migration to this part of the border.

Tijuana represents the first stage in putting down roots. Similar settlement is occurring in other border cities such as Ensenada, Mexicali, and Nogales. The first Mixtec migrants cite the 1960s as the time of their arrival, often after several shorter stays in the agricultural corridor of northwestern Mexico. The life stories speak of family migration taking place from the 1970s onward; at the end of the decade Mixtec weddings were taking place in Tijuana (Lestage 1998), which suggests a pattern of family migration or residence. On arriving at the border, these migrants organized their life around the search for a place to live and work and a school for the children, in that order of priority. The history of the Colonia Obrera in Tijuana documents this process.

By the end of the 1980s, the Mixtec family groups concentrated in the Colonia Obrera had already spent an average of eight years in Tijuana. The first residents arrived in this *colonia popular* in the early 1960s.[15] Only one-fifth of the families had lived in any other part of Tijuana before moving into the colonia. Like many other urban settlements in Tijuana, the Obrera neighborhood was established through a combination of direct purchase and simple acts of mass squatting. There was noteworthy participation by women in the urbanization of this zone in the mid-1980s (Lestage 1998, 20–21). The new residents built a school, constructed a ramp to create access to the colonia, and made roads out of the footpaths of the ravines that crossed the settlement, as well as built walls with old tires to prevent mudslides and landslides during the rainy season.

Projects carried out in the colonia marked steps in establishing permanent residence. The history of these settlements differs little from those of other poor or working-class neighborhoods in other Mexican cities. What seems unusual is the way in which these families sorted out their working life, blending the options they found on the Mexican side with those that they found in the California labor market. The local employment available to these migrants was concentrated in street trading, working as gardeners in Tijuana's middle-class suburbs, and working in the construction industry; they also found jobs as farmworkers and nurserymen in California's floral and greenhouse industries.

My husband is working *al otro lado* [on the other side of the border], and he goes back and forth every day. He's got his documents now, but it's true, he really suffered a lot until, many years ago, they sent people to take censuses here in the neighborhood in order to give him his papers.[16] He still has a lot of problems at work because he is a bricklayer in the construction trade [and sometimes he works in nurseries]. That boss of his shouts at them; he treats them badly. I told him, "Look, old man, think about how they are going to treat you, however they want, how they're going to shout at you; it doesn't matter if they pay you, but keep everything steady, you know. . . . No, it is really tough to go to the other side with those gringos! However, that's how it is, that's the struggle of our race, some of us here in Tijuana, and others over there on the other side. (Ofelia Santos 1994)

Like other residents on the border, the Mixtecos developed domestic and employment strategies not limited to the opportunities on the Mexican side.[17] In 1989, 44 percent of the Mixtec homes in this neighborhood of Tijuana had one or more family members working in the United States. They had a pattern of border crisscrossing that was more complex than implied by the terms *commuting* or *transmigration*. As individuals residing on the Mexican side of the border and working in the United States, they might cross and return daily, weekly, or more sporadically. Despite these different lengths of stay in California, what these Mixtec transmigrants or commuters have in common is that they identify Tijuana as home and California as their place of employment.

The option of cross-border employment is accompanied by other choices in the urban and industrial life of the Mexican border region. Some members of Mixtec households work in the United States, while others within the same family may combine cross-border employment with work in Tijuana. These migrants are most commonly street vendors, gardeners, and construction workers, or they do paid housework—always in the informal sector. The work of women and children in street trading, one of the most important household strategies, deserves separate consideration.

Tijuana: Working on the Streets and in the Gardens

In Tijuana, tourism provides employment for a large number of individuals occupied in street sales of craft products and tourist souvenirs. In 1988, a total of 20,120,308 border crossings were made from California to Tijuana, bringing close to $1 billion (Bringas 1991, 29). The number of border crossings remained close to that figure up to 2003 (Bank of Mexico 2003, cited by Bringas 2004). The relationship between indigenous street trading and tourism can be seen at the principal market sites visited by tourists and in the selection of goods the indigenous vendors offer.

In 1990 there were 5,234 street vendors in Tijuana, of which an estimated 500 to 700 were of indigenous origin (INI 1993, 38). Indigenous vendors in Baja California constitute a sector by themselves, in which a variety of migrant groups participate—including Zapotecos, Tlapanecos, Mazahuas, Purépechas, Nahuas, and Triquis—but Mixtecos form the largest component (83 percent).

According to some figures (INI 1993) and a case study carried out in Tijuana (Velasco 1996), commercial activity can be differentiated by gender and age: 69 percent of those who practice it are women, while only 31 percent are men; and almost a quarter of the vendors are children (between the ages of seven and sixteen).

For 1989, the case study cited above showed that 75.5 percent of the Mixtec women who were employed were working as street vendors (Velasco 1995a). Since the work schedule was designed to coincide with the flow of tourists from the United States, peak work times were on weekends and in the summer. This employment allowed women to combine their domestic responsibilities, including childcare, with work in the streets.

In 1994, the fierce competition in street trade was one factor that encouraged the organization of Mixtec women. They needed to unite in order to facilitate their work and reduce their disadvantages. One of the disadvantages of being indigenous—and this is especially true for indigenous women—is a lack of fluency in the Spanish language and inadequate reading and writing skills. They also lack business strategies in regard to tourism. Despite these limitations, in 1994 there were three organizations of Mixtec street vendors. These organizations succeeded in establishing permanent selling points and in gaining support for the purchase of equipment for their commercial activity (Velasco 1996).

Mixtec women occupied in the sale of craft products in Tijuana have an income of between $10 and $20 per day, a figure that increases on Sundays and during the summer. In 1994, they earned between $280 and $480 a month. From this sum they had to deduct the cost of the merchandise, which in most cases was financed exclusively out of their sales. Street vendors depend on tourists who have leisure time to visit Tijuana. Therefore, their income is sensitive to alterations in the flow of tourists and what goods tourists come to expect on the Mexican border.

In 1994, most of the female vendors had husbands. Those men worked as gardeners for Tijuana's middle class and were less frequently employed in California's nurseries. Their incomes ranged between $190 and $220 per month. They had been trained as gardeners when they worked for California's middle-class households. After years of living as undocumented workers in California, some of them decided to establish themselves in Tijuana. They were able to practice the same trade in the middle-class suburbs and to join their families who were established in the city. A systematic observation of the employment dynamic showed that, in some cases, children or groups of two or three adult family members assisted the men. These small groups often owned certain tools in common, such as an electric lawnmower. It is becoming more the norm for the workers to have vans to transport their equipment. As with street vending, this occupation follows a seasonal pattern. In summer the demand for gardeners increases, while during the autumn and winter it falls off considerably. This decrease in demand can be offset, however, by undocumented agricultural work on the other side of the border. Migrants may also take advantage of the idle months to return to their towns and villages of origin. It is a time to visit family and check on the condition of their own land.

There is evidence of Mixtec women working in maquiladora plants; these tend to be the younger daughters of the first generation of Mixtec immigrants in Tijuana. The women do factory work temporarily in order to deal with a particular family need (Lestage 1998, 22); however, this type of work is growing among the second generation of Mixtec migrants.

The above mentioned are the prevailing employment options in a majority of the border cities. Despite the lack of a general and systematic overview of informal-sector employment on the border, it is possible to point out certain characteristics of Tijuana (Browing and Zenteno 1993, 16–18; Zenteno 1993, 53). Tijuana presents a more heterogeneous employment market than Juárez and Matamoros, with an important informal and quasi-informal sector. This border city has the highest percentage of women working in the informal sector when compared with the other two border cities. In terms of employment, Tijuana has a unique profile among border cities. It has the lowest proportion of maquiladora employment (14 percent), the highest proportion of its workforce in the tertiary sector (62 percent), the highest percentage of its economically active population (EAP) in trade (21.5 percent), and the highest proportion of the population working in the United States (7.8 percent) (Browing and Zenteno 1993, 16–18).

Finally, as was mentioned before, Tijuana is a strategic point on the route of Mixtec migration along the agricultural corridor that runs through northwest Mexico into the southwest United States. Transnational agricultural markets attract hundreds of Mixtecos, who circulate between the new settlements on both sides of the border.

The Transnational Farm Labor Market: The San Quintin Valley and California. Transnational farm labor markets can be defined as a productive venue in which the three major elements of land, capital, and labor are provided within different national systems. According to Zabin (1993, 2), in the early 1980s there was an increase in economic integration between Mexico and the United States in fruit and vegetable production, specifically in the region of California and Baja California. In this period, foreign investment, trade, and migration had risen, yet at the same time wages had declined on both sides of the border.

Despite the fact that farmworkers on either side of the border carried out the same tasks, used the same technology, and worked for the same firms, there were differences in wage levels and stratification along gender and ethnic-group lines. At the end of 1980s, the fields of Baja California had a higher proportion of women and indigenous people, whereas mestizos and men made up a higher proportion in the Central Valley of California (Zabin 1993, 4). In the mid-1990s, men dominated the labor force (82 percent) in many rural counties of California (Martin and Taylor 2000, 21). Since that time, women and children have made their presence felt as relatives and as workers, though relative to the male labor force their numbers are small.

According to Morrison and Zabin (1994), the Mexican export agriculture of Baja California has played an important role in stimulating migration toward the agricultural regions of California. Once migrants reached San Quintin, transnational migration became a possibility because the distance of displacement was reduced and workers understood the agricultural production process. This was not necessarily the case when they left their places of origin.

This hypothesis about interdependence and hierarchization within and between agricultural markets in Baja California and California will be reconsidered in light of a brief description of the dynamics of the labor market in each area.

The San Quintin Valley: Economic and Ethnic Frontier. From the beginning of the twentieth century to the early 1960s, Baja California's main product was cotton. Toward the end of the 1950s, cotton production contracted worldwide. Thus, in the early 1960s, other crops, such as vegetables, began to increase as a production option in some regions along the border, such as the San Quintin Valley.

The valley extends across 36,941 km^2 of territory combining desert and seacoast on the Pacific shores of the Baja California peninsula. Since the 1960s, development and modernization have shaped the region. Large tracts of land are under irrigation, and the region benefits from its proximity to the United States. The farm labor market of this region has two main aspects: (1) California's consumer markets define the volume and quality of production, and (2) there is a flexible labor force—flexible in terms of when it can work and in its acceptance of the worst labor conditions. Until the 1980s, this labor force had been transient and willing to follow seasonal crops in northern Mexico and the southern United States, but ten years later settlement in the region changed the situation.

San Quintin Valley possesses fewer surface-water resources than the arid valley of Mexicali, and so its vitality is dependent on pumping groundwater from aquifers. The number one market crop produced in the valley is the tomato. Tomato cultivation uses the most acreage and employs the greatest number of workers during high season, May to August. Other crops cultivated include chilies, brussels sprouts, and, in recent years, strawberries (PRONASOL 1991; SAGARPA 2003–4). Technology is altering the customary relation between crops and seasons. For example, with large-scale nurseries, tomatoes are produced almost year-round.

During the 1980s, Baja California's agricultural economy boomed. The San Quintin Valley claimed 70 percent of the state's horticultural production, particularly tomatoes (Garduño, García, and Morán 1989, 43). Production increased throughout the 1990s, peaking in 1999; production was double that of 1992 (532,705 tons versus 267,996 tons) (SAGARPA 2003–4). In 1999 tomato production represented 79 percent of total production, leading the national output per hectare (PRONJAG 1999; SAGARPA 2003–4). In addition to benefiting from technological innovations, cultivation in the valley has the advantages of ideal climate conditions, water, government support, and a large labor force available to meet production requirements.

However, after 1999 the output of the San Quintin Valley decreased; in 2002–3, production fell by 39 percent. In addition, during this period the number of growers decreased 27 percent, from 691 in 1999–2000 to 502 in 2002–3 (SAGARPA 2003–4). In 2000, government officials pointed out that a decline in the availability of water was likely the primary cause of production decreases in the region. Some growers and farmworkers agreed with this assessment. Water is at the center of agricultural concerns in the San Quintin Valley. Everyone understands that the future of the region is tied to this resource. Responsible management of large-scale greenhouses means conserving as much water as possible. Greenhouse construction has increased in the last five years. Before 2000, only tomato production used nurseries; in 2003 new crops were added—cucumbers, strawberries, lettuce, chilies, squash, brussels sprouts, and flowers. As one drives along the transpeninsular highway, the line of plastic greenhouses seems to reach to the horizon.

Until 2003, the agribusiness in the valley relied primarily on immigrant and indigenous labor. This relationship began with the development of the San Quintin region. In the 1950s, migrants arrived from Michoacán, Guanajuato, Jalisco, Zacatecas, and Nayarit to pick cotton. Toward the end of the 1950s and into the early 1960s, as production shifted to the agro-industrial markets of fruits and vegetables, the origin of the migrants also began to change. There are reports that, from 1959 onward, the farmers of Baja California brought laborers from Sinaloa (Garduño, García, and Morán 1989, 39); most of these, in fact, were from the Mixteca Baja region of Oaxaca and had similar work experiences in Guerrero, Veracruz, and Sinaloa.

Starting in the 1960s, the principal type of housing for workers was camps. That continued until the beginning of 1980s when landowners gave small parcels of land to a few day workers; some groups of day workers organized colonias through land invasions. At the end of the 1990s, there were thirty-five labor camps registered, and only twenty-two were occupied by day workers. New colonias spread along the highway and across the San Quintin Valley. However, this settlement process did not change the link between export production and the indigenous migrant labor force. Actually, labor conditions in agriculture for migrant and ethnic groups continue to be a major concern. For example, in 2002, 86 percent of the indigenous-language speakers living in colonias within the San Quintin Valley were farmworkers. Farmworkers were approximately 50 percent of all people living in colonias. The percentage of indigenous-language speakers increases significantly among the inhabitants of farm camps, reaching 90 percent in some places (COLEF and CONEPO 2003). The Mixtec group continues to be the most important source of labor, even though Triquis, Zapotecos, and Nahuas have gained influence in farm labor activities over the last ten years. The settlement process has changed the migratory phenomenon. Although most of the farmworkers were born in other states, they can live either in camps or in colonias. Mixtecos were the pioneer settlers, and they are living mainly in colonias. In the farm camps, Triquis and Nahuas are increasing their presence, along with mestizos from Guerrero and Veracruz. Since the 1960s, growers have implemented a recruitment system that relies on the traditional networks of these migrant communities. They have used kinship, community, and ethnic ties to recruit hundreds of workers from their homelands. In 2001, it was possible to find groups of boys working in nurseries with contracts for less than six months. Some of them came from nontraditional areas of Oaxaca, like the coast, where they were hired for a specific time. Juan and Andrés, two boys in this group, describe themselves as unemployed in their hometowns. They helped their parents by taking care of the cattle or working in the fields. They don't expect to return to their homeland

and think that they will look for more work in the agricultural fields of La Paz, in southern Baja.

The settlement of thousands of migrants in different colonias has changed the way farmworkers are recruited. In the last three years, a complex system of worker recruitment has developed in the colonias through an independent transportation system. According to an independent bus driver, a grower may pay the drivers two dollars for each worker per day. The worker's assignments are flexible and based on the priorities of the growers. Paula, a Triqui woman, lives in the Nuevo San Juan Copala colonia with her husband in their own house; she left the Aguaje del Burro camp four years ago and still works for the same boss. Every morning she rides the bus to the strawberry fields. In February, when the interview was conducted, strawberries were not in season. Paula continued working but was assigned to pick cucumbers on another ranch. Her husband was working in California, and she expected him back home in a few months.

In both camps and colonias the farm labor contractor plays an important role in the labor conditions of the workers. Although most of the indigenous workers are bilingual, their command of Spanish is very limited; they depend on the contractor to evaluate them and their family circumstances and match them with the employer's requirements. Thus, this workforce is maintained by their own countrymen or the broker. This arrangement dilutes the responsibility of the boss toward the workers and often prevents contractual labor agreements.

In general, indigenous farmworkers occupy the lowest strata and perform the hardest tasks in the production process. They suffer from weak legal and trade union protection and have no job security (PRONJAG 1999). Since they are hired by the day or by the season, they receive only occasional work and can be fired without notice. Even after being hired by the same employer year after year, they do not receive any financial compensation when they are fired. Their period of employment depends on the type of crop, the availability of labor, and the mode of payment, which may be piecework, by task, or by day. In the case of piecework, payment corresponds to the worker's productivity. In one camp, I learned that a sixteen-year-old worker could pack twenty tins of tomatoes and a middle-aged woman could pack sixty boxes of cherry tomatoes in eight hours. The mayordomo told me: "If they work hard in the nursery, they can earn in one day the salary of one week in the field." In 2001, Fredy, an Oaxacan day worker who had lived in a camp for seven years, compared his work in a nursery to work in a field. He can pick tomatoes in a nursery for eight or nine months each year. In the field he worked only three or four months. Nursery production has a higher output per hectare, and it is organized in a consolidated space requiring a more intensive workforce. Fredy noted the higher salaries—one or two dollars per day more than fieldwork. Not only can he get more money per day, he can work more days per week. At the time, Fredy was working seven days a week. The high temperature inside the nurseries was mentioned by Fredy, and by other workers, as a great disadvantage. He complained of severe headaches. During the off-season, he works fewer hours at the nursery and has time to build houses in ejidos.

In 2002 farmworkers received $7–8 for an eight-hour day. Some workers and leaders complained about an arrangement in which the boss paid some fringe benefits each week along with the salary. This allowed employees to be terminated without notice and without financial compensation or termination benefits.

The permanent settlement in San Quintin gave the growers access to labor with permanent housing and better living conditions. Toward the end of the 1980s, colonias—subdivisions of house lots, which workers obtained through squatter invasions close to the farm camps—began to appear, along with two types of workers: those living in the colonias and those living in the camps. The residents of the colonias are no longer at the mercy of agricultural seasons. There are employment opportunities in services or in local trades, and they may also remain involved in agricultural production. As can be seen from table 2.2, the population working in agriculture has nearly tripled in the past decade. The table also shows that, in addition to the population increase in the colonias, other forms of housing have appeared that did not exist as an alternative a few decades ago—for example, cheap rooming houses known as *cuarterías*. The popularity of this type of housing can be explained in two ways. First, it is conceivable that growers established cuarterías as a way to evade the responsibility of permanent housing and the claims about poor living conditions in the camps. In 2002, an onion grower paid the farm-workers' cuartería rent as part of their wages in order to avoid complaints about the poor housing conditions in his camp. Second, cuarterías may be a strategy of the temporary workers, enabling them to work for different employers during the year. The appearance of both cuarterías and colonias marks a substantial change in agricultural labor relations and in the living conditions of the workers, as well as in the pattern of migration, since the demand for schools and health services indicates family migration. There are frequent references in the life stories to the difficulties associated with bringing the family to San Quintin. In 2002, 51 percent of the population living in colonias were women, and approximately 30 percent were under the age of 14 (COLEF and CONEPO 2003).

Interviews suggest that the changes in housing were the result of social mobilization. Sometimes this occurred through workers' initiative; at other

Table 2.2 Population Working in Agriculture in the San Quintin Valley, 1989–1999

Type of Population	1989		1999	
	Number	Percent	Number	Percent
Population living in camps	16,234	66.7	20,800	33.0
Population living in colonias*	8,120	33.3	35,820	56.5
Population living in cuarterías	—	—	6,650	10.5
Total agricultural population	24,354	100.0	63,270	100.0

Sources: 1989: INI 1989; 1999: PRONJAG 1999.
*For 1999 the figures include 3,380 permanent inhabitants of ejidos.

times, it occurred through a combination of initiatives by growers, *ejidatarios*, and workers, with government supervision. For example, in the mid-1990s, the colonia Nuevo San Juan Copala was founded by a small group of day workers at the Aguaje del Burro camp. Later, they were organized under Frente Indígena de Lucha Triqui (FILT). This new settlement of workers has mobilized to demand housing, services, and schooling for their children. At the present time, buses transport workers from the colonia to the agriculture fields. In addition, other types of employment have emerged within the colonias in the services and small trades. In 2002, 49 percent of the population in the colonias was working in industry and services (COLEF and CONEPO 2003). These new residents slowly reoriented their individual and collective life projects toward these new localities, leaving behind the image of the migratory day worker.

The seasonal migration to California from San Quintin, already mentioned by Morrison and Zabin (1994), is one of the aspects of regional mobility least documented in government sources and scholarly studies. Nevertheless, in-depth interviews with residents in colonias and in the farm camps indicate that mobility toward California is increasing regardless of the agricultural season. Florida and Oregon are frequent destinations for many husbands and sons. It was common to find that the parents of the middle-aged interviewees were in Oaxaca, while the sons were in California, Oregon, or Washington State. In 2003 approximately 8 percent of the people (primarily men) living in San Quintin were working in the United States (COLEF and CONEPO 2003).

The Fields of California. As mentioned previously, the Bracero Program was a milestone in the development of Mixtec migration toward agricultural California. As Stephen (2002, 92) stresses, despite the gap between the Mixtec bracero migration and the actual migration to the United States, for many inhabitants of hometowns like San Miguel Tlacotepec, in the Mixteca Baja, memories of pioneer braceros are still vivid. The old people remember those who went so far and came back to speak of "el otro lado" and dollars. Many migrants living in the border region remember stories about grandparents working or traveling to the United States. The word *bracero* appears in the accounts of women and men of different ages in different hometowns in Oaxaca. Although the flow of migration to the United States decreased at the end of the Bracero Program, there are many memories of that time.

Contemporary Mixtec migration appears to be linked to the transnational system of agricultural production established in the sixties. By the mid-1970s, the system had become centered in organizations like the United Fresh Fruit and Vegetable Association (UFFVA), which brought together agricultural concerns in the north of Mexico as well as in California, Arizona, and Florida (Besserer 1988, 130). An exemplary case is the tomato industry, which extends throughout the northwestern region of Mexico and across California and Florida. According to Krissman (1994a, 4), the transnational industry that produces tomatoes for the U.S. market extends across several states of northwestern Mexico (Sinaloa, Sonora, and Baja California), as well as to California and Florida. During the last three decades these states produced more than 90 percent of the tomatoes consumed in the United States.

At the close of the Bracero Program in 1964, a total of 50,000 workers, primarily Mexicans, were working in the annual tomato harvest. Nearly a decade later, in 1972, the number had fallen to 18,000. This figure was reduced even further in 1975 with the introduction of new technology in the production process, such as harvesters with electronic selectors (Friedland, Barton, and Thomas 1981, 41; Krissman 1994a, 5). Nevertheless, in the opinion of Martin and Taylor (2000, 20), the loss of jobs in California was offset by the growth of jobs in other farm commodities and by the substitution of hired workers for family workers on many farms. These scholars point out that technological innovation did not reduce the labor force, since workers were generally available and the cost involved in adapting plants and machines for the harvesting of some perishable commodities was prohibitively expensive (Martin and Taylor 2000, 20). It appears that the new technology has not been successful in reducing farm jobs in either California or Baja California.

During the 1990s most California farmworkers were Hispanic immigrants. The National Agricultural Workers Survey (NAWS) reported that between 1995 and 1997, 95 percent of the crop workers employed in nine California counties were foreign born, including 95 percent who were born in Mexico. During that period, these workers were, on average, male (82 percent), had a median age of thirty, were married (61 percent), with a family (60 percent), and had three children living with them. Approximately 53 percent of those interviewed had been in the United States for less than five years, and about half were unauthorized (Martin and Taylor, 2000, 21).

How, then, do Mixtec migrants fit into the farm labor market? As already noted, the presence of Mixtecos in the fields of the United States has been documented since the early twentieth century. Life stories gathered from interviewees confirm the findings of other studies on participation of fathers or other relatives in the Bracero Program (Besserer 1988; Kearney 1994; Stephen 1999). However, the mass presence of Mixtecos in agriculture—particularly in California—seems to date to the U.S. agricultural crisis of 1979–80. This crisis had the effect of reducing the nominal wage and increasing workloads and harassment of undocumented workers, which resulted in their displacement to other regions. According to Zabin (1992, 7) and Krissman (1994a, 10–13), a displacement of local agricultural workers was evident during the 1970s and 1980s. In agricultural states such as Florida, mestizo migrants, as well as white and Caribbean farmworkers, were replaced by undocumented field hands who had established a migratory pattern that tracked seasonal cultivation.

As has already been mentioned, Mixtecos have had an important presence in the tomato industry since the 1970s. They came to replace the mestizo migrant workforce, which shifted toward the Atlantic coast in an attempt to maintain wage levels (Krissman 1996, 3). In the 1980s Mexican workers (including Mixtecos) continued to move east, filling less desirable jobs when mestizos moved to better ones. Less experienced Mixtec workers, who tolerated poor working conditions, filled the jobs left by others (Krissman 1996; Zabin 1992, 2).

According to the *Survey of Oaxacan Village Networks in California Agriculture* (*SOVNCA*) (Runsten and Kearney 1994), in 1991 there were between 30,000 and 50,000 Oaxaqueños in California (excluding the Zapotecos and Mixtecos in Los Angeles). The survey estimated that 75 percent of the Mixtec population in California was employed in agriculture. It is possible that Mixtecos represented 5 percent of the state's agricultural workforce. Oaxacan migrants had diverse geographic origins; the source mentioned above registered 203 different sending localities from twenty-two districts of the Lower Mixteca. Juxtlahuaca, Silacayoapan, and Huajuapan districts accounted for 78 percent of the Oaxacan migrants in California.

Oaxaqueños in California are less dispersed than it appears. Although the same source registered an Oaxacan presence in 47 localities of California, with social networks extending to 100 localities, these migrants are concentrated in a few counties and localities. As table 2.3 indicates, approximately

Table 2.3 Location of Oaxacan Migrants in California

County	Percentage
Fresno	7.9
Kern	5.9
Madera	36.5
Merced	2.5
Monterrey	4.5
San Diego	13.3
Santa Barbara	5.4
Santa Clara	1.6
Santa Cruz	2.2
Tulane	3.5
Other locations	16.7
Total	100.00

Source: Runsten and Kearney 1994.

50 percent of the Oaxacan migrants in California reside in Madera and San Diego counties.

Madera County is located in the Central Valley of California. In 2000, with 123,109 residents, it was one of the less populous counties in the valley, with 44 percent of Hispanics. Martin and Taylor (1995, 7) state that since the mid-1980s, Mixtecos from Oaxaca have become the major group of entry-level workers, displacing mestizos from Michoacán who had worked in the vineyards. In 2003 Rogelio Méndez was living in San Diego and Tijuana. He remembers that in 1974 he came to Madera to pick grapes. "I learned English in Madera thanks to some *pochos.* I met them in the field and they taught me some English words; this was a tremendous advantage to me because later I found a better job in San Diego" (R. Méndez 1996).

Another interviewee, Rufino Domínguez, described the situation in Madera County a decade later: "In 1986 I arrived at Selma, close to Fresno because my fellow countrymen were there. They paid my 'coyote.' I was there three or four months, and then I moved to Livingston and to other rural towns. Madera was the heart of all this zone [Central Valley]. From there we moved to any place to find jobs in the vineyards or in the tomato fields" (Domínguez 1996).

On the other hand, San Diego is the most populous border county in southern California, with 2,813,833 inhabitants (2000). In the mid-1990s, the principal San Diego County farm crops were nursery products and flowers (55 percent), fruits and nuts (23 percent), and vegetables (11 percent)

(ACCR 1994, cited by Krissman 1996, 4). Annually, those activities occupied a workforce of approximately 20,000 people. Hothouse and flower
crops provided employment to both undocumented workers and documented cross-border commuters, whereas vegetable farming utilized undocumented workers who lived isolated in hidden ravines. The county of San
Diego requires approximately 11,300 workers for the harvest during May
and June each year. In the last decade the demand for workers has continued
owing to the increasing demand for ornamental plants, which represented 91
percent of the gross value of agricultural production in 2001 (ACCR 2001,
1). Many of the migrants moved to other states, such as Oregon, Washington, Florida, and New York; others settled in California or in Baja California. Fieldwork research has identified the commute from Tijuana or Ensenada to California fields or nurseries as an issue for the migrants. Francisco
is a Mixteco who has lived in Tijuana since the 1970s. For years, every day at
five in the morning he crossed the border to work in an Escondido nursery.
He used his brother's car each week for the round-trip and paid for the gas;
after the September 11 attack, he decided to live in Vista with relatives, thus
avoiding the congestion at the border and the increased scrutiny. Now he
visits his family in Mexico on weekends.

There is evidence that Mixtecos are concentrated in the least desirable
jobs, in terms of wages and working conditions, and not only in California but in Baja California (Zabin 1993, 125). At the end of the 1990s,
Sergio Méndez, an activist of FIOB, talked about labor conditions in harvesting the strawberry crop: "In Santa Maria (California), you can find about
15,000 fellow countrymen in the strawberry season. The town is about two
hours from Santa Barbara, on the coast, and it is very cold. Many people from
San Martin Peras go to pick strawberries; they speak a little Spanish, therefore it is very difficult to fight against the bosses. They said, 'We don't
want to earn $1.60, we want to earn $2.' Many of them left their relatives [wives and children] in San Quintin or Maneadero in Mexico" (S. Méndez 1996).

In the San Joaquin Valley, Mixtecos constitute the base and the nucleus of
piecework in the cultivation of citrus fruit, tomatoes, raisins, and wine grapes
(Krissman 1994a, 10). Rufino Domínguez talked about the problems of
piecework in the Central Valley: "In 1986, the minimum wage was $3.35,
now [1997] it is $4.25. However, when I say that they do not pay the
minimum wage it is because if you work by piece or by contract, you can do
twenty tins a day, one dollar each; you will earn $20 per day. The law states
that if you earn less than minimum wage, the boss must pay you the difference, and they do not do that. This is a minimum wage law violation"
(Domínguez 1996). In the mid-1990s, many farmworkers could earn between $5 and $6 per hour (Krissman 1994a, 10; Martin and Taylor 2000,

21). Interviewees constantly refer to real wages versus official wages. These complaints make more sense in the context of the differences in wages between sectors and the approximately 10 percent deterioration of wages between 1989 and 1998.[18] In San Diego, the average hourly earnings of farmworkers are about half of those performing manufacturing jobs, and they are employed for twenty-three weeks of farmwork each year (Krissman 1994a, 9). The rest of the year they need to move to find work in another place in the service sector, or return to Mexico.

Employment options beyond farmwork have become available to the Mixtec migrants. Information from the *SOVNCA* shows that some Oaxacan migrants work in restaurants and other industries (domestic work, ice cream sales, construction, gardening, hothouses, and factories). This is mainly the case in such counties as Los Angeles, Orange, Riverside, San Diego, San Francisco, Santa Clara, and Santa Cruz. Of the total of Oaxaqueños interviewed in 1991 (6,687), 61 percent were men, 17.3 percent were women, and 21.7 percent were children. It is unclear what family relationships these percentages indicate. However, the presence of children indicates either family migration is taking place or migrants are putting down roots, with a first generation of children being born in California.

Runsten and Kearney (1994) hypothesized that the Immigration Reform and Control Act of 1986 affected Mixtec mobility across the border before their settlement. While that hypothesis makes sense in general terms, it must be reviewed in light of the presence of women and children and the appearance of other informal occupations and of groups of residents of Mixtec origin in California. The ethnographic work accompanying *SOVNCA* about the networks of Oaxacan peoples revealed a nucleus of Mixtecos who had been living in California for more than twenty years, some with their own homes and some in the process of acquiring them. As Martin and Taylor (2000, 21) documented, between 1995 and 1997 approximately 61 percent of California crop workers were married, and most married workers had families, with an average of three children each. About 60 percent of farmworkers in the mid-1990s had their families living with them while they worked in California. Palerm (2000a) has described the settlement process in rural California. He found a process of colonization in McFarland (Kern County) by which migrants engaged the residents, participated in the local society, and transformed the old, rural California town into a new place. Although Palerm's research focused on mestizo immigrants from central Mexico, many of his findings correspond to the Mixtec experience. Since the end of the 1980s, some Mixtec men have brought their families to California under the family reunification program of IRCA. Maura Salazar, a Mixtec woman, arrived in California in 1987 with her husband and three children. The husband's relatives lent them a room in a *traila*.

In 1986 or 1987, we returned to California. This time, we brought four children with us, two boys and two girls, and we left three girls there in Mixtepec with my mama. We arrived in California, and we stayed in Arvin. . . . Because his niece and his brother-in-law were already living there, we went to the home of one of my husband's relatives. They let us stay in a small room, and there we were, all piled in together . . . it was a traila.[19] Then, little by little, we were working and putting together money to rent another house. . . . We all were working—adults and children alike. After a year, I began to worry about the girls who had stayed behind [in the pueblo]. I talked to my husband, and told him, "Either you go or I go, whichever of the two, one of us is going to go, and the other is going to stay here with the other children." Then he said: "I'm going to go because you can't, you're a woman. I'm a man, and so I can go. You stay with the children who are here." I told him, "Well, that's good if you go." (Salazar 2001)

The entire family worked pruning grapevines, and after a few months they were able to pay rent for a room. Three years later, Maura's husband died; she has chosen to continue working with her children in California. The legal situation of the family members varies. She and two children have resident visas; three others do not have any papers. Maura saved money and bought a small house in Lamont. Her expectations are to become a U.S. citizen and to have citizenship for her children as well. She does not want to return to San Juan Mixtepec, Juxtlahuaca. She thinks that there are more opportunities for her children and herself in the United States.

Maura's experience is common in the settlement process of many Mixtec families in California, confirming the findings of Palerm (2000a). In 2001, the Farmworker Women's Organization in California and the Indigenous Binational Front organized an indigenous women's workshop in Lamont, California. For two days, roughly eighty Mixtec and Triqui women discussed their needs as immigrants in California. They were living in Madera, Fresno, Arvin, and Lamont with their families, working on farms. They were as interested in housing, health, and school services as in the agricultural working conditions. A third of them had lived in the United States for eleven years or more. Language problems and legal status were two barriers to access to public services. A small group of indigenous English-speaking young women attended this meeting; they are part of the new, younger Mixtec and Triqui communities in California.

The preceding overview of Mixtec migration to California and Baja California has given special attention to transnational labor markets. The following presents another aspect of the transnationalization process involving

Mixtec migrants: the migration policies of Mexico and the United States, with particular attention to their impact on Mixtec migration.

Mixtec Migration and Policies to Control National Frontiers

Mexicans have been immigrating to the United States since the mid-nineteenth century, when the United States took more than half of the Mexican territory. On the new frontier, those who had formerly been Mexicans were now potential U.S. citizens, while those living further south found themselves converted into border inhabitants. Once the new political and administrative border had been established, a certain period of time and infrastructure were necessary to institutionalize it along the confines of the new frontier states. According to Durand (1994, 86), in 1884 the introduction of the cross-border railroad was a definitive step in the process of worker migration between the two countries.

In the twentieth century the border took on even greater importance with the consolidation of each nation-state. At different stages in the last century, each country assumed its distinctive position; but the image of the border as a "swinging door," as Durand (1994) describes it—with a constant to-and-from movement resulting from the combination of a demand for labor on one side and a labor source on the other—became more and more defined. In the United States, the national border acquired a political meaning as a region of strategic importance for national sovereignty, whereas the Mexican government adopted a laissez-faire attitude favoring free transit and nonintervention (Durand 1994, 65). Thus, government policies concerning the migrants who cross the Mexico–U.S. frontier have originated primarily in the United States, in the form of legal provisions on immigration and through policing and military activities, starting with the creation of the U.S. Border Patrol in 1924. Mexican policies concerning migrant populations go back only two decades. However, in 1917 Mexico entered into a bilateral agreement with the United States on the recruitment of workers. This was part of a package of decisions made in response to a formal request for workers, which the United States needed during the first half of the twentieth century. The following section examines how Mixtec migration was affected by some of the laws and programs implemented by both nation-states.

U.S. Migration Policies

The Bracero Program is an appropriate political and legal starting point for understanding Mixtec migration to the United States. This program was aimed at attracting temporary workers, principally for agriculture and the railroad. Under this program, the first pioneering Oaxacan migrants were prepared for life and work beyond the border; they established the basis for migrant networks (Besserer 1988; A. Flores 2000; Runsten and Kearney 1994; Stephen 1999; Velasco 1990, 1995a). However, Oaxacan migrants were not as numerous or as visible as those from other states with a migratory tradition to the United States going back to the beginning of the twentieth century. In 2001, almost four decades after the end of the Bracero Program, the participation of Oaxaqueños in the program became an issue, when 839 former Oaxacan bracero workers complained that their savings in the Peasant Saving Fund (Fondo de Ahorro Campesino) were not given to them at the end of program.[20]

The Immigration and Nationality Act Amendments of 1965 abolished the national origins quota system. But it placed a ceiling on Western Hemisphere immigration (120,000) for the first time. Further amendments in 1976 applied a limit of 20,000 immigrants per country to Western Hemisphere nations, including Mexico. In 1978 the quota was abolished again, and a worldwide limit of 290,000 people was established. In 1989 this ceiling was reduced to 270,000 immigrants (Vernez and Ronfeldt 1991, 2). During those three decades, Mexican migration continued. Some studies carried out in the 1970s report a significant presence of migrants from the states of Oaxaca, Morelos, Guerrero, Zacatecas, Hidalgo, and Michoacán in California agriculture (Commission on Immigration 1991). During the same decade Mixtec migrants became an increasing presence in California's agricultural fields, following a pattern of undocumented mobility organized through agricultural transnational systems (Krissman 1994a, 1994b; Zabin 1993); more recently this has been shown to be the case in Oregon as well (Stephen 2002).

Between 1979 and 1981 a U.S. Congress Select Commission on Immigration and Refugee Policy (SCIRP) carried out a wide-ranging public review of national policies on immigration. During the subsequent five years there were numerous attempts to turn the recommendations of this commission into law. Finally, these policies took form in the Immigration Reform and Control Act (IRCA) of 1986, also known as the Simpson-Rodino Act. Its main purpose was to reduce illegal immigration by means of three strategies: (a) legalizing those immigrants already in the country through two amnesty programs; (b) reducing the future flow of immigrants to the United States through the imposition of fines on employers hiring illegal migrants; and (c) strengthening the U.S. Border Patrol. The amnesty provided by this law made special provisions for agricultural workers under the Special Agricultural Worker (SAW) program, requiring of them an uninterrupted stay of five years in the country in order to qualify for amnesty (Bean, Edmonston, and Passel 1990, 3). This law had several observable effects on Mixtec migration. According to Runsten and Kearney (1994, 36), nearly half of the Oaxacan migrants legalized their presence in the United States under the law. The same authors note that—in contrast with what happened to other migrant groups from central Mexico (i.e., from Zacatecas, Jalisco, and Michoacán), who started a process of permanent residence under the IRCA—what the Mixtecos achieved was limited to the legalization of their circulation as migrants, facilitating entry and exit from the country corresponding to agricultural seasons. The law gave them greater opportunities of movement across the border, without improving the stability of their living or employment conditions. Runsten and Kearney conclude that the length of stay or establishment of migrants of Oaxacan origin in the United States has more to do with the vicissitudes of the labor markets than with their legal status. As long as their mode of incorporation in the labor market is through seasonal work, their long-term settlement is bound to be difficult. Nevertheless, as was noted in the previous section, the same survey in California showed that in 1991 there was a Oaxacan population occupied in work activities other than agriculture, even though urban areas were not included in the survey. The presence of children (22 percent) suggests migration patterns involving families, who require such things as permanent dwellings, health services, and education. During this period Tijuana served as a home for the families of Mixtec workers who were legalizing their situation in California. Wives and children waited in the Mixtec colonias in this border city, in the hope that their husbands would be able to get them across the border and reunite families in the new destination. The effects of these changes in the law are only now beginning to be evaluated. Stephen (1999, 124) believes that in populations of Mixtec and Zapotec workers in Oregon, such provisions set off legal conflicts among these indigenous migrant families, since not all members achieved the legal status of agricultural workers. The same scholar (2002, 109) states that the SAW program of 1986 had a gender-selective effect, as most of the agricultural workers were men.

The double logic, economic and political, governing the opening and closing of the door is exemplified by the simultaneous signing of the North American Free Trade Agreement (NAFTA) between Mexico and the United States and the initiation of Operation Gatekeeper in 1994.[21] The section in NAFTA on commercial exchange excluded Mexican labor, leaving the border open for capital and merchandise and closed—even through military means—to the flow of labor. Concerns about control of the border, and the electoral potential of the Mexican population in the United States, were expressed in the Illegal Immigration Reform and Immigrant Responsibility

Act of 1996. This restricted social assistance (medical services and social benefits, such as unemployment insurance and food and housing allowances) to U.S. citizens and withheld benefits from legal resident migrants and undocumented immigrants. The act does not modify the legal status of those migrants who obtained residence under the amnesty program for agricultural workers introduced under the IRCA; what it does modify is access to the federal and state welfare systems, thus eroding migrant living conditions in the United States. Because of the prohibition on obtaining legal status for undocumented relatives living in the United States, family members came to have unequal legal status.

At the end of 2000, President Clinton authorized a special "sunset provision," the Legal Immigration and Family Equity Act, which provided another chance to those who had a family member with legal status and who had missed the January 1998 deadline to qualify for permanent residency. Through a payment of $1,000, children and women could apply for legal residency (Stephen 2002, 107). At that time, some of the Mixtec families in the Colonia Obrera in Tijuana hosted relatives who were saving money to apply for residency and return to their California home.

Mexican Policies

The loss of more than half of its territory during the second part of the nineteenth century put Mexican governments in a state of alert over border issues. This alertness gave way to unconcern, even passivity, once the twentieth century got under way. The new posture was limited to fighting for free transit and not intervening into what happened to migrants in U.S. territory (Durand 1994, 87). From the 1920s to the 1960s, there were some government initiatives, such as programs aimed at facilitating workers' return and their monetary remittances, but these were not precise policies reflecting a long-term vision of migration. The question arises: Was the attitude of passive concern intended to improve relations between the two countries, or did it arise from Mexico's own internal dynamics? In any case, the attitude seems to have changed beginning in the 1980s.

In accordance with the Mexican government's desire to ensure the free transit of migrants, the Paisano Program was established in 1989. Recognizing the abuse and extortion to which migrants were often subjected when returning to Mexican soil, the scheme was intended to bring about fair and dignified treatment of Mexicans entering and leaving the country (Bustamante 1994, 260). It also dealt with the practical implications of the free transit of individuals accompanied by goods and merchandise. Automobiles were of particular importance since they tended to remain in Mexico after their owners returned to the United States. This apparently innocent flow of vehicles was, in fact, a means of creating fleets of automobiles available for legalization in Mexico. In the Mixteca, fleets of taxis materialized from vehicles brought in under the program and legalized collectively during the 1990s. In 1994, FIOB founded 8 Venado Garra de Tigre (the name of a Mixtec king) transport cooperative in Juxtlahuaca, Oaxaca, with fifteen vans from the United States (Pimentel 1994).

In that decade, the Program for Mexican Communities Abroad (PCME) was organized for the purpose of establishing or strengthening links between migrants of Mexican origin in the United States. This incorporated several subprograms aimed at workers, students, businesspeople, and general populations of different economic levels (Goldring 1997, 7). Until 1998 this program had created more than 300 clubs in ten U.S. states (Contreras, Sánchez, and Calderón 1999, 160). While the Paisano Program was focused on free movement, this later program (PCME) centered on the maintenance of links and cohesion among Mexican migrant communities through consulates in the United States. Both the scope and strategies of these programs maintained a traditional focus on territorial action of the Mexican state and evolved during a decade of earthshaking transformations that culminated in the 1988 presidential elections, as Durand points out (1994, 97). It was at that time that the political-electoral potential of the Mexican population in the United States began to be appreciated.

In the 1990s, the most radical changes came about in the attitude of the Mexican government regarding Mexican migration. The first occurred with the constitutional reform of 1995, which declared Mexican nationality by birth to be permanent and "non-renounceable." This reform, which went into effect in 1998, allowed Mexicans who had lost their nationality by acquiring that of another country to recover it; at the same time it permitted Mexicans living abroad to acquire the nationality of the other country in order to attain their rights in that country without automatic loss of Mexican nationality, as was the case in the past (SRE 1998, 41). This reform accorded liberty of transit on Mexican soil, labor rights, incorporation into the fiscal regime, social security, military service, and property-owning rights to persons of Mexican origin who had acquired another nationality (SRE 1998, 18). The second change was the electoral reform bill, which held out the possibility of migrants with Mexican nationality being able to vote in presidential elections while living in the United States. Although the proposal did not become law, it set off a wave of mobilizations by Mexican communities in the United States and a discussion at the national level in Mexico; an important precedent was established for future presidential elections. In 2003 President Fox made a commitment to approve electoral reform.

As Goldring has pointed out (1997), those programs and legal reforms, taken as a whole, express the will of the Mexican state to review its relationship with Mexican migrants outside the national territory. The government promotes migrant mobility beyond national boundaries, their residence abroad, and the recovery of lost Mexican nationality. The effects of these policies on the Mixtec migrant community are still being defined and require further study. It is a fact that no article of these policies has made distinctions regarding indigenous migrants. Neither in language nor in procedures have these programs taken into account that quality that, since 1991, the Mexican constitution has recognized as intrinsic to the Mexican nation: its multiethnicity.

Projects of a local nature have been added to these programs and legal reforms. Since the late 1980s and throughout the 1990s, the state governors of Oaxaca have visited the Mixtec and Zapotec communities in California and promoted the establishment of associations or the signing of cooperation and investment agreements between migrant organizations and state government institutions. In 1998 the Migrants' Support Trust (Fideicomiso de Apoyo al Migrante) was set up in Oaxaca with the participation of twelve Oaxacan migrant organizations in the United States, the Federal Ministry of Social Development (SEDESOL), and the state government of Oaxaca. The purpose of these organizations was to channel migrants' remittances to family members back home and to finance small-scale community development projects in the communities of origin (Contreras, Sánchez, and Calderón 1999, 161). In 1999, this institutionalization process was taken a step further. The Oaxacan government opened an office to attend to Oaxacan migrants both in Mexico and in abroad. In the opening years of the twenty-first century, the old image of migrants who abandon their land without a backward glance no longer reflected reality. The amount of migrants' remittances, and likewise the political capital it represents, has had a considerable impact on government initiatives involving Mexicans who reside and work in the United States.

Crisscrossing the Mexico–U.S. Border

The traditional image of places of origin as impoverished regions with few employment options and of places of destination as little more than workplaces may turn out to be far too simplistic. The migration process has modified the living conditions of the hometowns and has created a settlement process on both sides of the border. According to the hypothesis of the articulation of modes of production, the workforce bases its social reproduction on its places of origin and generates an economic surplus in the places of migration where capital is invested. Research on Mixtec migration does not completely support this hypothesis. The seasonal farm labor immigrant fits this hypothesis, but the settlement of thousands of Mixtecos in Tijuana, San Quintin, and different counties in rural and urban California contradicts it. At this time the new settlements in California are as important for the social reproduction of the Mixtecos as the hometowns. Despite allegiances to hometowns, the new settlers are making greater investments in their new locations by buying homes and cars. They are filing immigration papers and sending their children to school.

The story of Mixtec migration would be incomplete if one focused only on the dynamics of the labor markets, leaving aside the effect of migratory policies, particularly those of the United States. Policies affect frontiers that are economically permeable (and that tend to be increasingly so in the wake of recent international commercial agreements) but politically impermeable. This contradiction causes different transnational processes to be woven into the daily lives of migrants; both factors (the labor markets and the migratory policies) are structuring mechanisms of the migrants' social agency in that they affect the migrants' courses of action. We also need to ask how migrants themselves have experienced this process of transnationalization. How do they experience the contradiction between the logic of capital and government migration policies? What other contradictions do they experience, and how do they respond collectively? How do they generate knowledge in the course of such experiences? Who are they as a collectivity in historical terms? At the same time, how do they modify the frontiers of their ethnic identity? We are now in the terrain of what some authors have called "transnationalism from below" (Goldring 1997; Portes 1998; Radcliffe, Laurie, and Andolina 2002), meaning the process defined by the action of the migrants themselves as transnational agents.

It is perhaps too early to assess the effects of U.S. immigration legislation on Mixtec migration. For the moment, I shall merely sketch four possible lines of future research: (1) the process of "citizenization" that the new law is fostering as a condition for receiving welfare benefits, and the impact this process will have on migratory patterns and on the relationship these migrant populations maintain with their places of origin and arrival; (2) the deterioration in living conditions that will be brought about by the loss of health services and food programs for those migrants who fail to qualify or do not file their applications for citizenship; (3) the important process of Mixtec settlement on both sides of the border and its consequences for their future; and (4) the climate of racism and xenophobia that prevails, especially in California and particularly after the terrorist attack, and actions taken by organized migrants in their own defense.

After September 11, 2001, U.S. national security focused notorious attention on border enforcement policies. The 1994 trend to push the migration flow into risky areas, such as Arizona's desert, continued with more emphasis and resources. After the terrorist attack, some Mixtec commuters in Tijuana chose to move their homes to California to avoid the longer queues to cross the border. Mario, a Mixteco living in Tijuana, moved to Chula Vista in San Diego. Crossing the border every day had become more difficult even with a work permit. "It was a nightmare crossing the border every morning. I had to wake up at four in the morning to arrive at Chula Vista by seven o'clock and then went back to my home at night." In 2003, Mario and his wife decided to rent an apartment in Chula Vista but maintain their house in Tijuana. The family is separated. Mario, his wife, and one of their children live in Chula Vista. Their oldest daughter lives in Tijuana and cares for two younger children. Every weekend the California family returns to Mexico, where Mario, his wife, and all of the children enjoy being together for two days.

3

Crossing the Border
From Hometown Associations to
Transnational Organizations

Seen in the context of international migration, Mixtec migration is a recent phenomenon. The first generation of Mixtec residents on the Mexican border and in the United States has flourished only in the last twenty years. For this reason, the emergence of hometown associations and other forms of organization among the Mixtecos in the last two decades deserves special attention. This chapter will define another facet of Mixtec transnationalism: the migrants' ethnic identity project and their capacity to resist the structuring forces of the labor markets and the state policies of control.

The following pages offer an analysis of the emergence of the Mixtec migrant organizations and their alliances with Zapotecos and Triquis during the process of migration and settlement in California and Baja California. A longitudinal perspective on the group of Oaxacan migrant organizations under study allows us to appreciate the transformation of some hometown associations and project committees into more complex organizational forms and brings into focus the dynamics of the alliances and the key events in this process. Such a view may also facilitate a greater understanding of the leading role of various transnational pan-ethnic organizations.

A Genealogy of the Mixtec Organizations on the Mexico–U.S. Border

The systematization of written records, together with the biographical narratives, allows us not only to build a chronology of the migrant organizations but also to account for their emergence and their development into the present regional formation. The organizations are groups formed by migrants of common origin, in the sense either of coming from a particular locality or of having a shared ethnic identity; they may be Mixtecos, Zapotecos, or Triquis. In constructing the chronology of the development of the migrant associations,[1] the ethnic configuration becomes redefined in terms of participants' field of social relations and geographic locations. I define the ethnic configuration as a constellation of related social categories that are differentiated ethnically. As will be shown, social class and national differentiation introduce more complexity into that configuration.

The strategy adopted was to follow the life stories of the organizations' leaders, supported both by written records (internal documents of the organizations and newspapers) and participant observation. The chronology covers the period of the leaders' lives (with an average age of forty) and the existence of the associations from the 1980s onward.

The chronology is divided into five phases characterized by the specific direction of migration, adopted forms of association, and changes in ethnic configuration. For the first phase (1950–59), I reconstruct the significant events in the towns and villages of origin before the migration. The second phase (1960–85) is marked by departure from the place of origin—the experience of urban life in Mexico City or of agricultural work in Veracruz or in northern Mexico, and the beginning of migration to the southwestern United States. This period concludes with the appearance of the Comité Cívico Popular Tlacotepense (CCPT). The third period, characterized by migration to the United States, involves the experience of undocumented migrants and the emergence of the Caja Unidad Democrática and the Comité Cívico Popular Mixteco (CCPM) on California soil (1986–90). The fourth phase introduces interethnic alliances as a consequence of international migration and includes the formation of the Frente Mixteco-Zapoteco Binacional (FM-ZB) (1991–93). Finally, new forms of organization mark the fifth period, including an attempt to institutionalize the transnational on a political plane with the formation of the Frente Indígena Oaxaqueño Binacional (FIOB) (1994–97). Each of these chronological periods corresponds to the appearance of a new form of organization as well as a novel ethnic configuration. In early 2001, the Federación Oaxaqueña de Comunidades y Organizaciones Indígenas de California (FOCOICA) was founded in Los Angeles. Nineteen hometown associations and sports clubs took part in its founding—most of them Zapotec. Mixtecos were represented by the FIOB, the Nueva Alianza Oaxaqueña (NAO), and the Red Internacional Indígena Oaxaqueña (RIIO). There was one Mixtec-Zapotec confederation, the Coalición de Comunidades Indígenas de Oaxaca (COCIO), and one Zapotec, the Unión de Comunidades Serranas de Oaxaca (UCSO). Eight cultural and educational organizations with community roots also attended this meeting (Rivera and Escala 2004, 158).

The geographic dispersion of the associations across this region led me to seek an empirical thread with theoretical significance. Thus, of all the organizations existing in the border region in the mid-1990s, I chose the Frente Indígena Oaxaqueño Binacional (FIOB) as the most typical transnational migrant organization at that time. Nevertheless, at the beginning of 2000, FIOB suffered an internal crisis that affected its profile. The crisis was rooted in its organizational structure and new interests in a transnational context.

The work of reconstructing origins led me to research the founding of the Comité Cívico Popular Tlacotepense (CCPT), in San Miguel Tlacotepec in the heart of the Oaxacan Mixteca Baja in the 1980s. It is partly a matter of chance that my reconstruction centered on the organizational experience of the group of leaders who originated in that location and who took part in forming the CCPT. This committee can be viewed as like a lake from which a number of different rivulets flow and join another lake among many other lakes that are in the process of being formed; the second lake is the FIOB. For these reasons, the narrative begins with the evolution of the organization and migration experience in the town of San Miguel Tlacotepec, cradle of the Comité Cívico Popular Tlacotepense.

The Hometown: San Miguel Tlacotepec, 1950–1959

The name San Miguel Tlacotepec is a mixture of Spanish and Nahuatl, the indigenous language. (During the Spanish colonial period, towns were often named by combining words from both languages. Tlacotepec means "between hills" in the Nahuatl language.) By 1950 it had 2,695 inhabitants. It became part of the Juxtlahuaca district in the heart of the highlands of the Mixteca Baja at almost 2,000 meters above sea level. After five decades, the population had increased to 3,525 and included the inhabitants of the municipal agencies. In the year 2000, San Miguel Tlacotepec had the lowest percentage of Mixtec speakers in Justlahuaca district and one of the most stable population growth rates over the last five decades in the district.

In the 1950s, life in San Miguel Tlacotepec, according to the migrants' own accounts, showed a pattern of social differentiation between the indigenous and mestizo inhabitants and between caciques and landless peasants, similar to patterns documented for other indigenous regions of Mexico.[2]

> When my parents got married, for some reason my father went to live in my mother's village. From there, we left because my mother did not have a piece of land. My uncles were poor. It is correct to say that the owners of the lands were caciques, people of *razón*, mestizos, even direct descendants of Spaniards. No indigenous person had a piece of land in the village's downtown. The indigenous were in the communal lands on the hillside, where it was only rocks. . . . The houses on the main streets of the hometown were for mestizos or whites. (R. Méndez 1996)

The migration of families wends its way, like a procession of pilgrims, from one locality to another. The establishment of new villages throughout the region often resulted from the search for a plot of land on which to establish themselves with their cattle. The loss of lands owing to abuse from the wealthier indigenous, referred to as *caciquillos,* or from local whites or mestizos, is a constant theme in the stories told by the inhabitants of these localities.

Rogelio Méndez recounted a process of progressive indebtedness among some of the poorest inhabitants, as mestizo usurers gradually usurped lands, animals, and other property in restitution for unpaid debts. Méndez's accounts have been corroborated by studies in indigenous regions. Migrants often incurred debts by spending hard-earned money on civic-religious festivals. Such debts would eventually consume the entire family inheritance, with consequent loss of its land.[3]

Along with the plundering of land and, from the migrants' point of view, its inexplicable exhaustion, the interviewees recalled how official posts in the municipal authority were controlled by a small coterie, serving as pivots of domination and ethnic discrimination in Mixteca localities like San Miguel Tlacotepec. The posts of *síndico* (an officer with specific responsibilities), mayor, and, above all, secretaries[4] appear as a source of conflict among the inhabitants. Local administration has forever been recognized as the business of "people of reason," not suitable for "Indians." This gives us insight into the nature of the bureaucratic elite who ruled village life. Control of lands and authority along with mastery of Spanish as the official language in administrative procedures are the main instruments of discrimination and domination in the villages. Local government secretaries acquired an awesome power in the eyes of these migrants, who reconstruct them in their narratives as characters with a mastery of written and spoken Spanish.

> Mestizos always have had the power; they always take the síndico, president, and secretary posts. The rest of people used to be *regidores* of this or *regidores* of that, or mayor of the church key. It was compulsory to occupy those posts. . . . Mestizos administered and made decisions; they manipulated the indigenous *principales* [local gentry] to their own interests. . . . In Oaxaca, secretaries manipulated everything; they circulated the post between friends, cousins, and other relatives. It is like a little PRI (Partido Revolucionario Institucional). They never leave the power to the people. (R. Méndez 1996)

In this scenario, traditional authority appears in the figures of the principales, reconstructed paradoxically as instruments of the mestizo authorities and at the same time as figures of prestige in community life. In San Miguel Tlacotepec, as in most of the towns and villages of the Mixteca, the system of public responsibilities created individual and collective obligations, functioning as a mechanism of recognition and acceptance of the individual as part of the community as well as a system of parallel authority in the local or regional government.[5]

According to the life stories, forms of discrimination and domination are articulated not only within indigenous villages or communities like San Miguel Tlacotepec but in the framework of municipal or regional systems. The politico-administrative status of a particular town or village distinguishes the members of that community from others whose villages have a lower or higher position in the hierarchy of the region. To live in a small and less accessible town introduces another factor of discrimination, relegating its inhabitants to the category of "mountain-dwellers," "dirty," or "ignorant people."

> My town is San Miguel Cuevas in the Juxtlahuaca district. It is a small village in the middle of the hills, and when we—people of the town— came to Santiago Juxtlahuaca, we heard words like *indio huarachudo,* or "dirty people coming from the mountain" or "mountaineer." We felt despised, and for me it was so painful to hear the people say these words without looking at the cause. They named us "ignoramus, or ignorant person" or "dirties" just because they were mestizo people or even Mixtecos living in the head district. (R. Domínguez 1996)

There is also a religious hierarchy. San Miguel Tlacotepec was established as a head parish in the regional system (*cabecera parroquial*). It has a higher status than the other villages in the organization of the civic-religious festivals and in the administrative formalities of religious ceremonies. The missionary enterprise and its institutional geography also contributed to differentiating the status of the communities of the Mixteca, as did, in later times, the educational policies of twentieth-century Mexican governments.

Ethnic discrimination also seems to be tied to individual and collective loss of lands, election rigging by the local authorities, and the use of the Mixtec language. Two of these—loss of lands and use of the language— involve both the domestic and extra-domestic spaces, the public and private domains. Loss of land is mentioned in some cases as the cause of the disintegration of the extended family, the parentela (groups linked by a common surname such as Méndez, Sierra, Ramos). In other cases, loss of land refers to the cause of the people's peregrinations between different villages and towns of the region.

Leaders and other migrants recognize language as the most important element of ethnic differentiation in hometown life. The life stories frequently describe the many forms of discrimination resulting from use of the Mixtec language. The dilemma over use of the language makes itself felt in public spaces—for example, in elections for local authorities or in classrooms—and also in the private spaces of family life. The memory of discrimination associated with the language goes back to early childhood; this gives it an affective force.

Juan Lita remembers "Tlacotepec was a parochial and municipal center; therefore the Church and the educational programs came to disturb us. Both played a part in destroying the indigenous language. I remember when we were in Tlacotepec's school, the teacher said to us, 'You are not indigenous . . . here there are only mestizos.' The indigenous language was the loser" (Lita 1996). Such discrimination is revealed in the most vividly remembered childhood experiences: relations with other children, with schoolteachers, priests, family, and community members.

> I don't teach my children Mixtec because there was a time in the south—when I was a girl—that a teacher arrived, and he wouldn't allow us to speak Mixtec with our children. It was because he said that our children didn't need Mixtec. I believe he was thinking that they wouldn't ever use Mixtec, and it was better to teach them to speak Castilian or Spanish, or any other language. That's why all of us denied our language to our children; we didn't even talk about it. All my family were Spanish speakers; we didn't speak Mixtec. Only my mother spoke Mixtec, but she couldn't speak it with us—only with her brothers and sisters. (R. Hernández 1994)

In summation, examining ethnic configuration in the places of origin—specifically in San Miguel Tlacotepec—reveals a hierarchical social system organized around the control of land, election of authorities, use of languages, and the status of the particular locality in the political-administrative system. The indigenous and mestizo are positioned in terms of these factors. Other differences are subtler to the eyes of outsiders, such as the designations "mountain people" and "town people." Thus, the basic indigenous-mestizo dichotomy in the social universe becomes more complex as other shades of differentiation are introduced, such as identity expressed in spatial terms. The "mountain people" are more indigenous than the "town people," although they speak the Mixtec language; those from the town center are distinguished from those on the outskirts, although they live in the same town. Those living in the center of the towns, within the zone of the church and the municipal offices, are not only described as mestizo but are also regarded as direct descendants of the Spaniards. The hillsides flanking the towns, or their outskirts, are, on the other hand, the preserve of the indigenous people. The centralized areas under Spanish and mestizo dominion include the church, the municipal administration, and the commercial center. The life stories about the places of origin portray them as being extraordinarily complex, very different from the image of indigenous communities as possessing a high degree of homogeneity. The elements described are arenas for competition and social conflict, which occur constantly within and between communities. Political life is defined by the election of civil and religious authorities, the activity of the political parties, in particular the Partido Revolucionario Institucional (PRI), and the community works, giving rise to factions within the community that often affect family relationships.

Migration to Veracruz, Mexico City, and the Fields of Sinaloa: The Comité Cívico Popular Tlacotepense, 1960–1985

The journey to Veracruz is a recurring memory in family histories of migration. During the 1950s and early 1960s, the departure of parents from San Miguel Tlacotepec to Veracruz to cut the sugarcane was an event repeated again and again. In those days the asphalt road that now links Huajuapan de León and Juxtlahuaca did not exist. The journey along mountain paths from San Miguel Tlacotepec was made on foot or on beasts of burden, usually donkeys. Veracruz was an important city on the migration route of the Mixtecos who now inhabit the Mexico–U.S. border.[6] Actually, Veracruz forms part of the childhood memories of some Mixtecos who founded the Comité Cívico Popular Tlacotepense (CCPT). "When I was about seven years old, I had to go with my parents to the state of Veracruz. There I attended the first two years of grade school, and I cut cane and worked as a helper. At the time we left, there weren't roads [between the towns]; we had to go by burro for two days just to reach Huajuapan [de León] and then take the bus to Veracruz" (Pimentel 1995).

Some Mixtecos were born in Veracruz or spent time there when very young. Once migration to that state had become established, news about employment opportunities in Mexico City spread among the migrants.

> I feel like I'm from San Miguel Tlacotepec even though I was born in Omealca, Veracruz. . . . My parents are from San Miguel, but my mother was born in Soledad de Doblado, Veracruz. In my family, migration has been going on for a very long time, and that is why my mother was born there but my father comes from San Miguel Tlacotepec. When I was around twelve years old, I was in the school in my town. My parents took me to Veracruz. I stayed there until I was seventeen or eighteen years old. Homesickness for the land brought us back again to San Miguel Tlacotepec, to the Mixteca region. There, within a few years, we lost my father, and we had to emigrate. At that time, a new wave of migration was starting to the northwestern part of the country. In those days, the Oaxacans

were migrating to the states of Sinaloa and Sonora. We, too, followed that migratory flow, which took us to the state of Sinaloa, sometime around 1971. (Morales 1996)

Migrants tell of the journeys they made to Mexico City by train during the 1960s. In the same decade, the Pan-American Highway was extended, crossing the Mixteca Alta and the Mixteca Baja and connecting them with the most important cities in the country. Mexico City had a completely different layout than today; the peripheral ring road and the system of wide axial roads that cross the city had not yet been planned. The subway system was in its initial stage of construction, and it was there that many migrants from Oaxaca found work.

The stories of the migrants are rich in detail about return journeys to the hometown—to San Miguel—to visit family, keep an eye on the land, or assist in patron saint festivals. These journeys caused constant interruptions to children's education, but they also provided a way to stay in touch with friends and relatives in the hometown. Wage work began at an early age for the interviewees: whether cutting cane in Veracruz or working in the factories or bakeries of Mexico City. Various types of employment filled the workday of the parents. For example, fathers might find jobs as security guards, factory workers, or laborers; mothers might work as domestics. These jobs were indicators of the emergence of the middle class in Mexico City in the late 1960s and early 1970s. Soon the boss made his appearance as an authority figure and a fellow countryman (*paisano*). When a conflict arises in the workplace, paisanos are, by definition, allies, but in ethnic terms they are contrasted with "them"—scabs or opportunists who have no clear ethnic attachment and distance themselves from the paisanos. This same situation occurs at fiestas in the cities, in cooperative projects associated with the hometown, and in solving problems such as finding a place to stay upon arrival in the big city. In the memory of migrants, *here* and *there* often become confused. Geographic movement is a key element of the life stories, which describe travels between different places searching for a job, visiting relatives, or going back home.

I was the son of a poor indigenous family that spoke Mixtec, and, thanks to that, from the time that we were small children, my parents took us to Mexico City. We were there, in the Distrito Federal [Mexico City], a good while. My mother worked as a domestic and my father as a street musician. Around '63, my father got a job as a caretaker in a building in the Nueva Anzures neighborhood. I was in first grade. But, generally speaking, my parents were migrants who could never commit to forsaking their hometown. So, sometimes we were in Mexico City and sometimes in the pueblo [hometown]. This affected us in some ways because we were about to finish first grade and then we had to repeat it in Oaxaca. That was how we managed until we finished grade school around 1970. (S. Méndez 1996)

The cities of central Mexico and the fields of Sinaloa became an important destination for those who wanted steady employment during the 1960s and 1970s. In the 1970s, work as agricultural laborers was available to many Mixtec families. These were the boom years in the agricultural economy and also the beginning of the agro-industrial expansion into Mexico's northwestern region. At that time, this path was followed by young people who moved along routes established by their hometown networks. Journeys to the hometown or to Mexico City were frequent; in some cases, the purpose of the journey was to collect a young wife and children before returning to the north. The 1970s was the time of agricultural laborer movements in Sonora and the mobilization of students who supported the farmworkers' demands. The migrants' narratives offer colorful, almost chaotic images of life in the fields: short periods—often just a few months—of work in the camps and migration toward the south or toward the cities of central Mexico. For thousands of Mixtecos, the fields were stepping-stones to the border between Mexico and the United States. Barrón (1997, 119) describes the movement of agricultural workers in Mexico's northwest in the 1970s as having a circular pattern, encompassing Sonora, Sinaloa, Baja California, and the United States.

I arrived in Sinaloa in '85, which was the time of the Movement. There I met Benito [García] in the fields of Moroleón; he was a guard during the labor strike. I participated in some agitating with him there, and that was when they shot him. They left him looking like a colander, but he survived. There were many university students from Sinaloa who went into the fields and supported the workers. From there I went to Sonora, where I worked for two or three months just to earn enough money to eat and to be able to go on to San Luis Río Colorado. From there I went to Yuma, to the other side [of the border], where I didn't last long because *la migra*[7] [the border patrol] caught me and threw me out. Then I went to San Quintin; by then it was '86. I worked there as a mayordomo, and I began to see how badly they treated the workers—especially us, the indigenous people. They humiliated us a lot, just as they still do today. That was when Benito [García] arrived. Once again, I heard, Yup, Benito García's around here now, mobilizing the people. (Bernardino Julián Santiago 1996)

By the 1980s, migration from the Mixtec communities of Oaxaca was included in national statistics. In 1979–80, of the municipalities that form the district of Juxtlahuaca, San Miguel Tlacotepec lost the greatest number of inhabitants (Alcalá and Reyes 1994); by then, several groups of Mixtec migrants could be identified in Veracruz, Morelos, Mexico City, Sonora, Sinaloa, and Baja California, as well as in California. Within this pattern of mobility, associated with the rhythms of agricultural production, a gradual process of settlement at the points of migration can also be perceived; one of the clearest indicators that people were putting down roots was the emergence of migrant associations involved in matters related to dwellings, services (utilities, transport), working conditions, and migrant rights.

In 1985, a group of paisanos from San Miguel Tlacotepec met in Mexico City and founded the Comité Cívico Popular Tlacotepense (CCPT). As the founders themselves recounted, this committee came into being on the initiative of a group of migrants who were studying in the capital, and with the collaboration of companions who remained in San Miguel Tlacotepec. The experiences that led to the formation of the committee included migration to the city and to the fields of northern Mexico, the experience of being migrant children in school in the 1950s, and the emergence of a new generation of activists within the migrant indigenous communities.

The formation of CCPT occurred as the community was mobilizing around the construction of a secondary school in San Miguel Tlacotepec. However, a number of different collective experiences converged in this event: the communal tradition of the locality, the conflicts involved in election of the authorities, the experiences of the young people (the second generation of migrants in the cities), and the agricultural struggles in the north.

> In 1979, in San Miguel Tlacotepec, the caciques of the PRI [Partido Revolucionario Institucional], the traditionalists, always clung to power, and no indigenous person could lead the people—and most of us are indigenous! We saw the need to do something. What brought us together— it sounds like a lie!—was the project to build classrooms for a secondary school. To accomplish this required all the organized forces of the locals, those who had already started the Comité Cívico [the Tlacotepense Civic Committee], which had recently formed in Mexico City.
>
> The committee was founded by students from Oaxaca, and migrants in Sinaloa and Mexico City took part. Most of them were young people living in Mexico City and the young people and leaders in San Miguel Tlacotepec. That is, we wanted to rely on the experience of those who had been *presidentes municipales* or mayordomos, which are the highest officers in the pueblo. We relied on them in order to learn more about the

community's customs and how those who were governing were violating the customs. (R. Méndez 1996)

Leaders experienced, directly and indirectly, important regional and national events; some participated in those movements. In the national field, three events feature prominently in memories of that period: the student protests of 1968, the teachers' movement of the 1970s in Oaxaca, and the mobilization of agricultural workers in the fields of the northwest. These three arenas of social conflict permeated the political experience of the activists who founded the CCPT. For members of indigenous and popular organizations, the context of rural and urban struggles and the peak of the guerrilla movement in the early 1970s are important, especially in the wake of the repression of the student movement.[8]

A fundamental experience was the agricultural workers' movement in Sinaloa, out of which emerged the Central Independiente de Obreros Agrícolas y Campesinos (CIOAC) in 1975. During mobilizations in the fields of Sinaloa, indigenous migrants had the support of students from the Universidad Autónoma de Sinaloa.

As recounted in most of the migrants' narratives, the experience of political participation, beginning in the hometowns, included active membership in political parties—the Mexican Communist Party and subsequently the Partido Socialista Unificado de México (PSUM). This took place during the seventies at the height of what was called the "political reform" (the reform of the political parties and electoral processes), which sought to open a limited but institutional space for the opposition to cut away the ground sustaining extralegal and violent political participation (Meyer 1994, 172). Once migrants had arrived in Mexico City or the fields of Sinaloa, political participation was reinforced through mobilization in workers' organizations or involvement in the student movement.

As in other indigenous localities in Oaxaca, community service in San Miguel Tlacotepec was organized through a civic-religious hierarchy based on the mayordomía and the cofradía. These institutions, which organized political life in the migrants' hometown, were a traditional means for expressing and resolving conflicts that divided the community. The clash over the construction of the secondary school was a typical example of what confronted the members of communities in the region.

According to the migrants' narratives, those from San Miguel Tlacotepec were very much involved in the construction of the Mexico City subway during the 1970s. That experience drew them together and also made them aware of the workers' struggle in factories and in other establishments such as bakeries. In these industries, young migrants from Tlacotepec (fifteen- to twenty-year-olds) were working side by side with others who had been in the fields of the north and had participated in the agricultural workers' movement. Thus, when an opportunity arose to build a federal secondary school, these young people mobilized to make sure it was built with money earned in the places of migration. The construction of the school led to confrontations between different factions of the community; each group hoped to gain control of the construction work. In addition, factions fought and argued among themselves about the site selection. This project led to the formation of Comité Cívico Popular Tlacotepense, and it was the migrants who mobilized to raise money to buy the land and erect the buildings. (Later they had to deal with the director of the school, who was found to have embezzled funds contributed by parents for the purchase of school supplies.) In the negotiations, the young migrants joined with the older people and the traditional authorities of the four barrios of San Miguel Tlacotepec in an attempt to gain support for the project.

However, the participation of young migrants was not well received by everyone in the hometown. The problems lay not with the local authority, mayors or síndicos, but rather with the traditional authorities, who did not approve of the active role of these young people with urban ideas and a new policy. The life stories frequently refer to how difficult it was to get the principales of the town to listen to them. The accusation, "You youngsters don't know anything," was frequently heard.

The episode of the secondary school exemplifies the clash between generations. The male gerontocracy[9] was still dominant as a force to lead disputes, but the influence of young people with political ideals began to be felt. Resistance was directed not only toward their ideas and vitality but toward their capacity to financially back projects proposed by activists, who resisted the PRI's domination of the town. The leaders, who were at that time still in their youth, acknowledge that they adjusted their initiatives to the traditional ways of doing politics in their hometowns. Thanks to their financial capital earned through migration, these young leaders gained legitimacy. This fact turned them into agents with considerable influence on events in their hometowns.

On the Mexico–U.S. Border: The Caja Unidad Democrática and the Comité Cívico Popular Mixteco, 1986–1990

The generation of migrants who narrated their life stories arrived on the northern frontier in the 1970s.[10] Following a period of residency in the Mexican capital, migration generally occurred in stages, with migrants passing through the fields of Sinaloa, Sonora, and Baja California. Although some migrants from the Mixteca took part in the Bracero Program of 1942, the parents of the storytellers in the present work pioneered migration to Veracruz, Morelos, and Mexico City. From there, people migrated to the border. The experience occurred during these narrators' adolescence and in the company of an older family member. Those who went to Veracruz were the generation of migrants who established the route to the north and the first generation of migrant organization leaders in the border region. Migration to the northern border and the United States led to a new experience for undocumented migrants. A series of new agents and social categories appeared among them. Even within Mexican territory, they discovered that as poor, indigenous people they were vulnerable to the same discrimination and exploitation as undocumented migrants abroad.[11] Extortion, abuse, and racism began at their departure point and continued until their arrival in cities like Tijuana.[12] Soon they recognized the need to organize themselves as indigenous migrants and establish links with nongovernmental organizations that defended human rights and championed migrants in the border region.

> We crossed into the United States over the mountains. We can proudly say that, in 1974, when we tried to cross for the first time, we paid only $20 to the kid who was taking my brother, my father, and me across. . . . We went more than a month without working, until one day, la migra caught us and sent us back to Mexico. We went to San Quintin . . . but we stayed only a month, and then we again went al otro lado [to the other side of the border]. And this time, we crossed on our own. When we arrived there [in the United States], we had friends, relatives, and family members waiting for us. Later, when we returned during the eighties, it was as members of an organization that would not exploit its people. We brought our friends, our cousins, our compadres, whoever wanted to come, without charging them a red cent, but they had to understand that we are not coyotes,[13] only the guides of our friends. (Everardo Flores 1996)

The living conditions of these migrants on the Mexican side of the border mirrored their working conditions. On the U.S. side, legal status is part of the living and working conditions. In the 1970s, some Mixtec migrants established temporary shelters along the banks of the Tijuana River. They lived as a group in improvised dwellings informally named "Cartolandia" (Cardboardtown); on being evicted from the area, most of the migrants reestablished themselves in a colonia popular in Tijuana. This settlement is important because, according to another study (Velasco 1995a), this was an ethnic niche that functioned as a safe haven for family migration—a place where the women and children were safe. Males also stayed in the colonia before migrating to the United States. It was this core of residents—and some other later groups—that founded the various residents' and street vendors' organizations in Tijuana, such as the Comité Comunitario de Planeación (COCOPLA) and the three street vendors' organizations that were active during the 1980s. During the same period, as recounted in migrants' narratives, many Mixtecos from San Miguel Tlacotepec reached the canyon area of Vista, California. In settlements like these, hidden in depressions, the migrants carved shelters out of hillsides, which they covered with plastic sheets or cardboard containers to provide sleeping places. The discovery of these shantytowns in the 1980s caused indignation among human rights organizations on both sides of the Mexico–U.S. border. As described by migrants, conditions in the fields of California were not much different from in Sinaloa and Baja California: they lived on the boss's property and satisfied their needs in the shops or the *loncheras*,[14] with little or no mobility beyond the agricultural camps. During this period of considerable residential instability, the Caja Unidad Democrática appeared among migrants. This was an example of what are known as *cajas populares*. According to Florescano (1998, 314), "community chests" formed an essential part of the economy and were the base of social solidarity among indigenous peoples. They functioned like a savings bank where members of the community deposited funds to cover the costs of religious worship and other collective expenditures.[15] This organization, established in places of migration, fulfilled the same purposes as the ancient tradition of the *cajas de la comunidad* in the places of origin. According to the narrative of Rogelio Méndez:[16]

> In 1984, we started the Caja Unidad Democrática [Democratic Unity Savings Fund] because here in San Diego we began to get involved in the racism hassles—in hassles with *cholos* who were stealing from *la raza*, hassles with the [Mexican] judicial police, who were extorting money from us, and the [Mexican] customs agents, too, all along the way until we got here. The Caja was open only to members. At that time, we couldn't worry about the pueblo because there wasn't much dough. Among our own, we each chipped in $10 to have some savings to be able to deal with whatever situation might come up for us as migrants. (R. Méndez 1996)

The idea of community represented by the cajas is deeply engrained in migrant groups. Although they were not necessarily from the same hometown, all came from the Oaxacan Mixteca. While based on the cultural and social practices of colonial indigenous institutions, this form of association transcends the territorial limits of the village community and extends, thanks to the experience of migration, to the Mixtec ethnic condition.

During the 1980s, the change in migration policy had a notable effect on

Mexican migration to the United States. In the case of the Mixtecos, as the leaders' narratives indicate, the passing of the Simpson-Rodino Act (IRCA) in 1986 brought about important changes in their living conditions and their migratory mobility. "In '85 or '86 almost, there were not many people in the cities. I mean indigenous people because most of us come alone. After a few years, relatives began to arrive and the legalization was going on among the first families. Before that time it was one or another woman coming alone, but families were not coming" (Lita 1996).

When the Mixtecos left the canyons and began to live in cities, those from San Miguel Tlacotepec established themselves primarily in the northern part of San Diego County. New places of residence brought other needs: money for rent, water, electricity, and telephone, transportation, and appliances for food preparation.

In the new places of residence, just as in the ravines of the hillsides, the migrants found countrymen, not only paisanos from Tlacotepec but also other indigenous living under the same conditions. In the words of Juan Lita,[17] a new ethnic solidarity formed around Mixtec identity.

> I went to the United States, and there I linked up with people from my pueblo [San Miguel Tlacotepec]. At that time, I already had friends in California, in Carlsbad. We all started to talk about our situation. Living in the canyons . . . in such an inhumane way just knocked me flat, *eso me podía* [it was intolerable]. Around that time, we began to get word about the racist policies of Pete Wilson [then governor of California]. We held a meeting in the canyon, and we prepared a letter to the media about our political opposition. . . . As always, they accused us [the migrants] of being responsible for crimes and depravities against the people of California. . . . After that, we realized that our problems went beyond those of the Tlacotepenses. We couldn't accomplish anything if we stayed organized only at the community level, at the level of our pueblo. The need had arisen to widen our efforts, to encompass the Mixtec issue. (Lita 1996)

Still acting as the Comité Cívico Popular Tlacotepense—although now in California—they carried out other projects for the home community, such as an infrastructure project to make drinking water available. The activists from San Miguel Tlacotepec involved in the CCPT discovered other migrants who were also enthusiastic about their hometowns. Thus, relations were established with members of the Organización del Pueblo Explotado y Oprimido (OPEO), formed by migrants from San Miguel Cuevas, and the Macuiltianguis hometown association. Rufino Domínguez explains: "By 1986 I had arrived in Livingston, and a short time later I began to organize other committees in Madera and Fresno. I started to work not just with my hometown,

San Miguel Cuevas, but also with other communities or hometowns in Oaxaca that I never have been in touch with. The idea was to be more extensive as an organization, but still operate under the name of OPEO" (Domínguez 1996).

These movements have focused on migrants' problems as workers and residents in California. However, the organizations did not neglect issues in their hometowns, especially political ones. In 1987 the same nucleus of activists decided to change the name of the organization (CCPT) to Comité Cívico Popular Mixteco (CCPM), incorporating other hometown associations, such as those of Macuiltianguis and San Miguel Cuevas. Sergio Méndez recalls: "In 1986 the organizations began to rise. Then we were Comité Cívico Popular Tlacotepense in North San Diego County, but with the work of Arturo [Pimentel] in San José, other peoples or hometowns from the north joined us, and then we became Comité Cívico Popular Mixteco (CCPM). It was the only organization fighting for its indigenous brothers both in the United States and in Oaxaca. The organization did productive projects in the Mixteca region" (S. Méndez 1996).

Despite the homogeneous ethnic and class composition, this new phase of the organization addressed a variety of experiences, even among migrants from the same hometown. This heterogeneity grew out of unique migration experiences and participation in politics. The organizational nucleus of the young CCPM brought together people born in San Miguel Tlacotepec, San Miguel Cuevas, and Macuiltianguis, as well as in Mexico City or Veracruz. Almost all of them left for Veracruz when very young and later went to the capital. As urban and agricultural laborers, they had experience in workers' movements and, in some cases, students' or teachers' movements. They maintained a strong interest in the economic and cultural development of their communities of origin, while defending workers' and human rights in the United States. As the Mixtec CCPM, they set up an office in northern San Diego County with the support of the Lutheran Church, and organized the struggle for consular registration as a way to combat corruption and police harassment.

For the hometown associations brought together under the CCPM, the Mexican federal elections of 1988 marked an important stage in their development as a political entity. Although the elections were won (under suspicion of fraud) by the PRI candidate, Carlos Salinas de Gortari, the campaign by the candidate for the recently formed PRD, Cuauhtémoc Cárdenas, which included a visit to California, aroused considerable interest among Mixtec leaders. Many of the leaders tell of their mobilization and participation in the Cárdenas campaign tours, as well as their dismay at the election results. The participation in the campaign by migrants living in the United States made national headlines in Mexico. The political force represented by the migrants woke the government from its deep lethargy; an indicator of this awakening was the appearance of the Paisano Program in 1989 at the federal level and at the start of the Oaxaca state governor's tours to California in the 1980s.

A new stage in community organization development was linked to migration. The experience of migrants as both international and undocumented people modified the ethnic geography of the border region, prompting contact between Oaxacan leaders who had been isolated from one another. This new ethnic geography brought about renewed attempts to create political spaces larger than hometowns and their territories, reaching beyond the ethnic limits of the Mixteca. Fundamental to this transformation were both the constant movement across the border and the process of settlement of Mixtecos on both sides of the border.

The Frente Mixteco-Zapoteco Binacional, 1991–1993

More than a decade after the 1986 IRCA, the popularity of these migrant organizations and the interest of the state government (Oaxaca) in visiting them indicated a significant Oaxacan population living in California.

After 1986, migration by women and children increased not only on the Mexican side of the border but also to the United States. Creating a stable family life brought challenges:

> We left the ravines. We began living in the cities, finding ourselves with the hassles of having to rent, having to have a car, having to pay for tickets. And we found ourselves facing the really big hassle of double expenditure, paying here for food and housing, telephone, electricity, car, and having the family there in Oaxaca. So, in 1987, I went to get my wife and children. When they arrived, I had already rented a house in the city [one of the suburbs of San Diego]. (R. Méndez 1996)

With the migration of women and children, there were more workers to contribute to the family income and a reconstitution of what had been the basis of ethnic identity since the days of the Spanish colony: the parentela, or big family.

Between 1988 and 1991, relations with other organizations, such as the Asociación Cívica Benito Juárez (ACBJ), brought together Mixtecos from Juan Mixtepec in the district of Juxtlahuaca[18] and the Organización Regional de Oaxaca (ORO), Zapotec migrants from the Valley of Oaxaca.[19]

> Until about '87, all of us were Tlacotepenses. We began to look at incorporating other people into our ranks, people who were not from Tlacotepec. We saw the need to change the name to Comité Cívico Popular Mixteco. That was when we began to fight for registration in the consulates, to end the police harassment and the bribes. We wrote to Salinas de Gortari [president of Mexico]; we had sit-ins at the consulates, [like the one] here in Los Angeles. Meanwhile, we worked for the construction of a potable water system in the Mixteca region. That project, by the way, the governor of Oaxaca, Heladio Ramírez López, claims as his own work. (R. Méndez 1996)

Méndez's words are seconded by Arturo Pimentel: "Starting in '85 . . . we proposed two things: apart from being a community, like San Miguel Tlacotepec, San Juan Mixtepec, or San Miguel Cuevas, we also have common concerns. You can see that two factors intertwine: the question of the community, our identity as a people, and the question of our general problems as migrant workers" (Pimentel 1995).

Toward the end of the 1980s, the first visit by a state governor of Oaxaca to California took place. Various Oaxacan migrants and their organizations argued over how to receive him: whether to give him a typically festive Oaxacan reception, or to treat him as a foreign official from whom they would demand solutions to the problems of their hometowns and their problems as migrants.

> In 1989, Heladio Ramírez came to California, and he was confronted and questioned. Even little old men were saying things like: "Now that you've come, governor, we want to talk to you without having to bite our tongues!" And people let fly with some amazing statements. It was really beyond belief: Where had all these people come from? This gave us an incredible connection with many organizations. These meetings were used strategically as forums where we could also get to know one another. There was a lot of arguing. Perhaps by being outside of Oaxaca, the people were not afraid to speak frankly to each other. (Jesús Iñiguez 1996)

Such experiences nourished alliances and sharpened conflicts among organizations as they faced one of the most significant dates in the history of the indigenous movement in Latin America: October 12, 1992—the five hundredth anniversary of Columbus's arrival at Hispaniola. In view of the intention of some of the continent's governments to celebrate the "meeting of two worlds," the indigenous people of Latin America prepared their own celebrations in memory of five hundred years of indigenous resistance. It was in this context that, on October 5, 1991, the Comité Cívico Popular Mixteco, the

Asociación Cívica Benito Juárez, and the Organización Regional Oaxaqueña met in Los Angeles to create the Frente Mixteco-Zapoteco Binacional (FM-ZB). Rufino Domínguez[20] recalls:

> Before the five hundreth anniversary celebration of the Discovery of America, as the Spaniards call it, all the indigenous organizations on the American continent and, of course, in Mexico, united to refute the Spanish version. On October 5, 1991, five Mixtec and Zapotec organizations met in Los Angeles to establish the Frente Mixteco-Zapoteco Binacional. . . . The only objective was to work on the 500 Years of Resistance campaign. (Domínguez 1996)

The new Front was set up, bringing together a large number of the country's indigenous organizations in protest against celebrating the five hundred years since the discovery of the Americas.[21]

This stage was marked by interethnic alliances, incorporating groups both in and outside the state of Oaxaca. For the first time such alliances adopted the "binational" vision, incorporating communities of origin and those of destination in the United States. What had been a territorial community was reconstituted in the political sphere as a dispersed community, resulting from migration. At the same time, the sense of community was sustained by common origin, which was not only territorial but historical. The concept goes back to the experience of the Spanish Conquest and colonial domination. Mixtec-Zapotec ethnic belonging extends beyond national and regional boundaries: Mexico and Oaxaca.

The FM-ZB formed at a particular historic moment. This enabled an ideological encounter between the leaders of different organizations and different ethnic groups, specifically Mixtecos, Zapotecos, Native Americans, and Chicanos. In this context, the first Mexican pan-ethnic organization in California was founded.

> Then the Mixtecos and Zapotecos in Los Angeles got to know each other. . . . The Zapotecos and the Mixtecos here in California shared the experience of racism and exploitation: Oaxaquita-indio ["little Oaxacan Indian"]. This we redeemed and politicized, by saying we are going to affirm that, yes, we are indigenous peoples. But this time, it happens within the context of the continent-wide meetings, where the Native Americans from the United States are saying, "Hey, our brothers, this is great!" and the Chicanos, who are nationalists, are saying, "Hey! These are our brothers." This is good for the Mixtecos. (Iñiguez 1996)

According to Domínguez (2004, 71), an important achievement in the period was a labor training and education project with California Rural Legal

Assistance (CRLA). This project was staffed by indigenous speakers in California and extended to Oaxaca and Baja California. In the opinion of Domínguez, for the first time collective action assumed a binational scope.

As the FM-ZB grew and extended, internal conflicts and the intergroup alliances characterized a new post-1992 structure; little by little, different political strategies became defined, identified by their individual means and styles. However, two sources of conflict marked this phase: (1) relations with governmental institutions, specifically those representing the government of Oaxaca, and (2) relations with the political parties in the hometowns. In the migrant narratives, the ethnic configuration includes three new categories of identity: Zapotecos, "gringos," and Chicanos. The Zapotecos and Mixtecos share the experience of the Spanish Conquest and have a similar pre-Hispanic origin and the same Oaxacan government. The social category of "gringos" becomes the "bosses" in working life and are also seen as a dominant cultural group. The Chicanos are described ambiguously in respondents' accounts; the group is considered a political entity with whom the Mixtecos have a certain cultural affinity. But this cultural affinity—by its Mexican origin— represents an undesirable future.

The Frente Indígena Oaxaqueño Binacional, 1994–1997

By 1994, a new front had been established in Tijuana: the Binational Oaxaqueño Indigenous Front (FIOB). After a period of mobilizations and meetings in California, the organization shifted its attention to the Mexican side of the border. A brief look at that moment will help to situate the emergence of the FIOB.

A new phase of organization for the Mixtecos occurred in the 1990s. The hometowns were still the base of these organizations. FIOB activists and organizations became the essential link between hometowns and ethnic groups. The stage of hometown and ethnic alliances was followed by separations. The two sources of conflict referred to in the previous section—relations with Oaxaca's state administration and with the political parties back home—had their first consequences.

> The conflicts in the FM-ZB had a lot to do with the government—in this particular case, with the government of Oaxaca. Because we don't trust them. For example, when the governor of Oaxaca came here [to California], he sent the coordinator of advisers to tell us how to run the meeting, even where to put the podium. We said, "We aren't children; we are an organization, and we'll receive him in the way we want to, and not in the way you tell us to." At that point leaders rose up among us who were

staunchly on the side of the Oaxacan government, and we began to splinter. (Domínguez 1996)

As with any conflict that gives rise to factions, there were different points of view. According to the coordinator of the Frente Mixteco-Zapoteco Binacional, the cause of the Asociación Cívica Benito Juárez (ACBJ) separating from the FM-ZB was the holding of the first Conferencia Internacional sobre Migración y Derechos Humanos (International Conference on Migration and Human Rights) in Huajuapan de León, in the Mixteca, without the consent of the Front's board of directors. The governor of Oaxaca, Heladio Ramírez, in fact, promoted this conference, and some members of the Asociación Cívica Benito Juárez took part in its organization. A confrontation took place during the forum, with the result that leaders of the ACBJ were expelled from the FM-ZB.

> Some of the leaders in California were used to a relationship of negotiation with the PRI in Oaxaca. They were well-meaning people, who had learned in their pueblos how to negotiate to get things, like the fertilizer for their corn crop. They said, "Why should we go looking for trouble? They're going to win anyway." And here in California, they tried to continue that type of negotiated relationship. . . . Because of the governor's visits, there was reconciliation with the Oaxacan government. The relationships were getting tighter, and pretty soon they were trying to enter our ranks. There was a lot of arguing among us. Those of the PRD saw this, and well, they began saying that we had to join their party. A fight started and we began asking ourselves, "What do we want to do?" The project still isn't completed; we don't know what our relationship will be with the parties, with the state government, with the communities themselves. (Iñiguez 1996)

As this statement indicates, there is a strong link with home governments beyond Oaxacan territory. The mistrust to which Iñiguez refers is based on the former relationship between communities and the governing party (PRI). Conflicts in the place of origin were carried over to the new territory, not only between organizations but inside of organizations. In the 1990s a split occurred within the pioneer activists of the Front. A confrontation between leaders from San Miguel Tlacotepec resulted in the formation of two organizations outside the Front: the Vamos por la Tierra movement and the Coalición de Comunidades Indígenas de Oaxaca (COCIO). To get beyond what, at first, appears to be a leadership struggle, we need to analyze the leaders' viewpoints in forming the new organizations. The now defunct Vamos por la Tierra had a strong class outlook and, with the creation of the Partido Indoamericano, an agenda of indigenous political alliances going beyond national limits. The COCIO, on the other hand, has a predominantly cultural orientation and emphasizes strengthening Oaxacan identity in California rather than advocacy in the hometowns.

In this situation of political-organizational fragmentation, the Zapatist movement appeared in Chiapas and NAFTA was signed. On New Year's Day of 1994, the Ejército Zapatista de Liberación Nacional (Zapatist National Liberation Army) burst on the national political stage. The First Declaration from the Lacandon Rainforest (Declaración de la Selva Lacandona) announced in its opening lines, "We are the product of five hundred years of struggle," and finished by demanding "work, land, homes, food, health, education, independence, freedom, democracy, justice, and peace."[22]

This event seems to have had an overwhelming effect on the 1994 meeting of the FIOB in Tijuana. In the preparatory meeting of September 2, Arturo Pimentel stated:

> Owing to the events in Chiapas at the beginning of the year, particularly in the weeks following January 1, with all the influence and all the extraordinary importance these events had, not only for the indigenous movement in the country but on all sides—for the democratic and people's movement in Mexico, for this too—the Front's documents are now very outdated and leave many things out of account in the Declaration of Principles. We need to include various things, to look at the question of regional autonomy, . . . struggle for ecological preservation . . . or indigenous legislation . . . international agreements. We need to include our position on matters that have been presented recently in the indigenous movements: autonomous regions and indigenous authority. (Pimentel 1994)

Finally, a large number of organizations from Baja California, California, and Oaxaca took part in the constitutive assembly of the FIOB on September 3, 1994. Of the associations that originally worked to organize the Frente Mixteco-Zapoteco Binacional, the Asociación Cívica Benito Juárez of San Juan Mixtepec did not participate, and only a section of the Organización Regional de Oaxaca (ORO) participated, that organization having withdrawn in protest at the formation of the FIOB. Despite opposing viewpoints among the activists from San Miguel Tlacotepec, new organizations such as Vamos por la Tierra and COCIO were represented at the assembly and signed as members of the FIOB.

The FIOB began a new stage in its organization and in the reconstitution of its identity. It institutionalized its political action toward the Mexican border, in Baja California. After joint actions with workers' organizations from the San Quintin Valley, on the Mexican side of the border, it incorporated organizations such as the Central Independiente de Obreros Agrícolas y Campesinos (CIOAC), the Movimiento de Unificación de Jornaleros Independientes (MUJI) from San Quintin Valley, and also the Movimiento Indígena de Unificación y Lucha Independiente (MIULI) from Maneadero Valley, the Asociación de Vendedoras Ambulantes Indígenas de Tijuana, and the Coordinadora de Lucha Indígena de Nogales, Sonora. And while the previous Front had included Zapotecos, the new one took in the Triquis who worked in the fields of San Quintin and were affiliated with the Organización del Pueblo Triqui (OPT). For the first time, the Front incorporated organizations that consisted primarily of women, such as the street vendors' association. This group organized a preparatory meeting for the constitutive assembly and a short-lived committee of the FIOB.

Although contacts had already been initiated with several Oaxacan state administrations (since the setting up of the CCPM and FM-ZB), the FIOB institutionalized relations with these authorities and initiated a relationship with aid agencies.

These new directions were reflected in discussions at the preparatory meeting of the Constitutive Assembly held on September 2. With many of the future members of the FIOB gathered together, the new ethnic composition of the organization was discussed as a problem. Joining the Mixtecos and Zapotecos of the old Front were the Triquis from the San Quintin Valley and the Mixtecos from the Oaxacan sierra. Many of the participants devoted their addresses to the question of the new organization's name: " 'Frente Indígena Oaxaqueño Binacional' reinforces the indigenous issue, 'Oaxaqueño' identifies the place from where we came, and 'binational' speaks to our real situation because we are located in both countries" (Pimentel 1994).

This statement sums up a complex discussion between assistants at the meeting. A "front" was the right organization to coordinate the action of diverse groups and to maintain their autonomy. The term "indigenous" links the members to their Mesoamerican origin and the experience of the Spanish Conquest and colonial domination. The adjective "Oaxaqueño" identifies the citizens' place within the political administration of the government of Oaxaca; and "binational" reflects that the Front brings together Oaxacan indigenous organizations in two different national territories: Mexico and the United States.

This name implied a new identity, in an ever more complex organization. The structure proposed in the Front's founding had a transnational character, which is present even today.

Two legal entities had been used to obtain funds for community development projects: the Binational Center for Indigenous Oaxacan Development, in Juxtlahuaca, Mexico, and the Binational Center for the Development of the Oaxacan Indigenous Communities, Inc., in Livingston, California. In 2001, only the former was recognized by state and federal agencies in California. It is worth noting that the organizing process had the support of several U.S. scholars from the beginning. They had an important role as brokers to international funding agencies and to international human rights bodies. The relationship began with informal support, with advice or small amounts of money for some meetings or specific projects, and gradually it became a source of more stable financial support. At the same time, the scholars acted as sources of information and as agents to help make visible the indigenous movement in the United States. Later, this relationship was institutionalized through an Advice Council, which integrates U.S. and Mexican scholars.[23]

Each of the regional coordinating bodies had its own specific characteristics and form of organization. On the Mexican side of the border, domain organizations were concerned mainly with the improvement of residential services and the defense of agricultural workers' rights. Meanwhile, on the U.S. side, hometown associations were the basis of ethnic organizations focused on cultural concerns, immigrants' rights, and preservation of links with places of origin. In Juxtlahuaca, on the other hand, organizations included communities with a wide variety of demands related to housing, food, community development programs, and settlement of boundary disputes.

Between 1994 and 1997 some changes took place in the internal organization of the FIOB: COCIO and Vamos por la Tierra left the Front, although they have continued to maintain relations with specific organizations; the split within the ORO deepened and this group distanced itself from the FIOB. In 1995 the CCPM, funded by migrants from the Juxtlahuaca district living in California, dissolved, and its members became an organic part of the FIOB. The OPEO also dissolved, allowing its communities to assume direct membership in the Front and set up community committees of the FIOB in Oaxaca and in California.[24]

During this same stage, the General Coordinating Body of the FIOB concentrated its efforts on promoting community development projects and the defense of human and cultural rights. Financial resources began to arrive during this period that enabled the Front to develop a presence among communities in Oaxaca, Baja California, and California. However, these resources also became a cause of internal and external conflicts.

Two large-scale projects will serve as examples of the needs in the transnational space of these organizations.

The Forage Cactus Project (Juxtlahuaca). In 1994 a trust was set up in Oaxaca called Peso por Peso (the name implying that for each peso contributed by the people, the government would put up the same amount of money). The Nopal Forrajero project (to grow nopal cactus for animal feed) was carried out under this program. In 1996 the Programa Nacional de Jornaleros Agrícolas (PRONJAG, National Farm Workers Program) supported the FIOB by sowing 50 hectares with forage nopal for the use of ten communities; among these, five lay within the municipal limits of San Miguel Tlacotepec. As Sergio Méndez, the program's then administrator,[25] explained, the forage nopal is grown specifically for livestock. "It has no spines and, when finely cut, its juicy texture and nutritious content made it an ideal feed for pigs, cows, and goats." The forage nopal can be combined with "vegetable" (i.e., edible) nopal. According to Méndez, there is another type of nopal cactus ideal for growing on terraces, which helps to contain soil on sloping grounds and prevent wind erosion or runoff (S. Méndez 1996).[26]

The Interpreters Program (California). The Interpreters Program was set up in response to the needs of migrants belonging to Mexican ethnic minorities, thousands of whom do not speak Spanish well enough to exercise their most basic rights as citizens, such as legal defense. While Mexican communities in California had made progress in defending Spanish as their mother tongue, this did little to resolve the problems faced by monolingual indigenous migrants. In the United States their language problems were compounded, since they had little or no command of Spanish. Their inability to understand or make themselves understood in English left them vulnerable when they were faced with any type of legal proceeding. In 1997, the project of a transnational network of Zapotec, Mixtec, and Triqui translators was approved. Since then, the project has worked with financial institutions and the U.S. Justice Department in the country's law courts, supporting the indigenous of Mexican origin. In 2004 this program had fourteen interpreters of the Mixtec, Zapotec, Triqui, and Chatino languages working in the courts of United States.[27]

Given geographic dispersion, communication is fundamental to the functioning of the FIOB organizations. In this area, two developments are important: the circulation, from 1995 onward, of the magazine *El Tequio*—conceived as the "binational voice of Oaxacans"—and the creation of a Web site offering *El Tequio* in electronic format and providing information on the organization, the indigenous movement in Mexico, and other organizations in the network, as well as a brief description of the Centro Binacional para el Desarrollo Indígena Oaxaqueño (Binational Center for Indigenous Oaxaqueño Development) and a Oaxacan Indigenous Interpreters Directory.[28]

Two years after the formation of the FIOB, the advantages offered by this Front to organizations that had previously worked in isolation were obvious.

Between 1996 and 2000 a series of meetings and congresses took place between the indigenous migrant organizations, led by people from Oaxaca and with the support of government institutions in that state, Baja California, and California. The many meetings, congresses, and workshops at this stage were of great historical importance for the indigenous migrant movement. Indeed, they are likely to be included among the important events of the twentieth century in Mexico. Their immediate outcome was to greatly increase the ability of these organizations to make their voices heard. The actions of the FIOB and the organizations that, together with it, make up the indigenous migrant movement of the region, must be seen in the context of five major events of the last decade: (1) the Zapatist rebellion and the discussion of the constitutional modifications that must accompany indigenous autonomy in Mexico; (2) the NAFTA agreement and its consequences for agricultural labor markets; (3) Mexico's economic crisis—especially after the devaluation of the peso in 1994—and its consequences for unemployment and poverty (growth of the informal sector); (4) changes in the migration policies of both countries: Operation Guardian on the California border, the "responsibility law" regarding undocumented migration, and the new context created by U.S. national security policies against terrorism; and (5) the recent law saying that Mexican nationality cannot be renounced and the government interest in the vote from abroad.

Table 3.1 shows the chronological development of Oaxacan migrant organizations. It is difficult to establish a single chronology since organizations appeared simultaneously and in different places over the last four decades. The geography of the organizations may serve as a basis for reconstructing the regions of migration and for appreciating the spatial configuration of the Mixtec, Zapotec, and Triqui peoples beyond the territory of Oaxaca.

Although this research project came to an end in 1997, a follow-up on the organizations revealed a new stage of conflicts and alliances. This stage opened in the year 2000 and culminated in the FIOB assembly, which took place in Tijuana in December 2001. At this meeting the general coordinator, Arturo Pimentel, was removed from his position because of the absence of financial reports. This action was a breaking point for several reasons.

First, the decision to remove Pimentel was made during a peak period of tension between the main activists and the general coordinator of the Front. According to the records of the last FIOB meeting in 2001, Pimentel did not provide adequate information on the Front's financial resources. During the last half of the 1990s, significant funds were provided to the Front from Mexico as well as the United States.[29] Funds and political influence came together. In Juxtlahuaca, the FIOB, in alliance with the PRD, won a seat in the House of Representatives. The win handed a loss to the dominant PRI.

Table 3.1   Chronology of Development of Oaxacan Migrant Organizations

Date	Association or Organization	Place of Founding	Membership or Origin
1975	Central Independiente de Obreros Agrícolas y Campesinos (CIOAC)	San Quintin Valley, BC	Agricultural workers of mainly indigenous origin
1983	Organización del Pueblo Explotado y Oprimido (OPEO)	Sinaloa	Fellow migrants from San Miguel Cuevas
1984	Federación Independiente de Obreros Agrícolas y Campesinos de Sinaloa (FIOAS)	Sinaloa	Agricultural workers, with support of students from the Universidad Autónoma de Sinaloa
1984	Asociación de Mixtecos Residentes en Tijuana (ASMIRT)	Tijuana	Mixtec residents based in the Colonia Obrera, fighting for regularization of their services
1985	Comité Cívico Popular Tlacotepense (CCPT)	Mexico City	Fellow migrants from San Miguel Tlacotepec
1985	Asociación Mixteca Benito Juárez (AMBJ)	Tijuana	Offshoot of ASMIRT, formed by street vendors in the city center, mainly Mixtec women
1985	Unión de Vendedores Ambulantes y Anexos Carlos Salinas de Gortari (UVAM CS)	Tijuana	Another offshoot of ASMIRT, formed by street vendors, mainly women, from San Jerónimo del Progreso and San Francisco Higos, both in the district of Silacayoapan
1986	Comité Comunitario de Planeación (COCOPLA)	Tijuana	Another offshoot ASMIRT, founded by bilingual Mixtec teachers
1986	Asociación Cívica Benito Juárez (ACBJ)	Fresno	Fellow migrants from San Juan Mixtepec
1987	Comité Cívico Popular Mixteco (CCPM)	Northern part of San Diego County	Offshoot of the Comité Cívico Popular Tlacotepense, whose principal base was migrants from San Miguel Tlacotepec
1988	Organización Regional de Oaxaca (ORO)	Los Angeles	Founded by members of three Zapotec communities of the Valley of Oaxaca, involved with organization of the Guelaguetza
1988	Unión de Alianzas Huitepec (UAH)	Maneadero, BC	Offshoot of the SINGOA agricultural workers' trade union (Sindicato Independiente Gremial de Obreros Agrícolas) and the CIOAC, made up of families from San Pablo Huitepec, Zimatlán, mainly working as agricultural laborers

Table 3.1 *Continued*

Date	Association or Organization	Place of Founding	Membership or Origin
1990	Movimiento Unificado de Jornaleros Indígenas (MUJI)	San Quintin Valley, BC	Another offshoot of the CIOAC, grouping Mixtecs, Zapotecs, and mestizos working as agricultural laborers; in 1995 they set up the Casa del Migrante in the San Quintin Valley
1991	Organización del Pueblo Triqui (OPT)	Nueva Región Triqui colonia, San Quintin Valley, BC	Triques from San Juan Copala mainly working as agricultural laborers
1991	Frente Mixteco-Zapoteco Binacional (FM-ZB)	California	Consisting of the CCPM, OPEO, ACBJ, and ORO
1994	Movimiento Vamos por la Tierra	Vista, CA, and Tijuana, BC	Broke away from the CCPM; made up of indigenous migrants from Oaxaca, along with mestizos and people of other nationalities
1994	Coalición de Comunidades Indígenas de Oaxaca (COCIO)	Vista, CA	Broke away from the CCPM; made up of Mixtec and Zapotec communities
1994	Frente Indígena Oaxaqueño Binacional (FIOB)	Tijuana, BC	Brings together Mixtecs, Zapotecs, and Triquis; set up jointly by the CCPM and by OPEO, ORO, COCIO, Vamos por la Tierra, Asociación de Vendedoras Ambulantes de Tijuana, Comunidades Oaxaqueñas Independientes de California, Asociación de Residentes Mixtecos en Nogales, CIOAC, OPT, MIULI
1996	Coordinadora Estatal de Indígenas Migrantes y Asentados en Baja California (CEIM-BC)	Tijuana	Promoted by Vamos por la Tierra; groups the following: FIOB-Maneadero, OPT-San Quintín, Grupo Mixtecos de Tecate, Organización de Istmeños Oaxaqueños Guelaguetza, Sociedad Cooperativa Mixteca de Artesanías Mexicanas, Comité del Diálogo Zapata Vive
1998	Alianza Indígena Migrante (AIM)	Tijuana	Set up by the FIOB (of northern San Diego County), COCIO, CCPM, the representative group of the "danza de los chilolos," and the Vamos por la Tierra movement; its principal aim is the construction of the Albergue Temporal Indígena in Tijuana

Table 3.1 *Continued*

Date	Association or Organization	Place of Founding	Membership or Origin
1998	Red Internacional Indígena Oaxaqueños (RIIO)	San Quintin Valley, BC	Centro de Desarrollo Regional Indígena (CEDRI), Coalición de Comunidades Indígenas de Oaxaca (COCIO), Organización Regional de Oaxaca (ORO), Asociación Cívica Benito Juárez (ACBJ), Unidad Mixteca, and Mesa Directiva de Santa María Tindú
2001	Federación Oaxaqueña de Comunidades y Organizaciones Indígenas de California (FOCOICA)	Los Angeles	Formed of community associations and sports clubs of mainly Zapotec origin (and to a lesser degree Mixtec and Chinantec); includes the following organizations: Frente Indígena Oaxaqueño Binacional, Red Internacional Indígena de Oaxaca, Coalición de Comunidades Indígenas de Oaxaca, and Unión de Comunidades Serranas de Oaxaca; also a group of cultural and educational organizations; radius of influence is California

The aid institutions, on each side of the border, reacted in different ways to the lack of financial reports. In Mexico, government institutions such as the Instituto Nacional Indigenista (now Comisión Nacional para el Desarrollo de los Pueblos Indígenas), considered this an internal problem for the organization.[30] In the United States, the primary source of the money, the aid institutions, decided to cut funding to and relations with any organization in which the former coordinator was involved. The FIOB needed to regain credibility with foundations, which were reluctant to give more than $500,000 because, after the Pimentel crisis, they questioned the organization's capacity to manage any greater amount (Domínguez 2004, 79). The different reactions of the Mexican and U.S. institutions to problems of funds within social organizations led the former coordinator to found a new organization working only in Mexico—the Frente Nacional Indígena y Campesino (FNIC) focuses only on domestic migrants.[31]

Second, this change was of historic importance since it resolved the conflict without leading to a split within the organization. Nearly two years after the Front's reconstitution, the organization had made structural modifications

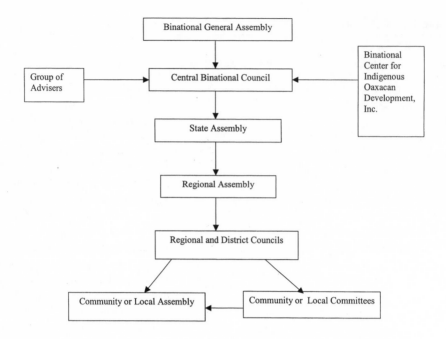

Figure 3.1   Organizational structure of the Frente Indígena Oaxaqueño Binacional, 2004.

Source: FIOB-Líderes Campesinas. 2001. "Mujeres Indígenas Colaborando y Transformando Vidas para el Bienestar de sus Familias" Plan of meeting. Bakersfield, CA. 16–17 February. Domínguez, Rufino. 2004:72. The FIOB Experience: Internal Crisis and Future Challenges. In Jonathan Fox and Gaspar Rivera-Salgado. Indigenous Mexican Migrants in the United States.

that involved strengthening collective decision-making procedures and replacing the personal influence that had been customary. These modifications included establishing the Consejo Central Binacional (CCB), as well as instituting procedures for the periodic submission of financial statements by the regional bodies. The conflict was openly discussed by FIOB members. The coordinator, Rufino Domínguez, even wrote an article on the issue. This demonstrated a shift in the way Mexican organizations handled internal corruption problems: no more secrecy. A year after the conflict began (2001), a new phase of alliances led to the founding of the Federación Oaxaqueña de Comunidades y Organizaciones Indígenas de California (FOCOICA) in Los Angeles, California (see Rivera-Salgado and Escala 2004). This organization followed the tradition of migrant federations from Zacatecas and Jalisco, which focused on the process of integration in the places of arrival as well as on developing hometown projects. A large number of hometown associations, mainly of Zapotec origin, responded to the convocation of the new Oaxacan federation, accompanied by other organizations such as the FIOB, COCIO, and RIIO of Mixtec-Zapotec composition, and a number of sports and cultural clubs. This new organization seemed to be more concerned with the process of integration into U.S. society, similar to other Mexican organizations in California, specifically in Los Angeles.[32]

Horizons of the Ethnic Reconstitution

In this chapter I have described the origin and development of the Mixtec migrant organizations and their encounter with Zapotecos and Triquis on both sides of the Mexico–U.S. border. This description shows the process of ethnic reconstitution during the experience of transnational migration.

Social classifications are transformed by the migration experience. In addition to ethnicity, class, and nationality, social and political participation impact the experience. For instance, the ethnic boundary of the Indian-mestizo dichotomy in the towns and villages of origin changes meaning in the urban experience. New class categories arise out of worker-boss relations, living conditions in the city, and alliances with other poor city dwellers. Agricultural employment in northwestern Mexico involves experience in trade unions or other workers' organizations. Life as farmworkers unified leaders' opinions about the exploitation of indigenous migrants in the fields of northwestern Mexico and southwestern United States.

The national frontier is a place of violence for migrants. Crossing the border entails risk and suffering. Accounts of international migration and its organizations rarely mention Mexican national identity. Despite the fact that international migration places Mixtecos, and indigenous migrants in general, beside other undocumented Mexican migrants, migrants from the same town or village of origin are the focus of solidarity. When migrants come from different towns or regions, their origin in the Mixtec region or Oaxaca state can be a source of solidarity, too. In the last two decades, homeland governments have had an important role in promoting solidarity between members of the same town, region, or state. Local Oaxacan governments promote a sense of belonging and commitment through their visits and transnational programs. At the same time, government policies are a source of conflicts between organizations, who compete for resources and for the right to represent indigenous migrant communities beyond the national border. The federal government has defined this population in terms of the economic and political meaning of Mexicans abroad, without ethnic distinction. In addition, indigenous organizations have established relations with federal, state, and local governments in the United States, mainly through the health, housing, or employment services of government agencies.

Presently, Oaxacan indigenous organizations in the border region are the result of diverse personal and collective experiences that frequently involve conflict. Nevertheless, leaders of those organizations share common experiences that define them as ethnic agents. In oral histories, leaders recall different sources of political experience: teacher and student movements in Oaxaca and Mexico City and the agricultural workers' movement in Sinaloa and Sonora—all occurring in the 1960s and 1970s—and more recently, the indigenous resistance and autonomy movement in Latin America. One experience seems fundamental: participation in the traditional community system in the places of origin. As a whole, these experiences define a new generation of indigenous leaders or activists who are constantly confronting the indigenous gerontocracy and beginning to look at conflicts involving male domination, as we shall see later in the book. As chapter 6 will show, gender differentiation is an unavoidable feature of the organizational fabric. Women have an active presence in many grassroots organizations or committee projects but have little decision-making power. However, the organizations are slowly involving more women in training programs and in executive positions of pan-ethnic and transnational organizations.

Finally, given the fact that this chronology has been constructed largely out of the narratives of those involved in the political field of indigenous migrant organizations, it constitutes a memory of migration to the Mexico–U.S. border.

4
Networks and Migrant Organizations
The Revitalization of
Community Experience

In examining the origin and evolution of the Mixtec organizations during the process of migration, a question inevitably arises: What made it possible for migrant organizations to emerge under such adverse conditions? It seems somewhat paradoxical that organizations of indigenous migrants with different interests and resources, and which cross national frontiers, should evolve in the shadow of such overwhelming macrostructures as labor markets and government migration policies. The literature on the subject points to several factors that may facilitate the emergence of such organizations or associations in different parts of the world (Hirabayashi 1985, 1993; Orellana 1973; Rex 1991; Rex and Mason 1986; Roosens 1994). They are summed up in the following list of assumptions proposed by Hirabayashi (1985, 580–581):

1. Migrants have previously experienced a strong communal tradition; in other words, they have participated in cooperative systems of a civic and religious nature based on a common identity and ethnic heritage.
2. Informal networks and groups are politicized, making immigrants ready to join in a formally organized people's association.
3. The associations constituted in the place of residence maintain a link with the social and political system of the hometown.

The previous chapter documented the strong communal tradition among Mixtec migrants on both sides of the Mexico–U.S. border, as well as the links the migrants (in the places of destination) have to the social system of the hometowns. Both of these features appear in the migrants' life stories. The politicization of the migrant networks or the informal groups is more difficult to discern in these stories. This may reflect the fact that political positions have not generated much conscious reflection, which may explain in part the scanty attention paid to politicization in the literature on migrant associations. Therefore, it is necessary to analyze the practical knowledge these migrants gained from the migration experience and their organizational duties. In analytical terms, both the migrant networks and their organizations are a product of social agency and may be thought of as mechanisms for revitalizing and reintegrating the sense of territory that had become fragmented during the international migration process. Despite this similarity, it is possible to differentiate networks from organizations following Giddens (1995), since such networks are, in effect, *unintended* consequences of the social action of migrants, and thus there is no explicit reflection on their meanings. This does not imply that in the ensemble of practices that sustain and produce the social networks there is no practical consciousness in the form of an accumulated knowledge regarding how "we" are different from the "others." The migrant networks enable the creation of new configurations of social relations—that is, organizations—that project themselves as forms of collective action with specific purposes. Historically, the migrant organizations could not have been conceived without the prior existence of the networks. Migrant organizations are political networks in which community relations are mobilized for the conflict as well as to create cohesion in the public sphere. Following Savater (1998, 28–32), I define politics as any kind of action that leads to change in public institutions through collective mobilization.

Reconnecting the Fragmented Experience of Territory

Migrant networks are structures of social relations into which individuals, families, or groups insert themselves. At times, the structures are relatively invisible, but they can be concrete. As total relational fields, they function as a space-time representation based on kinship relations and a common local origin (*paisanaje*). Migrant networks exist inside a broader system of social relations in which exist gender, social class, generational, and ethnic differentiation. As in any social network, some aspects of its structure can be distinguished.

The Geography of Migrant Networks: Circulation and Multilocality

Two principles of the geography of migrant networks are circulation and multilocality. Circulation refers to the necessary combination of two elements in the process of migration: mobility and permanence. The notion of mobility implies persons, but also comes to include objects, money, and information. The notion of permanence implies the consolidation of personal relations in time and space, making it possible to form residential nuclei, whether in the place of origin or in the places of migration. The principle of multilocality (Wilson 1998, 395) refers to the complexity of the network, which transcends the dual existence of origin-destination. The diversity of locations can be seen by following the migration flow from a particular place of origin through successive stages of the network's spatial expansion through time (Wilson 1998, 395–397). The multilocality of family life among residents of the San Quintin Valley, Baja California, is expressed in the following:

> I left my hometown [San Miguel Tlacotepec] sixteen years ago. I went to live in the San Quintin Valley, at the Vicente Guerrero colonia. I left for the same reason that other people did—because I did not have anything. My parents had [lands], but I didn't have anything. It was 1985. I have counted each one of those sixteen years. Then, I brought my sons when they were little children. There they grew up; they got a little school. . . . I have only two boys. The older one entered the army; now he is working in the Sonoyta customs [in Sonora, Mexico]. The other one, the youngest, is on the otro lado [other side, in the United States] with his family. (Antonio Reyes 2001)

Both principles, circulation and multilocality, enable us to understand the creation of a constellation of community nuclei dispersed in space that define a new spatial hierarchy among communities. Kearney (1986) takes up this idea when he distinguishes the mother communities—the places of origin—from the satellite communities. In the case of Mixtec migration, the latter multiply, following the various routes of migration. Satellite communities began to appear not only in the traditional agricultural regions of Sonora, Sinaloa, Baja California, and California, but also in Mexico City, Guadalajara, Nogales, Mexicali, Tijuana, and Los Angeles. As a result, Mixtec geography is characterized by a combination of urban and rural, national and international, and work locations, as can be observed in table 4.1.

The starting point for the development of networks is the mother community; hence, it is important to distinguish, within the districts shown in table 4.1, the towns and villages that are the sources of satellite communities in the border region. The place of origin is the basis for ethnic belonging during international migration. As migrants establish links along the way and in the places of arrival, they construct the network and the satellite communities, widening the geographical and sociological radius of the original community.

There are obvious difficulties in defining a "settlement" in terms of permanence. Nevertheless, when a nucleus of migrants—comprising families or not—establishes a relationship implying some degree of commitment to the places of arrival, the dynamics of the network, as well as the characteristics of the satellite communities, begins to change. Such commitment to the communities of destination is expressed in dwellings (rented or purchased) or

Table 4.1   Home District or Locality of Oaxacan Migrants by Present Place of
Residence

| | Present Place of Residence | | |
| | Tijuana (%) | Valle de San Quintín (%) | California (%) |
Home District or Locality in Oaxaca			
Silacayoapan	67.0	13.5	23.1
Huajuapan	4.9	7.9	16.1
Juxtlahuaca	12.2	29.2	38.6
Tlaxiaco	—	15.7	3.0
Other localities in the Mixteca	2.4	33.1	7.5
Other localities in Oaxaca			11.7
Other states (Sinaloa and Baja California)	13.5	0.6	—
Total	100	100	100
	N = 84	N = 177	N = 6,687

Sources: COLEF 1991; Runsten and Kearney 1994.

plots of land for building, and in more permanent employment and education for the children. Even in the camps (or "cantons" as they are called in the United States)—under difficult living conditions governed directly by the dynamics of work, and lacking any degree of independence—Mixtec men, occasionally accompanied by women and children, develop a social organization of their own that re-creates to some degree the traditional patterns of community life.

When the migrants leave the camps and move into rented houses, or onto a piece of land they have bought, or are in the process of buying, they face new expenditures and new dilemmas. Rogelio Méndez clearly identified the problems in chapter 3. When people left the ravines (after 1986) and took up residency in the cities, their daily life changed.[1] They faced the hassles of having to rent, of having a car, and even paying traffic tickets. Expenditures for housing and services changed their conditions and affected the frequency of their remittances back home.

These changes modified how the social network operated. The satellite communities moved on a temporary basis in accordance with the farming season, forming part of the circular flow of migrants. The new residential settlements, established as community nuclei, were forms of cohesion and solidarity that other conditions of life had not allowed to develop. The process of establishing a residence did not imply the end of migration, but rather—as Massey and colleagues (1987) affirm—served to strengthen the migrant networks and the reproduction of migration in different material and social conditions. These new nuclei facilitated the arrival of other migrants who formed the basis of a new generation of residents of Oaxacan indigenous origin, born or raised in these new places (see fig. 2.2).

A general overview of this new ethnic geography shows that the migrants settling in the city of Tijuana—specifically, the Colonia Obrera—were predominantly from towns in the district of Silacayoapan, such as San Francisco Higos, Nieves Ixpantepec, San Miguel Aguacate, and San Jerónimo del Progreso. Migrants from the Guerrero region of the Mixteca settled in the Colonia Valle Verde. The migrants in the Valle de San Quintin show greater diversity in place of origin; most commonly they were from the districts of Silacayoapan, Juxtlahuaca, and Tlaxiaco. On the U.S. side, the mother communities included San Miguel Tlacotepec, San Juan Mixtepec, Santiago Juxtlahuaca, and San Jerónimo Tecomaxtlahuaca in the district of Juxtlahuaca; Silacayoapan, Santiago del Río, and Nieves Ixpantepec in the district of Silacayoapan; and Tezoatlán de Segura y Luna and Santo Domingo Tonalá in the district of Huajuapan de León.

Migrant Networks: Everyday Practices and Social Links

Why do migrant networks appear? To answer this question we must consider the social action of migrants. The networks seem to be a classic example of the unintended consequences of social action, and therefore have a historic meaning. Given that networks emerge from a causal chain of individual acts in daily social practices, this section proposes to study the social links underlying such practices.

Social links give vitality to the networks and are expressed through a variety of social practices in family, community, and working life. Fawcett (1989, 674) proposes a schema that distinguishes different categories and types of linkage in the system of migration. Multiple links can be observed, from those in the sphere of action of national states to among the migrants themselves, whether via their agents or through family or individual structures.[2] Of course, links also exist on the macrostructural level, in the migratory policies of the Mexican and U.S. administrations: for example, those involving the integration of labor markets (supply and demand) or those of a financial nature (capital flow). Without ignoring such macrostructural links, this chapter stresses the social nexuses established in the migratory networks between individuals and families (Fawcett 1989, 674) and also between organizations.

In the next subsection, I analyze the social links present in the Mixtec migration network, following Fawcett's distinction (1989) between tangible, regulatory, and relational linkage. I use just the distinction between tangible and regulatory linkage to analyze individual and family networks. According to Fawcett's definition (1989, 675–676), regulatory linkage encompasses person-to-person obligations and community solidarities among relatives and or hometown acquaintances that help reproduce the migration. Tangible linkage refers to such things as monetary remittances, gifts, and written communication among network members that flow between origin and destinations. I propose another type of link that does not fit in the tangible or regulatory categories. It is a subjective connection: the migrant group's sense of historicity, its link with the origin. The ensemble of attachments to a common origin can be observed, in turn, as part of an ensemble of social practices that help to integrate territorially dispersed members into social units such as the family or the various groups of compatriots that form the ethnic community.

Regulatory and Tangible Links: Family and Community Ties

In the 1991 survey, among a sample of 261 indigenous migrants of Mixtec origin who settled in rural and urban locations in Baja California (Valle de San Quintin and Tijuana), it was found that 95 percent had a family member in the place of origin. In particular, 42 percent mentioned parents; 23 percent uncles, aunts, cousins, or grandparents; 20 percent the whole family; and 15 percent brothers or sisters. The family connection between the mother and satellite communities was important for maintaining active networks. In the year prior to the interviews, nearly one-quarter of the indigenous migrants interviewed had visited their relatives in the hometown.

Providing accommodations for relatives or visitors traveling from the same place of origin (whether with a fixed or unknown destination) was a common practice in the satellite communities, particularly the urban ones. The offering of hospitality was one of the unwritten laws of the migrant network and expresses the type of solidarity that sustains the network as a whole. The 1991 study showed that more than half of those interviewed had housed, on at least one occasion, some family member or paisano in his or her travels along the migrant trail. The link has two facets: one material, in terms of facilitating arrival, immediate survival, and obtaining employment; the other symbolic and affective, in terms of strengthening the sense of family and community belonging.

Another motivation for vitalizing the network was the migrants' relationship with their land. Of the total interviewed, 49 percent owned fields in their hometowns. Only a small number of these individuals had gone home to work their fields during the year prior to the interview (8 percent); nevertheless, the question of who was working and taking care of the land was an important topic in communications with relatives in the place of origin.

The civic-religious cargo systems, which Diskin (1990) and Kearney (1994) regard as the spine of Oaxacan ethnic identity, also function to vitalize the network. During my fieldwork in the agricultural camps and in the cities, I witnessed constant exchanges of fresh information about these systems and the responsibilities that go with them. Lists of the names of members of each local community were often sent from the places of origin to facilitate the collection of money for festivals associated with the ceremonial systems (mayordomías or cofradías), or alternatively, for the community works known as tequio. As the statement by Florencio Hernández below shows, migrants frequently return from the north to their hometowns to take part in the religious festivals (10 percent).

Migrants' concern with fulfilling these responsibilities can best be understood in terms of the importance of the civic-religious system to community identity. As Eric Wolf (1957) points out, the religious system serves to define the limits of the community and acts as a symbol of collective unity.

> In my hometown, we have a custom that consists of each person providing services to the community. That person has the right to invite someone like the president of the municipality or the mayordomo in the cofradía of the saint to participate in the community activity. Everything is done through meetings. There the people say: "This we will do, this we will ask the government, this we will do in this way." We do the same here in San Quintin. Only here there are many people from different states. Many of them don't like to participate because they are used to receiving support from the government; they don't need to do anything. We who are Oaxaqueños always have to participate. (F. Hernández 2001)

So far, I have mentioned practices that imply returns to the hometown to visit family, attend to community commitments, or take care of lands. The social links that sustain those practices may be classified as "regulatory" in the sense that they involve family obligations and community solidarity or commitments. Other kinds of flows vitalize the network as well; these include remittances of money and the sending of objects and exchanges of information, whether through electronic messages, telephone calls, or letters. The sending of money home from the satellite communities brings to mind the image of the hometown as a kind of mother community whose children are sent out to provide for it. Sending money home is also a clear expression of the basic motivation behind transnational communities: economic need. Migrants leave their villages and their homes for one simple reason: to earn money. To appreciate the depth of this commitment, one has to understand migrants' daily fight for survival in the host societies. To live on the Mexican side of the border is very expensive, even though wages are higher than in other parts of the country. However, living on the U.S. side is even more expensive. As the migrants themselves say, while you earn in dollars, you also spend in dollars. During the year prior to the interviews, 40 percent of the indigenous migrants who had settled on the Mexican side of the border had sent money to their hometowns, whether to help a family member or to support a community project. Their sacrifices show their commitment.[3]

Given the low levels of education among these people,[4] researchers have generally not inquired into their letter-writing activities. During my participant observation on farms and in the colonias, I discovered the existence of a network of scribes who often write letters for the migrants, particularly for those living in the agricultural camps. This finding led me to pay greater attention to letters as a form of exchange. Surprisingly, I discovered that written expression was one of the most frequent forms of communication; over 60 percent of those interviewed sent and received letters.[5]

Information is vital to the functioning of the networks. Knowing "what's going on" among relatives and loved ones is a way of being with them— "remaining at home" in the hometown, among one's own people—and sharing with them the experience of migration.[6] The way this medium of communication works is, in itself, an example of the collective construction of the experience of migration. I interviewed two scribes who explained how the epistolary network functions: a person comes to them and tells them in Spanish, Mixtec, or Triqui the nature of the letter; then the scribe interprets and writes. On many occasions, the actual words, which the scribe chooses, are not the precise ones stated by the sender. The act of interpreting occurs in the act of translating from spoken language to written; the target language is invariably Spanish.

All these exchanges—family visits, hosting relatives and friends from the hometown in the satellite communities, the maintenance and use of land, attendance and participation (even when one is not present) in civic-religious festivals, as well as the monetary remittances—show the same direction of movement across the network: from the satellite communities to the mother communities. So what exchanges move in the opposite direction—that is, from the mother communities to the satellites? Only family visits and the exchange of information by letters have a dual directionality. In general, both regulatory and tangible links play an important role in integrating migrants into transnational communities.

What lies behind these practices? Why do the migrants do these things; what motivates them to maintain the networks? The answer lies in ethnic identity, which functions as a moral horizon rooted in historical socialization.

Ethnic identity implies a subjective collectivity that shares a common sense of life. This collectivity pursues its own collective survival and enables its members to survive as individuals. Practices that foster the coming together of families and the strengthening of the community reproduce traditions that go back hundreds of years, like the agricultural practices mentioned by Florescano (1999, 314). The strength of the collective interest suggests that these indigenous migrants realize their individuality to a considerable degree in the framework of the community. This being so, the dynamics of recognition and conflict within the community are fundamental for regulating the practices that maintain the migrant networks.

The Link with the Place of Origin

Eugene Roosens (1994, 82), in a debate with Fredrik Barth, addresses the problem of defining ethnicity as merely a form of social organization. According to Roosens, Barth's definition is inadequate since it ignores the specificity of ethnicity. Referring to migrant populations, she reworks the Barthian concept and defines ethnicity as a form of social organization that functions through family links and principles of common origin. The author believes common origin acquires, in conditions of migration, an importance corresponding to the degree to which the place of origin is objectified as the migrants' homeland.

The social practices dealt with above—visits, remittances, hospitality, and mutual aid in general—illustrate both the practical implications and the symbolic importance of everything contained within the homeland; they also reveal the mechanisms—both in the original territory and abroad—that permit the reconstruction of the sense of "us."

According to Lejeune (1990, 244), as politico-administrative frontiers are weakened by the processes of global integration, the social and cultural matrices of different peoples become more clearly expressed. In these circumstances, the memory of places acquires greater importance as a mechanism for reorganizing the particular history of each nation. In the case of the migrants being studied here, the border is where they arrive; back there, in another place, is their origin. Thus, the origin becomes a reference through which the border is experienced. Whether thought of with longing or with a sense of rejection, the place of origin constitutes a central element in the ethnic identity of the migrants. The hometown materializes as a landscape, as a family home, as a place where a particular kind of food is prepared. There are childhood memories and emotional links. One's origins are remembered in rituals such as the Day of the Dead. Then too—and above all among Mixtec leaders—it is home to the political community that defines the meaning of their activism. The place of origin also conserves that otherness that defines them as indigenous people, distinct from the mestizo cacique, the landowner, or the PRI politician.

The origin, serving to maintain the sense of community in conditions of migration, has at its nucleus a set of blood relationships. However, these broaden out through links based on paisanaje or friendship; similarly those links based on family or community extend to other apparently weaker links of little importance in the hometown, such as sharing a language. The common phrase, "we are brothers from the same town," illustrates the way in which coming from the same town transforms the ties of paisanaje into blood ties; this metaphor seems to revive the ancient indigenous "big family," which included not only contemporaries but ancestors. The homeland functions as an anchor and as a center in a process referred to as deterritorialization or reterritorialization.

> There is a feeling when you are outside your hometown; you feel so unprotected. It is another world, a different society, so you feel the need to do something. Of course, I don't say this is a generalized pattern, that all the problems have arisen here on the border, and that those conditions haven't existed there too, in Oaxaca. I have become aware that on the border, for example, in Tijuana, you see the people grouped according to their hometowns, from Tepejillo, from San Miguel Aguacate. I don't know how it came about, but somehow in spite of their different hometowns they were fighting over the question of street vending. There are always groups of people from the same town; you never find yourself apart because there is a feeling of seeking each other out, as if you felt more protected. We are away from our villages. In the communities there are other things, stronger elements of cohesion: customs, fiestas, family, land, work. There are things you can take with you, others you can't. (Pimentel 1995)

Under conditions of migration, the frontiers of identity, at first associated with local belonging, begin to extend to regional belonging as Mixtecos. In the relational concept of ethnicity (Barth 1969), the origin is also reelaborated according to the others encountered on the road of migration. Thus, the homeland may be, under certain circumstances, the town of origin (San Miguel Tlacotepec), but may equally be the Mixteca as a region, the entire state of Oaxaca, or even all of Mexico.

> In street vending we buy from many people who come almost every day, their suitcases full of jewelry or piggy banks or leather wallets. They come from many places, from Tijuana itself, from Michoacán, Guerrero, Chiapas, and even from Guatemala. They nearly always trust us to pay later, and that is how we do it. Sometimes the selling does not go well, and

we tell them "there's no money, come back next week," and then the poor people come back; what else can they do? It seems there is war now in the south, because the people from Chiapas went back very quickly. They say they must go to be with their folks because the army is harassing the villagers. No, the struggle is on all sides. We're all being screwed, some by the gringos and others by the army. (Santos 1994)

The identity boundaries are wider since there are everyday contacts with people from different places. The restructuring of identity seems to combine territorial, ethnic, administrative, and class classifications (Tlacotepense, Mixtec, Oaxacan, and day worker). New boundaries form from these experiences, as shown by the following statement:

Why get together with Zapotecos, or with Mixes, instead of Huichols or people from Zacatecas? For a simple reason: the Oaxacan homeland, with which we identify very specifically. Look at us; it is a difficult thing to explain, especially from an anthropological point of view. We are, for example, from Tlacotepec. They call us *chacuanes*, which means people from very low down. The people from Macuiltianguis are called *chafanos*. When you are away from home, they continue saying: look at those from Nieves—Ixpantepec—or look, they are from San Juan Mixtepec . . . and so it is that everyone gets together with his own. But when there are problems, we realize we are all Mixtecos because after all we have the same language. We don't always understand each other because there are differences from village to village. . . . But then, when it gets to politics we find that we're all from Oaxaca . . . and so one thing leads to another like the steps of a staircase. However, I think that being from Oaxaca sometimes results in discrimination. "Oaxaquitas," that is what they call us, especially in Mexico City, and in Sinaloa, Sonora, and Baja California. (Pimentel 1995)

It seems clear that although the migratory network derives from the original territorial space, and from constructing another spatial environment, it transcends the original territory, which can be characterized as a transnational space. The hometown or homeland symbolizes the origin of the migrant people, but the process of deterritorializing and reterritorializing alters the ethnic and national boundaries.

The Multitemporality of the Migrant Networks

The migrants' experience of time is sensitive to the social changes that accompany migration. Mixtec migrants come from communities where the construction of time has become materialized in sacred rites and daily rituals related to the cycles of nature (in particular that of the cultivation of maize) and civic-religious events (election of authorities, festivals of the patron saint). For many centuries the civic-religious calendar has structured the routines of everyday life in accordance with certain key events that, as Bachelard (1986, 24) points out, bring time's existence into evidence. Such events have their own cultural logic for every group. According to Florescano (1998, 113; 1999, 297), the Mesoamerican Indians' ideas about time were founded in their worldview, which included conceptions of the creation of the world (cosmogonies), the composition and distribution of the universe (cosmography), the laws maintaining the equilibrium of the cosmos (cosmology), as well as the function of human beings on earth (history). Following López Austin, Florescano (1999, 317) tells us that the principal sources of the Mesoamerican worldview are the diverse everyday activities of all the members of a collectivity.

This helps us to understand the complexity of time systems among contemporary indigenous communities that link celebration rites for the dead and the land. Activities such as civic-religious festivals fit into a ceremonial system that joins pre-Hispanic and colonial institutions, the cycles of the harvest and the election of authorities.

The continuity of rites beyond the original territories may rearticulate the fragmented experience of territory and function as a temporal line of connection linking brief periods with cosmogonic time. According to Anderson (1993, 47), the nation, as an imagined community, only became possible when time became understood as empty and homogeneous, making it possible to imagine the new community in a framework of temporal simultaneity. This new apprehension of time, which, Anderson tells us, arises as the consequence of capitalism and the printing press, allows the construction of an imagined community with a common language. In Mexico, this community was imagined around the Spanish language, with the mestizo as the nation's ideal citizen. Some authors (Stavenhagen 1996) maintain that the indigenous peoples were excluded from this social imaginary, which has dominated Mexico since the nineteenth century. This exclusion was not absolute, particularly in the 1930s when Mexico developed its most important policies affecting the indigenous peoples—the bilingual education and training of hundreds of indigenous teachers. Many interviewers for my research benefited from the new educational policies and became teachers or cultural promoters, including Olga Quiroz.

> I was ten years old when I got to school. Two years later, I had finished the first, second, third, and fourth grade. . . . When I was in the fifth grade, my

parents told me that they must go to work in Sinaloa. The teacher told me that I was a strong and smart student and, if I wanted, he would propose me as a candidate to become a bilingual teacher. I spoke the Castilian and Mixtec languages, and they needed bilingual students. He told me that the government would pay me to study to become a teacher. . . . However, they wanted to send me so far from my home. I was afraid and I did not accept. My parents wanted to go to Sinaloa. They had a huge debt. It was two thousand or three thousand pesos. It was so much money. (Quiroz 2001)

How did the indigenous people think of themselves within this imagined national community? While there is certainly documentation about the adherence of the indigenous peoples to the different government plans carried out during the nineteenth century (Escalante 1993), it is also true that—as Manuel Gamio discovered in 1920 (cited in De la Peña 1994)—the indigenous population living in the valley of Teotihuacán had no word to express the concept of nation. It is not surprising that the indigenous people survived during all these centuries under closed and corporative forms of community, and at the same time were not wholly dissociated from the political and social system of Mexico.

I am self-taught. I began working as a teacher because I had the opportunity to get a scholarship since I spoke Mixtec. Then, they trained me to become part of a group of promoters of bilingual culture, in 1974, 1975. I got in, not because of my academic background, but because of my language skills. Possibly because I was working with the INI [Instituto Nacional Indigenista] and perhaps they could see the kind of person I am. Who knows what they saw, but they gave me the scholarship. I applied for it and took the examination. I passed and went to the course where they asked for good grades in the course. They gave me my diplomas, my certificates. (Gonzalo Montiel Aguirre 1996)

I wish to underscore that the comprehension of time did not change in a large part of the Mexican population. Change was particularly faint in the indigenous communities since they had no access to the decision-making processes that created the nation's social fabric, such as Spanish languages, education in schools, and communication outlets. Different temporalities seem to have continued to coexist through the centuries in the building of the cultural amalgam that, in 1821, became Mexico. I am inclined to think that the comprehension of simultaneous time was possible until the dissemination of mass media (radio and television), accompanied by large-scale migration both internally and internationally in the middle of cultures. Migration, in

Table 4.2 Places and Seasons of Work for Mixtec Migrants in Northwestern Mexico and the Southwestern United States

Place	Type of Crop	Season	No. of Months
Northwestern Mexico			
Sinaloa (Culiacán)	Tomatoes and green vegetables	January–April October–June	9
Sonora (Obregón and coast of Hermosillo)	Cotton, tomatoes, and green vegetables	July–November or December	7
Baja California (Valle de San Quintín)	Tomatoes, strawberries, and green vegetables	April or May–November	8
Baja California (Maneadero)	Strawberries, coriander, and flowers	April or May–November	8
Baja California Sur (La Paz)	Tomatoes, green vegetables, fruits (melon and watermelon)	April or May–November	8
United States			
California	Citrus fruits (oranges and grapefruit), green vegetables, potatoes, beetroot, artichokes, and flowers; wine grapes, tomatoes, and strawberries	March–October, August, March–May	1 3
Arizona	Peach and sweet potato	February	4
Washington	Pear and apple	July–October	4
Oregon	Cherries	April–July	6

Sources: Besserer 1988; Garduño 1989; Guidi 1988; Kearney and Stuart 1981; Krissman 1994a, 1994b; PIRCS-UABCS-SEDESOL 1998; PRONASOL 1991; Runsten and Kearney 1994; Velasco 1990; Zabin 1992.

Note: In the last decade technological innovation, mainly involving nurseries, has changed the work season. With winter crops, it is possible for a farmworker to find work during the entire year in the agricultural fields on both sides of the border.

particular, made it easier to conceive of the family or community as part of an ethnic or national entity that exists simultaneously across several territories.

Not only did migration to the cities or to the large agricultural centers incorporate new territories into community life, but the rhythm of production of the export-agriculture labor markets and the factories in the cities altered the Mixtec sense of time. Table 4.2, showing the seasons of agricultural work for Mixtec migrants, suggests how the migrants' incorporation into the agricultural labor markets of northwestern Mexico and the southwestern United States created new spaces and temporalities in individual and community Mixtec life.

> My hometown is Santiago Huaxolotitlan . . . only the community split up, and about thirty of us went to a *ranchería* [a hamlet] in a new community that we created, which is called San Juan Xochiltepec. It was founded in '70. . . . Well, I was an orphan, I lost my father. As a little kid, I did not know my father. I grew up living with an uncle who beat me a lot, and I left my hometown at the age of eight. I went to another town, called San Francisco Infiernillo. I grew up as a cowboy, and from there I went to Mexico City, in '67, where I lived for three or four years. . . . I worked in a factory that is called Mexicana de Envases. . . . I was working and studying. I went to school. In Mexico City, I made friends with paisanos from San Francisco Infiernillo. I began to socialize with them, and there I learned a bit about what a social movement is. In the factory, the union people from the CTM [Central de Trabajadores de México, Mexican Workers' Union] stole the savings account. We had to sue the company, and an independent union formed in the factory from the workers themselves. They appointed me as a union delegate. . . . I lived in Mexico City for eleven years. From there, I returned to my hometown. (Santiago 1996)

Table 4.2 shows the migration route of the Mixtec people in the agricultural labor market. That route includes places like Sonora-Sinaloa, La Paz, Baja California, and California. The Survey of Oaxacan Village Networks in California Agriculture (Runsten and Kearney 1994), for instance, reveals the seasonal movement of a contingent of Oaxacan migrants between California and Florida who follow the tomato harvest, or between Madera County (California) and Oregon following the strawberry harvest.

The systems of agricultural production and the consumer market consist of the different times of production, commercial, and consumption processes in Mexico and the United States as well as the crop production schedule that migrants follow in their places of origin. For example, in the villages of the Mixteca, most cultivation follows the seasons. In other words, the timing of the sowing cycles depends on the rains, while in the agricultural regions of the Mexican northwest and the U.S. Southwest the agricultural cycle has become less dependent on rainfall. Most crop production relies instead on the technology of irrigation and the accumulation of water in aquifers. For the Mexican or U.S. consumer market, timing is critical. Labor managers must anticipate their workforce needs and the best time to hire workers. These factors add complexity to the migrants' annual decisions about mobility. The dislocation of time appears in the dynamics of the networks. According to Speck and Attneave (1990), in the migrant networks the extended multigenerational family represents longitudinal time, while friends of the family, parents, and neighbors represent transverse time. In other words, such networks encapsulate longitudinal past, present, and future time and transverse simultaneous time, both *here* and *there*.

To the temporal logic of work both in the places of destination and of origin, we must add the temporal logic of the civic-religious ceremonial system to which each community adheres. Finally, family events, which correspond to the cycles of family life, must be included.

> We were in Sinaloa for about three months, and then we went to the village to sow the fields. We spent six months in the village and six months in Sinaloa. That is how things were; in this coming and going my children were born. From there, we returned to the village to celebrate the saints. For example, celebrations happened on October 4 for the local patron saint, Francis of Assisi; on December 12 for the Virgin of Guadalupe; and then the celebration of the Nativity. For each religious feast, we get together six or seven people to celebrate. It is necessary to celebrate, to organize our community. After this, we can be free, but not before. So, wherever we happen to be, we have to go back. It was like that during all that time. We could not make money, not only me, but other Mixtec people as well. There were also problems with the schooling of the children, because we had to take them away, go back, and fulfill this commitment. We cannot miss out on those things. (R. Hernández 1994)

The constant back and forth, and the exchanges of objects and information between members of the community, structures a social network that, in turn, structures other social relations. These exchanges give an immediacy to events taking place elsewhere. They permit a continued feeling of belonging to the same community, while they also update cultural traditions. The construction of the community now no longer depends only on direct interpersonal interaction over short periods, but is aided by the exchange of objects, electronic or postal messages, and phone calls. Through the networks, it is possible to be aware that while I am here, in the hometown or in some other place, such and such an event is happening, and that my people and my friends are there. Time is no longer just linear. Traditional time and modern time coexist in the migrant networks; the calendar of capitalist agricultural production overlaps with sowing for personal consumption in the places of origin. In addition, traditional practices are revitalized by other modern practices within the networks—what can be described as the co-existence of multiple nonlinear times.

Many men, women, and children have not yet made the crossing and have only a vague idea of those new places—the "other side" is only an imaginary place. The same can be true of the place of origin. The home-town inhabits the imagination through personal and collective memory and through nostalgia. Thus, the migrant networks allow the symbolic rearticula-tion of known, imagined, and reimagined places, within a worldview whose spatiality is altered by migration.

Politicization of Migrant Networks and Organizations

Migrant organizations are collectives formed voluntarily for several reasons. At their base are the criteria of shared local origin (*paisanazgo*) or shared regional-ethnic or national-ethnic origin, with these institutionalized to vari-ous degrees. The migrant organizations include hometown associations, resi-dential committees, workers' organizations, and inter-hometown and inter-ethnic organizations (see table 4.3).

Although diversified in their missions, the organizations are sustained by the strong community traditions of indigenous Mexican peoples. The axes of the social and political life of Oaxacan indigenous communities are the civic-religious institutions and those based on cooperation (mayordomías, cofra-días, and tequio). These institutions mediate disputes about the fundamental areas of community life, such as land issues and the election of authorities; their functioning principle is reciprocity. As described in the previous chap-ter, Mixtec migrants participate actively in the political life of their commu-nities of origin, while creating new forms of reciprocity as migrants in the cities or on the farms of northern Mexican or in the southwestern United States. Even though Mixtec migrants engage in political activity at a distance through the medium of migrant networks, that activity is effective.

> As a matter of fact, if you go to the canyons of Vista, in one place there are people from Tlacotepec, and in another from Santa Rosa, and in yet another from Yucuyachi, and so on—little groups from different commu-nities. In fact, you have no choice but to share an apartment because they are so expensive. There are those from Juxtlahuaca who stay in one group

Table 4.3 Oaxacan Migrant Organizations on the California–Baja California Border, by Ethnic Component, Social Base, Objectives, and Orientation

Organization/Place	Ethnic Component(s)	Social Base	Type of Objectives/Orientation*
(1) Frente Indígena Oaxaqueño Binacional (FIOB) / California, Baja California, and Oaxaca	Mixtec, Triqui, and Zapotec	Communities, organizations, and activists	ABCDE / transnational
(2) Asociación Cívica Benito Juárez (ACBJ) / California and Oaxaca	Mixtec	Communities and activists	ABCDE / transnational
(3) Coalición de Comunidades Indígenas de Oaxaca (COCIO) / California and Oaxaca	Mixtec and Valley Zapotec	Communities and activists	ABDE / transnational
(4) Red Internacional Indígena Oaxaqueña (RIIO) / California, Baja California, and Oaxaca	Mixtec and Zapotec	Organizations	ACE / transnational
(5) Organización Regional de Oaxaca (ORO) / California and Oaxaca	Zapotec and Mixtec	Communities and activists	AE / transnational
(6) Vamos por la Tierra / San Diego and Tijuana	Mixtec and mestizo	Activists	CE / crossborder
(7) Coordinadora Estatal de Indígenas Migrantes y Asentados en Baja California (CEIM-BC) / Baja California	Mixtec and Triqui	Organizations and teachers	D / local
(8) Unión de Vendedores Ambulantes y Anexos Carlos Salinas de Gortari (UVAM CS) / Tijuana, BC	Mixtec	Street vendors	B / local

Organization	Ethnic group	Target population	Activities / scope
(9) Unión de Comerciantes Benito Juárez (UCBJ) / Tijuana, BC	Mixtec	Street vendors	B / local
(10) Comité Comunitario de Planeación (COCOPLA) / Tijuana, BC	Mixtec	Residents and teachers	DE / local
(11) Movimiento Indígena y Lucha de Unificación Independiente (MUJI) / San Quintín, BC	Mixtec, Zapotec, and mestizo	Activists and agricultural workers	B / local
(12) Federación Oaxaqueña de Comunidades y Organizaciones Indígenas de California (FOCOICA) / Los Angeles	Zapotec, Mixtec, and Chinantec	Communities and organizations	ABCDE / national
(13) Central Independiente de Obreros Agrícolas y Campesinos (CIOAC) / San Quintín, BC	Mixtec, Triqui, and mestizo	Agricultural workers and residents	BD / national
(14) Movimiento Indígena de Unificación y Lucha Indígena (MIULI) / Maneadero, BC	Triqui and Mixtec	Agricultural workers and residents	BD / local
(15) Unión de Alianzas de Huitepec (UAH) / Maneadero, BC	Mixtec	Communities	AD / local
(16) Organización del Pueblo Triqui (OPT) / San Quintín, BC	Triqui, Mixtec, and Zapotec	Agricultural workers and communities	BDE / local

* Note:

A = cultural

B = workers' and human rights

C = political

D = residents

E = community development

and those from Silacayoapan in another, but there are fewer of them. The same thing happens, but each [group] stays in its own apartment. If there is a roundup [by the border patrol or INS agents], it is going to touch everyone who is from Juxtlahuaca. This regrouping can both make things easier and be more limiting [for the organization]. . . . Easier because there you have the people, all of them together. But limiting because you, as leader, have to be very up front. That is, you cannot hide information. You can't be *gacho* [slang for inconsiderate or rude treatment]. I think one of the bad things we face sometimes, indirectly, is about drinking. If they think you are a big drunkard, they won't have anything to do with you. I mean, they won't take you seriously, even if you are really *grillo* [literally "cricket"; in the political sense it means someone very active and informed]. It's as if all of them have every one of our life stories, and that's a limitation. (Lita 1996)

To repeat, the formation of a social group is facilitated by the proximity of individual agents in a social space (Giménez 1997, 18). Yet migrant networks create a social space that transcends, in geographical terms, the numerous places of migration and the original territory, creating a sense of proximity among geographically distant people. The organizations are the network's political space, or are themselves a politicized network. The migrant networks are the result of social practices that, on becoming routine, give rise to organizational institutions with different structures of rules and resources. Such structures produce and reproduce a social order. They both facilitate and limit the actions of the agents. When these networks function as channels and structures of collective action, the network is politicized, accompanied, reflexively, by the production of meanings. Once politicized, networks channel participation toward a specific aim, and hometown committees or organizations appear, creating a specific field of political activists with the capacity to influence and mobilize interests and resources through the migrant networks (see fig. 4.1).

Once migrant organizations are established, they become important agents in the reproduction of fundamental rituals (such as in the civic cargo system) and in the defense of the workers' and human rights of all Oaxaqueños; this enables them to be activators of what Speck and Attneave (1990) call the process of "retribalization." These authors define the "tribe" as a network of networks, and see it as conferring meaning on many individuals through a chain of relations that bestow identity and the feeling of belonging to a greater whole: the imagined community. In the process of retribalization, cohesion is not so much a prior condition but the result of a shared experience symbolized by specific rituals. Such a common experience includes not

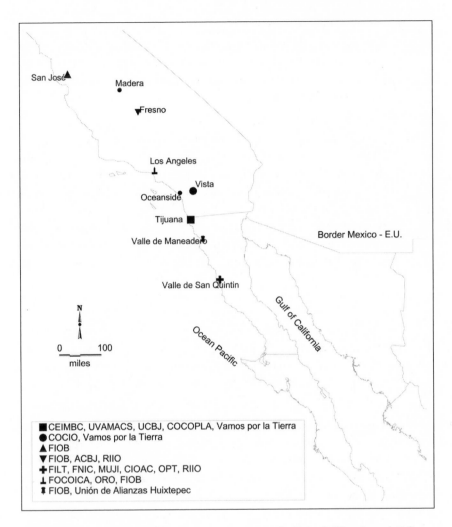

Figure 4.1   Indigenous migrant organizations on the Baja California and California border (Mixtecos, Zapotecos, and Triquis). (Map by Luis Francisco Lares Serrano and Laura Velasco.)

only concerting actions, as we observed in the last chapter, but also resolving conflicts.

Conflicts between different factions are common to community life. Given the closeness of social relations, it is not surprising that such conflicts cut across family ties and that—once outside the hometown—they extend across the links of paisanazgo. Frequently, a disagreement between leaders can unify the members of each person's family and even involve those outside the hometown. Conversely, a conflict arising in a place of migration may reach back to the place of origin. Internal disputes have continually caused splintering and the creation of new organizations. As Juan Lita stresses, internal conflict is intrinsic to community.

> We are also confronting another detail: We do not have the same community issues. We come here and live together in the same city or town; but we are different in the hometown. There are very humble people living with wealthy people; both are immigrants, but in the home community we have different economic and political positions. That makes [organizing] difficult; the issue is not to see the community as a homogeneous entity, because there are divisions and categories, since some people are very reactionary. In Vista, for example, there are people who are enemies of the democratic movement, if it can put that way. And, here, [in Vista] there is a difference between the racists, those who are *de razón* [a sixteenth-century term, "people of reason," or in other words, of European blood], and us, indigenous people. In Tlacotepec, there are those of razón (mestizos) and the indigenous people. These differences are present, and it is very difficult to reunify, for example, those from Tlacotepec. Even the super-tiny communities have these differences in mentalities and they are *grueso* [tough or ugly]. That is why, sometimes, we support a certain section of a community, the most progressive one and not the reactionaries. (Lita 1996)

In my opinion, these conflicts by no means paralyze organizational life but rather energize it. As can be seen from table 4.3, the entire set of organizations constitutes politicized networks in which alliances between hometowns take shape around a series of needs specific to the migrant populations in the Mexico–U.S. border region.

Diversity, Differentiation, and Constants in the Migrant Organizations

Taken as a whole, these organizations constitute forms of association with a more diverse and versatile profile than the classic hometown associations, clubs, and federations documented in the literature on internal and cross-border migration up to the mid-1990s in Mexico. The geographic framework is the border region between California and Baja California and its connection with the Oaxacan Mixteca, and Oaxaca as a whole. If, as Melucci says (1999, 11), collective action is a kind of premonition of future social tendencies—prophesying social change, so to speak—certain features of these organizations foreshadow a process of differentiation in indigenous migration: in ethnic composition, in patterns of mobility, and in new identities. As seen in table 4.3, within this ensemble of organizations are important differences.

The Multiplicity of Ties in the Organizations

The relationship between the migrant networks and the emergence of social organizations is evident in the history of these organizations. The original social nucleus of mobilization was family and community solidarity. These ties generated alliances in the various workplaces and contributed to the formation of Mixtec colonias on the Mexican and U.S. sides of the border. Wilson (1998, 397–398) observed that the constitution of a network is similar to that of a large family that spreads out to many places away from the hometown. The associations form in much the same way. The politicization of the networks follows the course of family and community relations. Individuals, families, and communities as a whole take part in the hometown associations. The hometown comprises family, friends, and paisanos. In reviewing the formation of the organizations listed in table 4.3, one can see a typical three-stage development process.

The first stage corresponds to the setting up of the hometown association or works committee in the hometown itself. This organizational nucleus, defined through belonging to a particular town or village, functions on the basis of strong ties of family or community.[7]

The second stage corresponds to the setting up of inter-hometown organizations, characterized by weaker ties such as being part of the Mixteca region or use of the Mixtec language.

In the third phase, these inter-hometown organizations based in the United States establish themselves as interethnic or pan-ethnic organizations with links to the state of Oaxaca and other parts of Mexico where nuclei of indigenous migrants have appeared. In this phase, ties to U.S. organizations have greater importance, particularly organizations that support human rights or the binational civic movement of Mexican immigrants (Fox 2001, 245). The ties at this level are of a national-ethnic nature, based on the category "indigenous," which acquires new meaning in the context of the Mexican community abroad and within the United States.

Once a field of hometown associations, inter-hometown organizations, and pan-ethnic organizations is established, a space for political action is created in which individuals and collectivities participate on an occasional basis. Thus, diverse organizations may be operating simultaneously in a political field. Group efforts are not always clear and concise; misunderstandings occur. For example, the two base organizations of the Frente Indígena Oaxaqueño Binacional are the Organización del Pueblo Explotado y Oprimido and the Comité Cívico Popular Mixteco; both were set up at the initiative of a nucleus of activists originating in San Miguel Cuevas, in the first case, and San Miguel Tlacotepec, in the district of Juxtlahuaca, in the second.

This pattern repeats itself in the history of the formation of street vendors' associations, which began with a nucleus of women mainly from San Jerónimo del Progreso and San Francisco Higos—villages in the district of Silacayoapan.

It is important to note that the relationship between hometowns and organizations is more evident on the U.S. side than on the Mexican side. Place of origin is also the basis for community solidarity in the colonias and the camps (expressed in money collected for the hometown or for the celebration of saints' days). These forms of support are not clearly defined in organizations south of the border. For example, the street vendors' associations and the Tijuana Planning Committee (Comité de Planeación de Tijuana) limit themselves to issues of worker representation and community development, respectively, leaving the establishment of links with the places of origin in the hands of the traditional authorities, whether directly or symbolically. It is those in the Mixtec and indigenous identity categories who are most affected by the line that demarcates the exterior, *the others.*

In general, on the Mexican side, the formation of groups by place of origin is related more to patterns of urban and agricultural settlement than to the actual aims of the organizations. Currently, the organizations of the San Quintin Valley or Tijuana focus more on ethnic components. In the San Quintin Valley, we find the Central Independiente Obrera Agrícola y Campesina, which is mainly Mixtec, and the Organización del Pueblo Triqui, which, as its name implies, serves the Triqui population of the valley. In Tijuana, two types of organizations exist: those representing residents and those set up by vendors. There are three residents' organizations and three indigenous street vendors associations associated with tourism; the Mixtecos of Oaxaca and Guerrero dominate these. On the Mexican side of the border, organization membership is based on ethnicity rather than place of origin.

On both sides of the frontier, one can observe how the migrant networks have prompted the emergence of social agents of various types. The difference between them lies in the way the agents explain the meanings of the collective action. I shall take up this point in the next chapter.[8]

Transnationality and Links with the
Community of Origin

Another way to distinguish the collective agents is by their degree of "transnationality." The links between different organizations cross the national border; nevertheless, the organizations are not necessarily transnational. Fox

(2001, 243) says that most of the immigrant clubs and federations participate in translocal Mexican policies but are disconnected from U.S. civil society. The organizations listed in table 4.3 vary in their degree of organic connection with their communities of origin and in their binational orientation. Organic connection refers to organizations in new territories explicitly offering assistance to, and participating in, the communities of origin. The purpose is to put many organizational strategies into effect; the clearest examples are the Asociación Cívica Benito Juárez and the Frente Indígena Oaxaqueño Binacional, which have organizational agencies in both the places of origin and migrant territories. Just as migrant networks (places of origin and destination) have multiple interests and resources, the organizations have multiple orientations.

The narrative of Sergio Méndez, activist of the Frente Indígena Oaxaqueño Binacional, describes how during the 1980s—following a period of political upheaval and attempts to construct interethnic fronts on behalf of Oaxaqueños in California—people began to appreciate the need to look south.

> I had the responsibility of working in the Mixteca, where before we had no basis; we lacked roots. We used to say we were like a plant without roots because there [on the northern border] we were very strong, but down there [in the Mixteca] we had nothing. So my visit to the Mixteca made it easier to organize in other towns where . . . on several occasions I had the bad luck, or however you describe it, of always being at the front as a coordinator, until finally I came to be regional coordinator. I'm talking about thirty communities in three administrative districts. (S. Méndez 1996)

Moisés Cruz, of the Asociación Cívica Benito Juárez, describes setting up the organization and the transnationalization of the struggle in the same decade:

> Then [each paisano] contributed around $350 in total. This is what I had taken to Mixtepec. I had already said good-bye to my companions; we agreed that the struggle we were carrying on in the United States was the same one that was going to be fought in Mixtepec. We began our struggle in the United States . . . to organize. We were going to need their support to organize in Mixtepec. They were going to do the same in Mixtepec. It was going to be the same struggle. The situations were very much related; we said to the people who were going to the United States: "Go to the association and give your support." And so, it goes spreading a little and there is already more communication. (Besserer 1988, 232)

The street vendors' associations in Tijuana represent the other extreme—that is, lacking a transnational orientation. Other examples are the Central Independiente de Obreros Agrícolas y Campesinos, the Movimiento de Unificación de Jornaleros Independientes, and the Organización del Pueblo Triqui. They lack organizational programs in the places of origin and in their satellite communities in the United States. Local awareness arose in the present CIOAC, which as a trade union organization is now more oriented toward solving the problems of new residents in the San Quintin Valley.

> We can consider ourselves as residents of San Quintin Valley because we have been here for twenty years, not six months. Of course, we are a product of migration. I am a migrant, but a "resident migrant" like many people who arrived between 1975 and 1978. It is worth mentioning that we are not people who come and go; we've established ourselves in this region. This is a struggle with the government of Baja California because of its plan for the Valle de San Quintin. During the last period [six years], we were considered migrants, not residents. They just don't take us into account. My proposal is to create representation within the cabildo [county chamber] for not only migrants but indigenous residents. We were migrants, but now we are residents with a common origin, which makes us indigenous. (Rojas 1996)

The link with the place of origin seems to be instrumental in the new places of residence. New residents negotiate with the local administration of the places of origin and destination for some rights such as ownership of land or local representation based on indigenous identity.

Finally, we must recognize the work carried out by the state of Oaxaca to strengthen the links between these organizations and the villages, region, and state of origin. Visits by state governors during the last twenty years, particularly to Baja California and California, have strengthened these ties. Most beneficial of all has been the investment of funds in local and regional development projects. Governments, recognizing these organizations as social and political interlocutors, have become greater participants in the creation of coalitions of Oaxacan migrant organizations.[9]

Multiplicity of Interests and Institutionalization of Organizations

A common characteristic of the organizations is their low level of formal structuring. In general, these organizations are in a stage of emergence. The FIOB and the COCIO are two exceptions. Over a twenty-year period, numerous organizations have appeared, disappeared, or combined with others at such a rate that, at times, they can only be traced by their activists or leaders or through scholarly documents on the subject. Only two of these organizations possess an informational bulletin: the FIOB publishes *El Tequio* (described as the Binational Voice of the Oaxaqueños), and the COCIO produces *Alma Oaxaqueña*. Only the FIOB has a Web site and offices on both sides of the border (California, Baja California, and Oaxaca), as well as a mission statement and bylaws.

The weak institutionalization of the organizations is explained, in part, by the mobile nature of their members. This feature, so highly valued in the international agricultural market, has enabled them to set up binational or transnational organizations. The process of institutionalization must be viewed in the historical context of all the organizations and the consolidation of a few. It seems to me that the Frente Indígena Oaxaqueño Binacional has seen the most consolidation in that historical struggle.

The life stories of the leaders and activists of these organizations, and the assortment of internal documents and scholarly literature describing the leaders and activists, support the hypothesis that organizational activity did not begin in the satellite communities. Community organization and participation in local and regional struggles formed a foundation of experience and knowledge that the migrants continually enriched with their struggles as workers in the cities, as laborers on the farms of the north, and as undocumented workers in the United States. Oaxaqueños organized themselves for festivals, did tequio (community work) in different projects, and participated in elections of local councils and in the regional movements during the 1970s. What the "Mixtec regions" of Mexico City, Baja California, and California did give birth to were the specific hometown associations, organized around the patron saint festivals or particular infrastructure projects. Also born in these regions was the need to integrate different organizations for the defense of workers' rights, residents' rights, and human rights, under a binational interethnic front or coordination.

> The group we set up, the Comité Cívico Popular Mixteco . . . we were about ten people—myself, Algimiro, Gregorio, and others, all from Tlacotepec. We met each other going from one place to another. We formed a sports club in the process of going to and from the hometown. In the mid-1980s we began to set up the committee because we saw problems in the hometown; they wanted to impose candidates for mayor. This committee got strong in California, but it really solidified between the village and Mexico City with people who went to work on the construction of the Metro. Originally, it was just the Comité Cívico Popular [Tlacotepense]. . . but afterward when we met up again with the same people in the

fields of the north and began . . . we shared the labor problems in the agricultural camps of Sonora and the San Quintin Valley. . . . Well, then it changed to the Comité Cívico Popular Mixteco. . . .

It was at that time that the reforms to the U.S. laws came in—the Simpson-Rodino Act. At that time the people from my village were in northern San Diego County and were already organizing themselves to send money to the village to support the mayoralty. . . .

We, as the Comité Cívico Popular Mixteco, succeeded in making this project grow. We incorporated people from other communities and we were, ourselves, the promoters [of the process] to seek out other organizations like the Asociación Cívica Benito Juárez [people from San Juan Mixtepec], and finally those of the Organización del Pueblo Explotado y Oprimido. Mixtec people were the embryo of the Front. As the committee between 1985 and 1987, we worked for a meeting with some advanced communities of Zapotecos in Los Angeles. . . . And so, in 1991 we set up the Frente Mixteco-Zapoteco Binacional. . . .

Since 1985, we have had two concerns: to learn English and to become informed about legislation . . . also the human rights problems. The paisanos arrived saying, "they took my money." So we thought, well, apart from the fact that we are from the communities of Macuiltianguis, San Juan Mixtepec, Nieves Ixpantepec, and San Miguel Cuevas, we have other interests in common . . . we are Mixtecos. That helped because we definitely didn't want to go in with the people from Zacatecas and Michoacán. In Sinaloa, our fellow Mexicans discriminate against us a lot; they call us Oaxaquitas. . . . So there are differences in customs, too. They don't have that identity that is within the Oaxaqueños. For us, things like community, identity as a people, and the general problems of being workers are very important. (Pimentel 1995)

This statement describes the formation of a pan-ethnic Mixtec identity and the pan-ethnic indigenous identity in the transnational process. A transnational ethnic subject is a result of the activism in this new political field. Another indicator of institutionalization is the legal constitution of the organizations. Until 1998, the Front was in control of two legal entities through which financial resources were collected: the Centro Binacional para el Desarrollo Regional, in California, and the Centro de Desarrollo Regional, in Juxtlahuaca, Oaxaca. This situation changed after the 2001 internal crisis described in chapter 3; in 2002, the Juxtlahuaca office became the Desarrollo Binacional Integral Indígena in Oaxaca City.

The organizations are transnational to different degrees in their interests and resources. Undeniably, the political component, which has been developing over the last two decades on the Mexico–U.S. border and in Oaxaca, has permeated all levels of organizational activity. While some organizations are more oriented toward the place of arrival, all participate in a transnational political and discursive field, as can be seen from the leaders' life stories. A fundamental example of this is the discussion among the organizations as to what relationships they should establish with local governments (mayors of municipalities of origin and arrival), regional governments (governors of Oaxaca and Baja California, or California), and with the federal governments of the United States and Mexico.

Networks, Migrant Organizations, and New Experiences of Community

In the migrant networks, multiple places, social links, and temporalities coexist, as in the reticulum metaphor proposed by Michael Kearney. The network, or rather the ensemble of superimposed networks, in the border region between Mexico and the United States is not constructed merely by the migrants' efforts to promote their social and cultural reproduction. The network also develops through the logic of capital, which imposes a particular spatial and temporal pattern on the network. At first the migrant networks served to facilitate the creation of a collective experience of migration, developing a collective knowledge about routes, seasons, employment conditions, dangers and risks, climatic conditions, contacts, forms of behavior—in short, a basis of knowledge that could be considered "cultural capital" (produced by migration, and which has been absorbed by even nonmigrants in the towns and villages of origin).

At this point, it is useful to recall Kearney's emphasis on the importance of information in the social networks, or "migrant reticula" as he calls them. If social practices are fundamental to creating and maintaining these networks, it is also true that such practices basically produce information about the community as a collective consciousness, which enables community life to be imagined as it is mediated by what others say (whether paisanos, television, videos, photographs, etc.) about what is happening in another place. In this way, the networks permit the creation of the simultaneous time to which Anderson refers, and also the rearticulation of the fragmented experience of territory as the material basis of the imagined community.

The hometown associations function as networks of migrants with a specific territorial base and a well-established relationship with the governing officials and also enjoy recognition from their hometowns. Thus, the results of the present research agree with the findings of Hirabayashi (1985) and Orellana (1973) for the Zapotec and Mixtec organizations in Mexico City:

the hometown associations that I studied had a well-established relationship with the systems of authority and recognition in their places of origin. At the same time, the research revealed that collective mobilization around interests associated with the places of arrival often revitalized the relationship with the places of origin. This turns out to be especially true among organizations functioning in California, which have entered into a quasi-competition to collect funds for their hometowns and to define the terms of their relationship with the municipal administrations and the Oaxaca state government. The same has not been true in the organizations established on the Mexican side of the border. They mobilize around labor, residential, and human rights, and maintain their hometown committees or associations independently of workers' or residential organizations.

The organizations' social fields of action constitute a heterogeneous political space with regard to (1) their local, cross-border, or transnational orientation; (2) their rural or urban environment; (3) their focus on residence on the border or in the places of origin; and (4) their emphasis on cultural affairs or the struggle for sources of employment and better wages.

The organizations that have emerged differ in their level of organization, which implies different forms of representation. A coalition, a coordinating body, an association, a front, or a federation—each has a different meaning in terms of representing its members. Some organizations represent individuals and other corporate bodies, whether hometown, community, or organizations. They can also be differentiated as multi-hometown and multi-ethnic or multi-hometown and mono-ethnic. The composition of the base represented may differ according to the analytic perspective one adopts.

The variety of organizational practices (mobilizations, demands, types of relationships with local administrations, and alliances) distinguishes these organizations as agents, while showing the ethnic consciousness of the migrant populations. There is no denying that within the organizations a constellation of leaders function as intellectuals. They may be bearers and creators of a discursive ethnic consciousness. This chapter has examined the social practices that sustain the migrant networks and organizations. The next chapter will focus on the discursive ethnic consciousness constructed by the leaders of these organizations. As we shall see in the next chapter, these intellectuals are also the result of the institutionalization of international migration and are privileged agents who re-create cultural contents of the community in multiple territories.

5

Indigenous Intellectuals

The Political Construction of the
Transnational Ethnic Community

The previous chapter analyzed migrant networks and organizations as mechanisms of the revitalization of the dispersed community. During and as a result of migration, migrants' experience of territory became fragmented. The geographic dispersion of hometown members required a reconstitution of ethnic boundaries and ethnicity's basic emblems (languages, civic-religious festivals, territory). To analyze the latter processes, we need to understand the role of particular agents who work politically to create the new frontiers of the ethnic community within organizations.

Despite an increasing number of studies that examine the formation of new social spaces and the actors associated with international migration (see Mummert 1999; Portes 1998; Smith and Guarnizo 1998), the formation of individual agents—such as intellectuals—in the framework of ethnic identities and Mexican migration to the United States has scarcely been addressed. It is of great interest to study the emergence and inner strength of indigenous intellectuals in migrant organizations in the California–Baja California area. This chapter concentrates on the ethnic identity project elaborated by these individuals, as important agents in the construction of the ethnic community.

To understand the influence of indigenous intellectuals, the life stories of twenty-four leaders of Oaxacan migrant organizations were examined. The focus was on the experience of social conflict, with attention to three vital dimensions: ethnic belonging (whether Mixtec, Triqui, or Zapotec); migration and the crossing of national frontiers; and political participation. Analyzing conflicts in those three dimensions helps to organize the biographical trajectories. The following brief discussion of the concept of the intellectual will clarify the role of intellectuals as makers of ethnic identity.

Political-Cultural Representation and Intellectuals

There is common agreement in the theory of social action that not all the individuals involved in a collective action have the same role in defining the collective project. This means, as Bourdieu explains (1982, 154), that in collective action as symbolic struggle, there are those who inevitably come forward to speak on behalf of others and construct the group that makes them its spokespersons. These spokespersons have been referred to, variously, as intelligentsia, the elite, or intellectuals. The present work opts for the latter term, following studies of nineteenth-century national elites (Anderson 1993) and Gramsci's (1998) concept of the organic intellectual.

According to Gramsci (1998, 9), all human beings are intellectuals, but not all have the function of intellectuals in society. Organic intellectuals do not form a class as such; rather, each social group has its own stratum of intellectuals or tends to form one. The legitimacy of the intellectuals does not lie in eloquence but in active participation in practical life as permanent persuaders, as well as in their capacity to guide and represent the aspirations of the class to which they organically belong (Gramsci 1998, 10).

In studies of the construction of nationalisms and ethnicities in modern states (e.g., Anderson 1993; Hobsbawm and Rangers 1983; and Sollors 1989), issues of representation become a central concern in the Gramscian definition of the organic intellectual. The Gramscian definition considers the two meanings of representation identified by Heller (1998, 341): the political and the cultural. The success of intellectuals is assessed in terms of their capacity to synthesize the group's historicity and to provoke a crisis in the hegemonic order, in which one class or ethnic group dominates. The latter capacity distinguishes the intellectual from the broker, who may act in the political field but not necessarily in the cultural and historical fields. Intellectuals are implicated personally by their adherence to the historicity of the group. Intellectuals can assume the role of broker, but cannot be the only broker since their identity is at risk in the social movement.

Specialists in indigenous matters in Mexico and Peru have not remained unaffected by this discussion. According to Bartolomé (1997, 170), the ability of indigenous leaders to represent migrants must be considered in the framework of the political practices of the indigenous communities. He finds a confusion in the academic literature between traditional authority and community leaders. The latter have the role of "cultural brokers," intermediaries between external agencies and the communities. They represent the community in the political arena. The traditional authorities, on the other hand, are guides or regulators of social, political, and economic relations. They do not possess a delegated authority that permits them to modify the behavior of other members of the community or to represent them in the outside world. Their power derives from the power of the word: the capacity to act as communal orators (Bartolomé 1997, 169). Although this is a clear distinction, Guillermo Bonfil (1995b, 122–124) has identified a new kind of leadership and a change in the function of traditional leaders. This author even proposes a typology of leadership, which includes the traditional figure with a political leadership role; the local leader emerging because of external pressure on the Indian communities; the Indianized intellectuals and militants; and the recuperated or re-Indianized leaders. The latter took part in the early migration process of their communities and were immersed in a non-Indian world. At the same time, they maintained social, economic, and/or symbolic relations with the community of origin and contact with the political militancy of nonindigenous sectors. Both Bartolomé and Bonfil stress the importance of reopening the debate on representation in indigenous history. That implies that ethnic relations be considered in the context of the struggle between social classes and the struggle over citizenship in postcolonial states. Therefore, the role of the ethnic intellectual is played out partly in the framework of economic relations and partly in the struggle for citizenship in the multiethnic nation-state.

As Mallon (1995, 12) pointed out about local intellectuals in Mexico and Peru, the role of intellectuals on the symbolic plane can be called strategic, since they labor to reproduce and rearticulate local history and memory. Similarly, Gutiérrez (1999) found that indigenous Mexican intellectuals participate actively in the construction of ethnic consciousness, as both destroyers and founders of myths. This activity is no less political since its role is to construct areas of positive distinction in relation to a multitude of "others" through an ethnic discourse.[1]

From my point of view, migration across the national and state border has brought new challenges in representation in the indigenous community. Community has been transformed: it is no longer a group of peasants living in a common territory. Community is dispersed across national and international territories; its members are class workers, day workers, vendors, undocumented people, and U.S. citizens. Political and cultural representation and the definition of who represents the community are also changing. Before focusing on the ethical and political discourse produced by leaders, I will profile these leaders.

Who Are the Indigenous Migrant Intellectuals?

The leaders profiled here do not constitute all the Oaxacan migrant leaders in the Mexico–U.S. border region; nor are they a statistically representative sample. As a stratum of intellectuals, their point of reference is the peoples of the Mixteca Baja region of Oaxaca, as well as the nuclei of Mixtec residents in Baja California and California. All of them belong to some organization active in the border region.

Their role as intellectuals is defined empirically by the fact that they occupy posts in the formal structure of an organization or are recognized as persons of influence in the associations and organizations. As can be seen from table 5.1, there are substantially more male than female leaders:

Table 5.1 Sociodemographic Characteristics of Interviewed Leaders

No.	Sex	Age	Education	Marital Status	Language	Place of Birth (District)[a]	Organization[b]	Occupation
1	M	40	Master's	Married	Spanish-Mixtec	San Juan Yolotepec (1)	UPN–Comité de San Juan Yolotepec	Teacher: first-degree level
2	M	31	Doctorate	Married	Spanish-English	Santa Cruz, Rancho Viejo (2)	FIOB	Student; assistant lecturer
3	M	39	Pre-bachelor (unfinished)	Married	Spanish-Mixtec	Huixtepec (6)	FIOB	Agricultural laborer
4	M	43	Primary	Married	Spanish-Mixtec	San Juan Xochiltepec (6)	UAH	Agricultural laborer
5	M	49	Primary	Married	Spanish-Mixtec	Santa María Yucuyachi (2)	MUJI	Agricultural laborer
6	M	24	Secondary	Married	Spanish-Mixtec	Santa María Asunción (3)	CIOAC-INI	Radio presenter
7	M	38	First degree of bachelor	Married	Spanish-Mixtec-English	San Juan Mixtepec (3)	ACBJ-INI	Radio presenter
8	M	22	Primary	Married	Spanish-Triqui	San Juan Copala (8)	OPT-INI	Radio presenter
9	M	49	Secondary	Married	Spanish-Zapotec	Tlacochahuaya (7)	ORO	Private chauffeur
10	M	32	Secondary	Married	Spanish-Mixtec-English	San Miguel Cuevas (2)	FIOB	Legal adviser in California; agricultural laborer
11	M	38	Secondary	Married	Spanish-Mixtec	Santa María Asunción (3)	CIOAC	Agricultural laborer
12	M	41	Pre-bachelor (unfinished)	Married	Spanish-Mixtec	San Miguel Tlacotepec (2)	FIOB	Profesional leader (teacher)
13	M	38	Bachelor	Married	Spanish-Mixtec	San Andrés Tonalá (1)	SEP-COCOPLA	Teacher
14	M	43	Primary	Married	Spanish-English	San Miguel Tlacotepec (2)[c]	COCIO	Agricultural laborer
15	M	35	Pre-bachelor	Married	Spanish-English	San Miguel Tlacotepec (2)[d]	MVT	Industrial worker
16	M	37	No schooling	Married	Spanish-Triqui	San Juan Copala (8)	OPT	Agricultural laborer

17	M	42	Primary	Married	Spanish-Mixtec-English	San Miguel Tlacotepec (2)[e]	FIOB	Legal adviser in California; agricultural laborer
18	M	30	Secondary	Married	Spanish-Zapotec-English	San Jerónimo Xochina (7)	ORO	Sales clerk
19	M	40	Primary	Married	Spanish-Mixtec-English	San Miguel Tlacotepec (2)	MVT	Industrial worker (in U.S.)
20	F	51	Primary	Separated	Spanish-Mixtec	San Francisco Higos (3)	AMBJ	Street vendor
21	F	41	Primary	Married	Spanish-Zapotec	San Jerónimo Xochina (7)[f]	ORO	Domestic worker
22	F	35	Pre-bachelor (unfinished)	Separated	Spanish	San Marcos, Guerrero[g]	COCOPLA	Dressmaking teacher
23	F	33	Primary	Married	Spanish-Mixtec	San Pedro Chayuco (2)	MIULI	Agricultural laborer
24	F	52	No schooling	Married	Spanish-Mixtec	San Francisco Higos (3)	UVAM CS	Street vendor

[a] Districts of Oaxaca

(1) Huajuapan de León, (2) Juxtlahuaca, (3) Silacayoapan, (4) Coixtlahuaca, (5) Tlaxiaco

Other regions of Oaxaca

(6) Zaachila (Valley Mixtec), (7) Valley Zapotec, (8) Triqui region

[b] Abbreviations of organizations

ACBJ	Asociación Cívica Benito Juárez
CIOAC	Central Independiente de Obreros Agrícolas y Campesinos
COCIO	Coalición de Comunidades Indígenas de Oaxaca
COCOPLA	Comité Comunitario de Planeación
FIOB	Frente Indígena Oaxaqueño Binacional
INI	Instituto Nacional Indigenista
MIULI	Movimiento Indígena de Unificación y Lucha Independiente
MUJI	Movimiento de Unificación de Jornaleros Independientes
MVT	Movimiento Vamos por la Tierra
OPT	Organización del Pueblo Triqui
ORO	Organización Regional de Oaxaca
UAH	Unión de Alianzas de Huitepec
UVAM CS	Unión de Vendedoras Ambulantes y Anexos Carlos Salinas de Gortari

[c] Born in Omealca, Veracruz. Mother also born in Veracruz. Father and grandparents came from San Miguel Tlacotepec.

[d] Born in Mexico City to parents from San Miguel Tlacotepec.

[e] Born in San Mateo Libres, but father was from San Miguel Tlacotepec.

[f] Born in San Diego and brought up in Mexico City, but parents are from San Jerónimo Xochina, and she describes herself as a "descendant."

[g] Her husband is from San Andrés Tonalá in Huajuapan de León. Since marrying, she has participated in the Mixtec communities.

nineteen men to only five women. Their average age is thirty-nine, the youngest being twenty-two and the oldest fifty-two. In general, this generation grew up and had their first domestic migration experiences in the 1960s and their border or U.S. migration during the 1970s and 1980s. Their marital history was difficult to reconstruct, as some of the leaders had a series of separations and unions.[2] All of them had had some kind of matrimonial experience, whether in the form of common-law marriage or one sanctioned by church or state. Unlike the women, all the men who had separated from a partner had a partner at the time of the interview.

Their level of education differentiates this group of leaders from the general population. I chose not to measure education in terms of the number of years of study, since many of the leaders pursued their schooling under conditions of migration. Migration often obliged them to carry out their studies in an open system of education, through the bilingual program in their community of origin or through special educational programs for migrants in the United States. Table 5.1 shows two people with no schooling, nine with studies at the primary level, five with a secondary education, four with studies at the bachelor level, two with bachelor's degrees, one with a master's degree, and one with a doctorate. Given the small size of the sample, the percentages may lack statistical value. It is worth noting, however, that half of the group in the sample had studied above the primary level and a third as far as the senior high school level or beyond. In 1991 (Velasco 1991, 98), 20 percent of the Mixtec migrants living in Baja California had no schooling, 72 percent had some degree of primary schooling, while only 8 percent had received schooling beyond the primary level. The sample of leaders shows levels of education that are above the average for indigenous migrants in Baja California.[3]

As for the use of indigenous languages, the extent of bilingualism among the leaders interviewed is noteworthy, as is the incipient trilingualism. This polyglotism is defined not so much by use of Spanish and several indigenous languages (Mixtec, Triqui, or Zapotec) as by the inclusion of English, whether as a second or third language. This development seems to be a fundamental change among the migrant indigenous populations, especially among the transnational agents. Of the eight leaders, three are bilingual in Spanish and English and five are trilingual in Spanish, English, and either Mixtec or Zapotec.

The activities of these leaders are based on the type of organization to which they belong. The occupations among the leaders interviewed are day workers (most of them), street selling, announcers on the bilingual indigenous radio station La Voz del Valle (The Voice of the Valley), legal advisers (originally farmworkers), teachers, industrial workers, service-sector employees, professional leader (originally a primary school teacher), and doctoral student. These occupations include both urban and rural environments on either side of the border. Some leaders found employment with cultural institutions, government agencies, or NGOs (nongovernmental organizations). They worked as legal advisers in California, as announcers on bilingual indigenous radio, as bilingual teachers in Baja California, or on the staff of Frente Indígena Oaxaqueño Binacional.

The leaders' place of origin was determined by their birthplaces, the birthplaces of their parents, and the places they grew up. The birthplaces did not always coincide with the place where the leaders felt an attachment or what they point to as their place of origin. The Mixteca Baja region of Oaxaca dominates as the place of origin for the leaders—nineteen of them come from there. Others come from Guerrero, in the Zapotec region of the Valley of Oaxaca, or from the Triqui zone of the same state. Of those from the Mixteca region, most are from the districts of Juxtlahuaca and Silacayoapan. Five are from the town of San Miguel Tlacotepec, and three others are from towns in the same area. The leaders had similar childhood experiences and in migration, work, and political participation, which unites them either directly or through relatives or acquaintances. Their shared background reinforces a network of municipal and regional political influences.

In regard to hometown, a particular pattern merits attention. In the life stories, I found five instances where leaders were not born in the places they recognized as their hometown. In other words, they were born in a place to which their parents had migrated. Nonetheless, they took part in the hometown network while still children, moving back and forth between the hometown and places such as Veracruz and Mexico City. Their dual allegiance permitted them to join or participate in communal work projects in their new community and to identify themselves as still belonging to their respective hometowns.

Table 5.1 shows the leaders' characteristics. Some leaders are involved with community-based associations, such as interviewee 3, a leader of the Unión de Alianza Huitepec; interviewee 12 is coordinator of several organizations and communities in different places in the border region and in the Oaxacan Mixteca; interviewee 14 is the coordinator of the Coalición de Comunidades Indígenas de Oaxaca, which is similar to the Organización Regional Oaxaqueña. Both organizations link various communities, and thus the organization leaders are organically linked to those communities. Interviewees 20 and 24, on the other hand, are leaders of street vendors' associations in Tijuana, and their role as intellectuals comes from their work as street vendors. The same is true for interviewee 11, who is also the leader of the CIOAC. Interviewees 1, 6, 7, 8, and 13 are leaders in the sense of being activists for their respective communities as radio announcers or as influential teachers in the indigenous migrant community. In general, these intellectuals are married men with above-average education and are multilingual. At the same time, they vary in occupation, hometown origin, and transnationalism.

Transnationalism is of particular relevance given the framework of international migration that defines the activity of these intellectuals. Transnational not only refers to the crossing of national frontiers but also identifies individuals who exist in different state and national contexts simultaneously. It may be said that transnationality is an experience that results naturally from international migration; however, it is when this experience is translated into these agents' political fields of action that its significance is revealed. Although their spheres of action are local, these intellectuals act in a transnational arena owing to their political connections on both sides of the border. This small group of leaders can be divided into six groups along a local-transnational continuum.

First group: Indigenous migrants with a high level of education, generally a fully trained primary school teacher, trained under the "cultural action" program of the Instituto Nacional Indigenista during the 1970s, with experience in the bilingual teacher movement in the southern part of the country; did agricultural work during childhood and youth and experienced urban life in Mexico City; migrated under an educational program to meet the needs of Mixtec populations on Mexico's northern frontier.

Second group: Differ from members of the previous group on the basis of sex and experience in urban spaces, particularly on the border; indigenous women with little or no schooling; experienced family migration to the agricultural camps of Sonora and Sinaloa; bilingual and organized around problems of community services and street vending in border cities.

Third group: Migrants with extensive experience as farmworkers; education up to the primary or secondary level; work experience in the agricultural camps of California but established as residents in the San Quintín Valley and in Maneadero; participating actively in workers' representative movements and in urban development of this agricultural region; bilingual in Spanish-Mixtec or Spanish-Triqui.

Fourth group: Defined by experience in agricultural work; have a broad base of international migration experience and a background in the farmworkers' movement in Sonora, Sinaloa, and Baja California; education not beyond secondary level; bilingual speakers of Spanish and an indigenous language such as Mixtec or Triqui; established in California.

Fifth group: Intellectuals with a high level of geographical mobility and considerable political participation in the rural and urban environments, both in Mexico and abroad; level of education is high secondary; Spanish language is mother tongue; born in Veracruz or Mexico City and migrated as young children.

Sixth group: In process of emergence; indigenous migrants who arrived as small children or were born on the Mexican border or in U.S. territory; have had access to formal education up to professional or postgraduate level in U.S. universities; have few memories of their hometowns and do not know them as adults; bilingual in English and Spanish, or trilingual in Mixtec, Spanish, and English.

Out of this group of intellectuals, a generation of administrators or other professionals has gradually emerged. Over the last decade, they have found their way into institutionalized areas established by nongovernmental groups or by the governments of either country. This group of intellectuals works on bilingual indigenous education, bilingual indigenous radio, and the administration of justice to indigenous migrants in Baja California and California.

Leaders, mostly men, function as mediators between government institutions and the community nuclei, a task in which their ability to negotiate in the various languages—Mixtec, Triqui, Zapotec or Mixe, Spanish, and English—has been essential. What cultural feature better indicates the transnationality of these voices than their polyglotism? The present and future existence of the indigenous migrant communities depends not only on migrants' languages of origin (pre-Hispanic and Spanish) but also on their ability to express themselves in English.

Social Conflict and the Emergence of Indigenous Intellectuals

Although some of the intellectuals have memories of hometowns, memories marked by ethnic discrimination, poverty, and authority abuse, most of them trace their first experiences of collective action to the places of migration: Mexico City, Sinaloa, Sonora, Baja California, and the city of Oaxaca. The intellectuals have enriched experiences of hometown community life and urban knowledge gained in factories, the construction industry, or agriculture.

The life stories show the late 1960s to the early 1980s to be the period of initiation into politics. The intellectuals identify poor working conditions, mistreatment, and substandard living conditions in the agricultural camps as the catalysts of their discovery of the "badness," the "injustice," of the migrants' situation. There seems to be a basic experience of conflict— varying only according to the space of relations in which it appears and is confronted—prior to that experience reaching full consciousness. The leaders' narrative reconstructions of their hometown life, before migration, are marked by a central conflict involving as their historical adversaries the "people of reason" (i.e., the mestizos), the caciques, the local authorities, and the government. Experiences of conflict during migration, in the workplace and in living conditions, delimit the *others* as adversaries, while "we" are seen as allies, in a network of social relations much more complex than the simple us-them duality. Whether these experiences happened in the agricultural camps or in cities like the Mexico City, the new condition of workers propelled some leaders into collective action. At the same time, conditions identified the boss as adversary and the paisanos and other workers in the factory or the agricultural camps as allies.

Migration to Sinaloa created lasting, vivid memories among the indigenous. Antonio, a Triqui leader in the San Quintin Valley, left his hometown (San Juan Copala in Oaxaca) when he was very young. He remembers the labor and living conditions in Sinaloa.

> After two years in Cuautla, Morelos, we went to Sinaloa. And well, you know, in the Sinaloa valley life was very hard. Many of our people died. They got ill and broke out in spots because the canal water was quite dirty. There, upstream, people were bathing, washing clothes, and down there a dog died and they threw it in the canal. Cows and so on, all in the canal, and there the people were drinking the water. In Sinaloa, we were there about six or seven months. Then we came to the coast of Hermosillo; we lasted nearly two years because Hermosillo was more or less clean. There we drank pumped water like here [San Quintin Valley]. The problem was that it was very hot. The boss treated us badly and, well, that is how it is. You had to work real hard there, and then when you got your pay, it was hardly worthwhile. If you missed a day, you didn't get paid and you always had to work like mad; if not, he gave you three, four days rest. If you didn't work at all, then he told you straight out you're fired. (Antonio López 1996)

Memories related to health were common among the women interviewed too. In addition, long journeys and intense activity day after day are two of the most powerful memories of these people.

> And well, it was from that time that I took up the struggle. It was around '77, '78. It was a very hard life because we spoke just the Triqui language and the other fellow spoke just Mixtec. To understand each other, it was difficult and even more so in Spanish, for in those times . . . I left [the village] when I was eight years old, I was very little. I still didn't know what reading was or what it was to speak Spanish, no. So it was here that I learned and, thanks to God, not long ago, maybe two or three years; now I can speak more. I speak some words badly but that doesn't worry me. I

recall that around '78, '79, and '80, there was a planting of flowers with an American called Roberto there at Guerrero beach. We were working, and there was a man called Cruz, who was kind of the general [foreman]. We weren't all Triquis. There was this ranch where we were working. He was telling us to get lost because we weren't doing the work. The man, well, he treated us however he felt like doing. So from that year on, I started to look for the solution and how to go about the struggle for my people. (López 1996)

The preceding statement shows how a sense of injustice is rooted in the working conditions of agricultural workers and in the community. A lack of communication between countrymen was one of the main problems. In order to form alliances with other indigenous people and fight injustices, a common language was needed.

In 1978, I met Félix Vega; he was working in the Human Rights office in Ensenada. . . . This person and his job caught my attention. At the beginning, I didn't know how to speak, but after I joined him, I learned how. So, my heart was being built up, was being born to the struggle, and from '80 to '84, that was when Benito arrived. I already knew how to speak a little and I already felt a bit of courage. I had already searched out . . . other companions. We knew each other to look at but didn't talk because I . . . for some reason thought that we didn't understand each other. I began to talk to my parents, my paisanos from Copala, and from there in the Triqui region . . . community. . . . They have a lot of courage. What happens is that they don't know how to speak. They don't know Spanish, and that's the only problem. As long as we are united. . . . So, when this man arrived [Benito García],[4] well, he gave us more courage to fight. All my people got stronger then. (López 1996)

Antonio López's statement shows how institutional or politico-cultural figures open the possibility of changing living and working conditions and building organizations. The experience of migration led to pan-ethnic alliances between Triquis and Mixtecos through community networks. But language is a significant barrier and a sign of indigenous subordination.

Organizational experiences under migration also vary according to sex. Conscious collective action by women began with the struggle for schools, services, and work, particularly on behalf of the street vendors in Tijuana.

In the beginning, there were few of us in the street. There were fewer vendors than now, around thirty. The problem was the whole colonia, the school, electricity, the access road, water, food, and the work. . . . I began to struggle for schooling. When we arrived in Tijuana, they wouldn't take my children anywhere; we had no papers, neither birth certificates nor even our own marriage certificate. Well, how could we, with so much coming and going? The children weren't able to study, hopping from one place to another all the time. So we had to talk to the authorities, with René Treviño, for them to register our children. Then he said to us, "Okay, how shall we go about it?" Many of our children don't speak Spanish, and in the schools, they were always scolding them. Yes, it was [René Treviño] who sent to the Mixteca for teachers. Fourteen of them arrived, but the Mixtec women didn't want them. They said, "Why do we want them [the children] speaking the language [Mixtec], if they already know it?" That was around '83; all of us were working to build the school. (R. Hernández 1994)

Language appears as a problem again in the context of urban settlement. The women needed schools for their children and jobs for themselves. Their ethnic background created the conditions for social and economic vulnerability. These conditions are the root cause of collective action on behalf of indigenous people. As earlier statements have shown, they needed to emerge as agents, in addition to being aware of the basic conflict. They also needed to forge links with other people who could serve as guides or mentors for action, other leaders or role models. They had to develop the necessary skills and the ability to perceive courses of action not previously envisioned. Such skills are prerequisites for action and gradually develop in the course of migration and in the collective action process.

Examining the life stories of these indigenous migrant intellectuals and analyzing their basic conflicts reveals various spaces of social relations, whether in the hometown or places of migration. Along with these spaces, different forms of expression and different adversaries come into focus (see table 5.2).

Table 5.2 shows the different spaces of conflict: community relations, linguistic relations, relations of authority and government, relations with migration officials, labor relations, and relations within and between organizations. In each of these spaces of social relations, conflict is expressed differently and with a different set of adversaries. These manifest a highly complex set of ethnic configurations, not because each of these adversaries has an ethnic character—like the "people of reason," the Mexican Americans, the mestizos, and the "gringos"—but because the other types of adversaries strengthen the ethnic dynamics. The different sources of conflict—from the despoilment of arable lands to the absence of indigenous representation at local and national levels—have common features. They are organized around three basic mechanisms: domination, discrimination, and resistance.

In the hometowns, discrimination against indigenous people was institutionalized in the despoilment of lands, the imposition of the Spanish language, and religious conversion. The mechanisms of domination that sustained these practices were reinforced by the disarticulation of the material base of production and the exclusion of indigenous people from the structures of state political representation. It is important to note that the leaders were aware of those mechanisms of discrimination and domination. Although most of them left their villages as children, the leaders have kept in touch with political events in those places, thanks to frequent return visits and the establishment of migrant networks.

Once the indigenous began the process of migration, their experiences of discrimination and domination in the towns and villages of origin were repeated in other social spaces. The factories and the fields became a new stage on which different forms of discrimination and domination were enacted. Once the indigenous cross the national border, their ethnicity and social class as an impoverished and undocumented workforce come into play. The relationship with the boss and migration authorities becomes an arena of conflict.

The third mechanism, resistance, will be covered below, along with the formation of the politico-ethnic project. This section will conclude with the idea that analyzing the experience of conflict is fundamental to understanding the social construction of ethnic identity boundaries. Identifying the different spaces of social relations in which conflict occurs—along with the particular adversaries in each space—enables one to conceive of malleable frontiers between the multiple "us" and "them" in the process of collective agency. These boundaries arise from conflict not only with those who are ethnically different but with those who are ethnically equal. The statements of Antonio López and Rafaela Hernández refer to this simultaneous inclusion and exclusion.

In the struggle between unity and diversity, mythical common ancestors and basic events in the history of the group become very important. These elements function as cultural capital with which contemporary differences are faced and with which the struggle is waged to reconstruct the subject as an agent of its own history. Cultural practices such as the civic-religious festivals, the cofradías, the mayordomías, and the tequio are areas of symbolic struggle to strengthen the "us" linked to the ancestors. Those cultural practices are part of mechanisms of inclusion.

Taken as a whole, these two paths of ethnic identity, inclusion and exclusion, transcend Barthian situationalism and come close to the conceptual approach of Roosens (1994, 82) and Bartolomé (1997, 125). The authors insist on considering not only what distinguishes the group from others but what members of the group hold in common over a long period. Roosens and

Table 5.2 Spaces of Conflict, Forms of Expression, and Adversaries in Migration and Collective Action

Conflict Space	Form of Expression	Adversaries*
Community relations	Appropriation of arable lands	Landowning caciques
	Differentiation in the use of space	Townspeople, town center folk
	Practice of usury and indigenous indebtedness	Moneylenders
	Performance of the cargos	Traditional leaders
	Inequality of participation in the cofradías and mayordomías	
	Struggle for dwellings and community services	Government officers
Linguistic relations	Stigmatization of the indigenous language	Spaniards, "people of reason"
	Schooling in a nonindigenous language	Teachers, local government
	Schooling in English	Secretaries, literate people/lawyers
	Legal procedures in English and Spanish	Mexican Americans and the gringos
Relations of authority and govern-ment	Control of positions of authority	Political caciques
	Intermingling of civic and religious authorities	Members of the PRI
	Absence of indigenous representation	Government
	Struggle for the consular registers (*matrículas*) in the United States	Government officers
Relations with migration officers	Extortion and abuse of migrants by the Mexican migration authorities	*Bajapollos*
		Cholos
		Police
		"La migra" (immigration service agents)

		[*]
	Robbery and assault by criminals along the migration route across Mexican territory and on the border crossing to the United States	Thieves
		Polleros
	Ill-treatment and violence by the border patrol	"La migra" (immigration service agents)
	Ill-treatment and persecution by civil or paramilitary anti-immigrant groups	Skinheads
Labor relations	Ill-treatment and overlong working days	Bosses
	Benefits and working and living conditions associated with work	Foremen and labor contractors
		Migration officials
		Municipal officers
	Struggle for urban space	Police officers
	Obtaining of permits from state governments for street selling	Other street vendors
		Mestizos
Relations within and between migrant organizations	Disagreements about strategies	Government officials
		Scabs or "collaborators"
	Differences regarding needs and interests	Migrant leaders
	Dealings with the Oaxaca state government	
	Relations with political parties	
	Leadership styles	
	Handling of resources	Corrupt leaders or caciques

Source: Analysis of the paths of migration and participation of fifteen migrant leaders, from their life stories.

* This column contains examples of "thesaurus language" (Poirer et al. 1983) used by the narrators themselves.

Bartolomé refer to the relevance of a common past (myths of origin) and the profound links between the idea of the original family and the ethnic identity project. Such contrastive and identification mechanisms are present in the discourses of leaders about the community beyond national and state frontiers.

A New Ethnic Community? The Ethical and Political Dimensions

The ethnic project, the ideal state pursued by the mobilized group, can be analyzed in its dual ethical and political dimension (Alberoni 1984). The project never arises independently from the interests and solidarity of the movement's members. It is a synthesis of the internal dynamics of the mobilized groups and the pressures of the external system that try to control the movement in different ways. Therefore, the project has two interlocutors: the members of the ethnic or pan-ethnic group and the agents of the external system with whom negotiations are carried out in the political field.

First, one must stress the heterogeneity of that political field. The organizations and communities that make up the politically transnational indigenous community are differentiated not only by their ethnic composition and their residence in different national territories, but also by their interests and the type of resources they mobilize. The Organización Regional Oaxaca (ORO), for example, is based in Los Angeles and in 1997 united thirty-four Zapotec towns and villages in the Sierra de Juárez, Oaxaca, and communities in California; its central aim is to preserve cultural roots in the United States and in Mexico. The Pueblos Mixe organization in Oaxaca, on the other hand, brings together four thousand coffee growers and focuses on the problems of marketing. These two organizations represent the poles of heterogeneity that nourish the cultural-political project. The diversity of interests means leadership practices and discourses will vary. Leaders have to give answers when a plan is put forth for the construction of dams in the towns of the Mixteca Baja or the central valleys of Oaxaca, or when a battle is being fought for recovery of Mexican nationality for indigenous Mexican residents in the United States.

In view of such diversity, how and by what strategy can unity be achieved? For Alberoni (1984), each social movement gestates in a basic contradiction that sets the long-term life project of an individual or group against actual experience. This theoretical assumption challenges us to trace—in the discourses, demands, and practices of our group of intellectuals—the ethical and political contents of the ethnic identity project of a community dispersed across the border. Ethical and political facets cannot be separated in that ethnic project; ethical refers to the proposal to transform the position of "Mixteco" or "Oaxaqueño" within the system of social relations as well as the structure of opportunities in a transnational context; "political" refers to the degree to which control of the institutions of domination—such as family, school, local powers, and finally the state—is aspired to.[5] It would seem that both facets of the project seek to construct both the "us" and the "others" simultaneously as interlocutors. In this current of transnational indigenism, we find—as Le Bot (1997, 23) found for the Zapatist movement[6]—that affirmation of the indigenous subject is juxtaposed with the demand for ethical and political recognition, but in a context that transcends national frontiers.

Indigenous Being Beyond Hometown and Nation: The Ethical Dimension of the Ethnic Identity Project

The search for strategic unity is reflected in the emergence of a vanguard group consciousness that functions as a meta-narrative of the competent and revalued "us." This can be seen in the narrative of the former coordinator of the FIOB:

> In gringo society questions of race are very clearly defined, and that's where the impulse came from. We over there ask ourselves, "I'm Mexican, but Mexican from where? I'm from Oaxaca, but from where? I'm Mixtec, but Mixtec from where? I'm from Tlacotepec," and so you go prioritizing. You realize that here is what you have recourse to because you're stuck in an amalgam of things. If you don't get smart, you risk losing out and becoming a nobody. You feel the need to protect not only your traditional food and way of dressing but also what you have inside.
>
> That's why it's important to have a project of organization and a cultural policy that recovers your identity . . . so that our children are able to keep it alive. If not, we too are in danger of getting lost and ending up being nobody . . . like the Chicanos who are neither gringos nor Mexicans. . . . With a project of recovery we can stop that. . . . I wouldn't like to see my children growing up as Chicanos, because I think the identity we have is better. (Pimentel 1994)

In this statement, Pimentel defines an "us" facing new categories of identity. The first identity category, "gringo," is quite dominant or hegemonic; the second one, Chicano, appears as a possible menace. There is a kind of revindication of "purity" and a criticism of the hybridization that Chicanos can represent.

In the following I present a narrative matrix with the main elements of the ethical dimension of the ethnic identity project. These elements function as emblems or symbols of ethnic identity and are organized around origin as the main symbol of "purity" or "the genuine."

Indigenous Being Without Land: The Relation with the Hometowns. There is a conception of the indigenous as people who belong to a community located in a specific territory. Based on my reconstruction of the experience of migration through examining the life stories of migrant leaders and the actions of migrant organizations in the region, "being apart from your community means ceasing to exist as a person." The community expands territorially with the migratory experience; it preserves, however, a symbolic center in the state of Oaxaca. This requires the rearticulation of the fragmented experience of territory through practices that reproduce family and community links. Holding festivals in the places of migration, sending money to hometowns for community projects, and even directly meeting civic-religious obligations mandated by the communal authority are important to maintaining the sense of community, even in situations of dispersion.

Genuine Indigenous Being: The Critical Reconstruction of Traditions. Festive music and dance traditions are looked on critically by some of the leaders. The historical role of the indigenous people in these forms of representation is being questioned. For example, some leaders criticize certain cultural practices reproduced by indigenous organizations in California; interpretation may alter the original form of traditions represented by festivities such as the Guelaguetza or the Danza de los Rubios (literally, Dance of the Fair-haired People) from the Mixteca. These are just two examples of questions about and concerns for the way in which the "indigenous" has been reconstructed.

> I think that if some members of Vamos por la Tierra had remained in the management of the FIOB, its policy would have radically changed. We don't agree with giving people everything that they ask. The people have been looking for someone to give them a tank of water or support to continue with the custom for a dance . . . which is all very good, the business of traditional culture . . . promoting it. I think that before dancing, we have to see first where we are going to get the resources to work with, and after that put on fiestas and traditional dances. Apart from that, we have differences with the Comité Cívico [COCIO]. . . . For example, they promote the Danza de los Rubios, when the Rubios is not an indigenous dance.
>
> We think they [COCIO and FIOB] have gotten it wrong.[7] Our position is that if we promote the traditional fiesta, we indigenous people

ought to have good relations with religions as religious people, but not cease to be Catholics or get into some other religion until we've researched the history of our religions. I proposed it in the documents that were presented at the first encounter. We should at least be sure which gods were ours before those Spanish sons of bitches came and got us into their thing. We ought to have the strength of knowing who our gods were and what they were like; we are indigenous people. I very much respect the beliefs of my mother, and so I keep the Virgin of Guadalupe. (R. Méndez 1996)

Rogelio Méndez's statement presents a complex idea of tradition. He recognizes these festivals as part of the migrants' identity, but he also considers festivals to be means of impoverishing and maintaining control of the indigenous. His statement suggests a search for historical, nongeographical ethnic origin. Nevertheless, his and Arturo Pimentel's views coincide on the central question: "Who are we?" Méndez questions the "genuineness" of the past represented by festivals. He says something like, "We are not that," whereas Arturo compares "us" with "otherness." Both seem to be aware that traditions (festivals or customs) are a source of legitimacy in the political space. Pan-ethnic encounters have facilitated the diffusion of some traditions, which gain a new meaning in the migration context. The following statement by Algimiro Morales illustrates this:

The Guelaguetza in Oaxaca has become an official event. It has been above all a matter of promoting profit-making companies through the Office for Tourism. . . . The communities take part, but in a bad way. For example, the whole region from La Cañada to the Coast, all the regions are called on to bring their dances, their cultural expressions. The Tourism Office promotes the event to support its own interests. In California [Vista] the opposite is taking place. I believe it has real popular content; it has a genuine collective content because here in the community, we do not accept donations from companies. And it is going to remain that way. The communities themselves put up all the resources they need for all the expenditures needed by a Guelaguetza. Anything from outside has to come with no strings attached, just with the intention of helping. . . .

We Mixtecos don't know much about the Guelaguetza. I'll be frank with you; it's a tradition from the areas around the city of Oaxaca, from the valley; it's a tradition most deeply rooted in those areas. We Mixtecos know, from hearsay, that Tlaxiaco goes, sometimes Juxtlahuaca, which are our most important districts, and Silacayoapan, from the Mixteca Baja region; but we don't know any more than that they go and participate. We're a bit far away from all that. Most of what I know about the

Guelaguetza I've learned here in California. For six or seven years now we've been following the ORO organization's experience with La Guelaguetza in Los Angeles. We think this work should be repeated in different areas; it should be done here and in the north of California. (Morales 1996)

As Morales's remarks suggest, genuineness is related to the sense of community, which rests on commitment and service. Community is constructed as an entity that encourages its members' participation in the festivals. In addition, service is seen as the opposite of commercial endeavors. Materials and services should not be controlled by money interests. The ideal community member gives without expecting any reward.

The Indigenous Family: The Indigenous Being as Family. Throughout the life stories of the intellectuals there is a positive valuation of family ties and of the responsibilities and commitments that arise from these ties. From their point of view, the new identity categories do not value family in the same way. Esteem for the family reaches into the past through relations with parents and elders and into the future through brothers and sisters, friends, and paisanos. For the indigenous, family ties are being expanded to include friendship, paisanaje relations, and ethnic relations within the political sphere. In some ways, the indigenous extended family mentioned in chapter 2 appears in the discourse of leaders.

We place great value on friendship and fraternity. They arise from the family, where there is the deepest relationship. When I stop to think about how the Oaxacan countryman deals with other cultures—such as the gringo culture—it surprises me. When I first arrived in America, I was amazed to see how a healthy family forsakes its parents, relatives, and elders. They are sent to special homes. To us, they are abandoning a beautiful thing—the warmth and love of the grandparents, the father and mother. We see with a great sadness how the gringos abandon something that we would not, even in a critical situation. We don't abandon our fathers or brothers, because we know that old age is the time when they need more protection, support, and love. (César Sánchez 1994)

César Sánchez rediscovered his values when he encountered a different social category and compared himself to the "other." Migration introduces dissonance into the indigenous social order that is rarely documented in the literature on transnationalism. This is particularly true with family relationships and older family members. During a period of fieldwork in San Miguel Tlacotepec, in the summer of 1997, I was able to draw up a list of more than a hundred people over age sixty who were alone because their families had emigrated to the United States or the north of Mexico. Few of them had news or received financial support from their distant family members. This led me to inquire whether the same thing was occurring in other villages. The delegate for the FIOB in Juxtlahuaca remarked that indeed this was the case in other villages of the district and that it was regarded as a chronic problem. On my second visit to San Miguel Tlacotepec (1998), I found that the Committees of the Third Age [the elderly] were devoted to raising chickens and pigs. They had been set up by the FIOB and remained very active.

This situation led me to notice contradictions between the ethical content of the narratives of intellectuals on the northern border and what was happening in the hometowns. These contradictions should be viewed in light of Alberoni's observations (1984) on the identity project of mobilized groups. For Alberoni the project is a set of ideal values to guide action, which remains independent of what actually happens in daily life. The project functions in the long-term future. In other words, despite the abandonment of the old people in the hometowns, the family unit continues to be valued, perceived by indigenous migrants as part of their identity. Family is also valued within the second generation as a temporal extension of the ethnic group. In the discourse, children and young people represent the future in a new land where ethnic identity is threatened and dependent on adult actions. In the following, Rufino Domínguez answers my question: What about the future?

> The future presents a great challenge. What will happen is a big question for which I don't have an answer. Really, we are in a country where the culture feels threatened, and it is taking measures to survive. As a Front, our wish is that each member take it upon himself to teach his family the language, the culture, the stories about who we are. It is all we can do; more than that is impossible. For example, I'm requiring my children to learn Mixtec, Spanish, English, and as many languages as need be, and to learn where we come from. I know that they are not going to feel it the way I do. They're growing up in a different environment. (Domínguez 1996)

The migration experience brings uncertainty about the future. Family links are a safeguard to deal with the new conditions. Children are growing up in a new society with new opportunities not imagined by their parents. The idea of family, and its value for ethnic identity, may change.

The elements mentioned, such as the relation with the hometowns, the genuine traditions, and the indigenous family, define being indigenous in a positive way. However, another set of elements characterizing the collective project of the indigenous puts a more negative value on the present indigenous state of being: poverty, the use of the language, and education. With these core issues comes a struggle to cease being poor, illiterate, and stigmatized speakers of a language without an official status.

Poor Indigenous Being. Poverty, regarded as a historical condition and associated with both colonial domination and the modern Mexican nation-state, shows different facets depending on the angle from which it is viewed—the hometowns or the places of migration.

In the hometowns, poverty is associated with the poor quality of the soil, the lack of means to exploit the land, the scarcity of jobs, the corruption of government officials and authorities, and the appropriation of lands by land-owning caciques. In the places of migration it is associated with capitalist exploitation, the voraciousness of the bosses, Mexican and U.S. racism, and the weakness of state and national governments in ensuring the labor rights of migrant workers in Mexico and the United States. In an overall vision, present-day poverty is the sum of specific situations at different geographic points and at different times. In other words, the reconstruction of conditions of poverty in the field of politics follows multiple causality: colonial model + modern state model + local *caciquismo* + migration in search of work + waged work in poorly paid jobs + racism + exploitation of the indigenous workforce throughout Mexico and the United States. Thus, the condition of the impoverished migrant worker is merely a present-day expression of a "historically poor indigenous being."

Poverty is a condition of "indigenous being," but unlike the positive elements mentioned above, it is something to struggle against and is perceived as a condition that damages the image of "indigenous being." The strong impulse to rid the indigenous identity of these conditions is observed in the constant struggle to promote and foster projects of community development, with the objective of improving living conditions. Among those interviewed, opinions varied about the best social practices for the migrants as poor people.

> Around '92 or '94 the Vamos por la Tierra movement, of which I am now a member, came into being . . . but within our organization we view the customs of celebrating the saints as very bad. I work here eight or ten months and go back there to give recognition to a compadre because he's taking my child to her First Communion. Such a fiesta! A great big fiesta where our relatives arrive and other people arrive saying, "Christen my baby." Large sums of money are spent. There are very bad customs like those I'm telling you about. We feel that this is one of the causes of our poverty, apart from the fact that the system doesn't allow us to earn a decent and just income. Besides that, there are no jobs in our hometown.

Tlacotepec has a lot of land. However, the government does not invest in the land. They prefer that we leave and work for them up in Sinaloa or in maquiladoras, working for a little money. We leave there with the little we earn. We go back to our hometown and spend it in two or three days. This is one of the ways we are different from the Cívico [COCIO]. We would like things to change more in the south. People should stop seeing the feasts of the patron saints as an obligation. They can do these things if they want to, but it should be on a voluntary basis and without spending so much money. . . .

I know people who, in order to serve at a saint's festival in San Miguel Tlacotepec, spent so much money that the debt itself made them leave for Baja California. Generally, the mestizos were the strong people. They're the ones who say, "Leave me your deeds as a deposit and I'll lend you so much. When you pay me back, there's your land. But if you don't pay me, I'll have your land." Here [in northern San Diego County] there has been a problem because they say, "You're Communists." They try to discredit us with that kind of talk. Some people think it's not fair that everything we earn in the north goes to build big churches in the south. The hometown authorities already rebuilt an enormous church in Tlacotepec that was damaged in the earthquake. At one time we opposed the reconstruction because we thought that it was more important to have the irrigation work done. Now we have some 50,000 new pesos, which are the result of a three-year drive to establish a fund to counteract the enemies who wanted the church at all costs. Then we said, "If we have money and if the government doesn't want to do the irrigation project, we will pump the water. Let's make the lands productive. Let there be life and work. When there is work and there is money, we'll build a church on every street corner. How's that? Not just one. If they want a church in every section of San Miguel Tlacotepec, we'll build a church, but first things first—work opportunities. Although most of the indigenous people agreed, the people with power said: "No, that's all wrong. The people want a church and a church is what they'll have." (R. Méndez 1996)

Rogelio Méndez discovered in the religious system a root cause of poverty, added to which was the government's failure to create job opportunities and social programs. He emphasizes how saints' festivals and the cargo posts added to the structural problems of poverty. Investment in the festivals becomes a major point of contention between community members in the place of origin and the place of arrival. This type of conflict spreads into family and community life, as in the San Miguel Tlacotepec example. After a few meetings, the Tlacotepec people decided to eliminate eleven festivals of saints from the festival calendar. The decision to change the calendar took place in the political space and led to a confrontation between members of the community and organization leaders. Criticism of the role of tradition in the life of the poor divided the leaders and community members into two groups: those who focused on cultural meaning, such as festivals, and those who gave priority to economic consequences, such as indebtedness and migration.

Ignorant Indigenous Being: Language and School. Indigenous condition has two major elements: (1) use of the indigenous language and limited use of other official languages (Spanish and English), and (2) low levels of schooling, which result in indigenous people being seen as ignorant and illiterate. These elements are a constant topic in the voices of all the indigenous migrants. These negative elements of identity are the basis for campaigns by organizations and the intellectuals. The learning of other languages is promoted— Spanish and English—but also the reevaluation of indigenous languages. The status of the indigenous languages—generally and incorrectly described as "dialects"—is also being revised. The right to education in the family and at school in the mother tongue, without prejudice to the learning of other languages, is being reaffirmed.[8]

> I believe that indigenous education could in some way enhance these differences. That would mean finding a way for the children of indigenous communities to improve their level of education without detriment to their culture. That's important! There are towns in Oaxaca—I could name them—where the more visible aspects of indigenous culture such as the traditional customs and the language have disappeared. Why? Because of the idea that if one ceases to speak the indigenous language, that's an advance, an improvement. It is as if one were to blame our language and our culture as the causes of our marginalization. I think the causes are other things. The problem of undernourishment, alcoholism, and so on. It isn't just the language; maybe it's the lack of opportunities and education. Maybe it's the system itself that we've suffered from. We are the product of history. It's not just a matter of chance that people turn alcoholic, that people don't bother with hygiene. There are a number of circumstances to explain this, not just the language. In Oaxaca, with the idea of "forget your language, forget your culture, and you'll progress," they've already forgotten part of their culture as an indigenous people. They look much more like other rural communities, not indigenous ones. And, what do you know! The economic circumstances haven't changed. There is still hunger. There is still poverty. There is still abandonment. There are still many negative things. An example is our language: learning Spanish is no guarantee of advancement. We need most of the people to

speak Spanish to be able to communicate with others, especially within the official institutions. Besides, I feel that it's good to teach our pupils what Mexico is, what Mexico has been. I think it is important to foster, to some extent, our identity as a country. (Tiburcio Pérez 1996)

This statement is from a bilingual teacher who has many years of experience in teaching indigenous children. He explains that indigenous language, when used in school, is a symbol of stigmatized ethnicity. The challenge is how to value and honor indigenous languages in schools and in the culture. Professor Pérez points out that the devalued position of indigenous languages is part of ethnic prejudice.

The ethical component of the ethnic identity project refers to indigenous being in the context of social relationships and opportunities. The elements are positive and negative symbols or emblems. To sum up, among the positive is the idea of the *indigenous being linked to the land*: migrant life is not viable without a relationship to the hometowns; hence the interest in investing in them, particularly on a political level and in festivals. The second, *genuine indigenous being*, refers to the reconstruction of ethnic history and the meaning of traditions. A third positive symbol is *indigenous being as family*. The relationship with the hometown and its traditions presents a contradiction to migrants. They may be critical of traditions. Yet they believe their essential nature comes from commitment and service to family and community. From these two entities, they seek and receive recognition.

These ethics of the collective are also expressed in family values, as a self-attributed characteristic normalized in the phrase, "that's the way we are," with the effect that the family metaphor extends to all those whom we regard as like "us." Ethnic identity is also defined by negative symbols. The poor indigenous being, the ignorant indigenous being (who is illiterate and speaks Spanish poorly), and the indigenous being without voice are stereotypes that take on meaning in the historical relationship between the indigenous populations and the state. In their discourse, leaders assert that the negative symbols are not primordial, but attributed and assigned by a social order of domination and discrimination in which the state has a leading role. In the emerging ethnic consciousness, there is a dual process of primordialization and decolonization of ethnicity as a narrative construction, centered on the critical reconstruction of its cultural nucleus. This emerging ethnic consciousness condenses what is recognized as actual "being" with what is "wished to be," so that this ethnicity is an unfinished process by its very nature and felt to be transitory. The wish "to be" or the will to find the means to be lends strength to a project that is expressed in political terms, no longer as a set of emblems but as a strategy.

The Will to "Be": The Political Component of the Project

The intellectuals interviewed have stressed the ethical facet of the identity project. On the basis of analytical questions alone, the project is clearly anchored in the political dimension. No ethnic identity project exists that does not include political strategies to bring the individual closer to the "indigenous being." Thus a web of power woven internally and externally in the ethnic community defines the political field. The kind of discourse that is recognized as political does not refer directly or exclusively to single situations; its aim, on the contrary, is to be as universal as possible.

Within the political field, constructing the unity of the ethnic project is strategically useful to political struggle and a way to bring nearer an ideal state of "being indigenous." As César Sánchez Liévano pointed out before an FIOB meeting in Tijuana: "What unites us, for example, as Zapotecos with the Mixes or the Mixtecos is that we are Indians, poor and exploited, who have had to leave our lands" (C. Sánchez 1994). The political is analyzed on the basis of elements that appear in the discourse of leaders, assembly discussions, and organization documents.

Political Representation and Relations with the National States. There has been much discussion of the way in which the relation of the indigenous communities to the state is mediated through corporate mechanisms of "control" or "co-optation." Such mechanisms are one aspect of a relationship of domination by the Mexican government, which has also manifested itself as a patron-client relationship. While the theme of indigenous autonomy appears in the background of leadership discourse, the dominant debate concerns representation of these people not only as indigenous but as migrants. The political representation of indigenous migrants appears in two spheres.

The first sphere is the local and regional one, where negotiations take place with the municipal governments and the state administration of Oaxaca and certain types of relations have been established. There have been examples of homeland mayors traveling to migrant settlements in order to set up municipal committees or hometown associations that extend the authority of the hometowns and also give a voice to migrants. Since 1986, several governors of Oaxaca have made periodic visits to California and Baja California to address issues related to indigenous migrants from Oaxaca, such as the Peso por Peso program.

> In the case of Tlacotepec, the link with the hometown has changed recently. For instance, in Mexico City a committee that has municipal authority represents indigenous people. It also coordinates and attempts to solve the problems of its community in Mexico City. Here in Califor-

nia, the path is the same, particularly in Vista where there are a lot of Tlacotepec people. The municipal mayor is coming here to establish a representative committee like the one in Mexico City. (Morales 1996)

The second sphere of political representation is in the national arena. The issue of the irrevocability of Mexican nationality—at times confused with that of dual citizenship—became a polemical issue along with related questions concerning migrants' right to vote outside national territory and the right to property, social security, and access to schools and work inside Mexican territory. A lack of representation of indigenous migrants and residents in the structure of the local and federal governments is a concern among leaders.

Forms of Political Representation: Parties, Associations, and Organizations. Concerns about political representation, accompanied by concerns about which forms of political representation are most adequate, arise in a project of ethnic identity. There is debate among the intellectuals on this issue, which divides along class and cultural perspectives.

In the case of political representation within the national state, one group of voices supports the creation of an Indian or indigenous party. Others prefer representation via the holding of posts in the existing structures of government, whether at the local or national level.

If one conceives of the indigenous as agents, several forms of representation at the local and regional levels are possible. One group argues for respecting and fostering the traditional forms of organization, such as the hometown associations, which reestablish in new communities the ancient customary law or forms of civic-religious authority from the communities of origin. Another group opposes party-related positions and argues for more diverse forms that facilitate alliances with other mobilized categories, whether of ethnicity, class, or another emerging category. The possibilities may be schematized as follows:

a. Hometown committees, such as those of Santa María Tindú, San Miguel Tlacotepec, and San Miguel Cuevas, operating in the state of California.
b. Ethnic and interethnic alliances, such as the Coalición de Comunidades Indígenas de Oaxaca, which includes approximately twenty communities of Mixtec and Zapotec origin in Vista, California, or the Frente Indígena Oaxaqueño Binacional, which brings together organizations and communities from both the hometowns and the places of migration.

Both forms of association on the Mexico–U.S. border influence the basis of recognition by which a person becomes a leader or community authority, as we will see in the next section when Algimiro Morales refers to the role of indigenous leaders.

A further area of disagreement is how to transcend the representational arenas of the national political system—political parties and state and federal legislative chambers. A consensus favors working through political alliances or forming an Indian-American party rather than formally joining any of the existing parties. As Lita suggests:

> Our interest is in building an organization in which the people can participate. It does not matter if we are a minority people with a political project. For example, our project Vamos por la Tierra [Going for the Homeland] seeks to solve the indigenous problem with strong leadership [ruling class]. I argued that fronts are the right way because they will permit community organizations to build a party with real power. We do not want quasi-leaders. The work will be nonstop with such types of organizations, like alliances or coordinations or fronts; we are looking to build the Indo-Mexican Party. Maybe it is a crazy idea, but ever since CCPM we have been thinking about it. Meanwhile we are working on political training. (Lita 1996)

The fight for representational quotas in the federal and local house of representatives and in the senate is one of the most important topics of argument and activity. In 1997 the Frente Indígena Oaxaqueño Binacional, in alliance with the Partido de la Revolución Democrática, fielded a candidate for deputy to the Oaxaca State Congress. The victory of this candidate in the local house of representatives brought the first representative to the cause of migrant communities. In 2000 a dispute arose in the FIOB when the former coordinator tried to run for the deputy post in alliance with the PRD. Nevertheless, there was a change in the organization's attitude toward party alliances; it remains independent of the political party affiliations of its member organizations.

The Role of Indigenous Leaders or Intellectuals. On this same subject of political representation, we encounter another concern among the organization leaders: the question of who represents whom. Does one want traditional leaders or modern ones, one of "us" or one of "them"?

These possibilities, which are not mutually exclusive, offer different ways of viewing the role of leaders. In the controversy over whether the subject of the struggle is an individual or a collective, opinion inclines toward the community as a corporate entity. The leaders or intellectuals must accurately interpret the will of the corporate entity. Their mission is to read the feelings and wishes of the community and to attend to them. Conflicts between leaders are generally symptomatic of a disjunction between leader and community, where the status of the leader has grown out of proportion as a charismatic figure—indeed, in response to the demand for such a figure.

On the other hand, there are controversies about the leaders' basis of legitimacy; at stake is the relative usefulness to the community of the traditional leaders' domain of wisdom versus the new approaches taken by the younger leaders. Disputes between migrant leaders and the principales have occurred constantly since the beginning of the migratory process. While the basis of legitimacy of the principales—their historical position in the system of traditional authority—is acknowledged, they are also regarded as a gerontocracy out of step with the current generation.

> Mexico City's experience is a milestone, and we would like to repeat it here. A committee was founded made up of representatives whose authority did not derive from the traditional forms of recognition. They won their posts based on their social activism and their willingness to fight in new places. Maybe this is because some communities have no elderly people capable of handling individual, family, or community problems. No, here it is personal efforts and facts; rarely are we going to delegate authority in the traditional ways. (Morales 1996)

Algimiro Morales's statement supports Bonfil's findings (1995b, 122–124) that identify a new indigenous leadership emerging from the migration process. Bonfil stresses a rising phenomenon among migrant communities: a new form of authority resulting from new political conditions for migrant and working-class indigenous people. Under these conditions other skills become important: mastery of Spanish and English, knowledge of the Mexican and U.S. political systems and immigration law (particularly U.S. legislation), and higher education.

Juan Lita, leader of the Vamos por la Tierra movement, believes that the main obstacle to founding an indigenous political party (Partido Indo-Americano) is the absence of "theoretical indigenous minds with the ability to read and write" (Lita 1996).

> Vamos por la Tierra is in a hurry to launch a project. We are documenting our experiences because many people, mostly in the cities, think that we shouldn't join the parties. Even though there are indigenous inside the PRD, some say our customs don't belong in that kind of organization. We need theoretical indigenous minds with writing and reading skills to build our party. I think that it is possible. I trust that we can organize a political group that blends our customs with those of the migrants. (Lita 1996)

Communities and individuals, in Mexico and the United States, value skills that respond to needs. However, skills are ambiguously valued in the organizations because the leadership is regarded with mistrust.

The subject of cultural and political mediation—or intermediation, as it is referred to in the life stories and during discussions in meetings and assemblies—arises in connection with the ethnic belonging of the leaders and their legitimacy as spokespersons for the indigenous community. In the preparatory meeting to founding the FIOB, this was discussed by the new organization staff: "We are considering making a proposal about ethnic representation at tomorrow's meeting. We are concerned that each indigenous group should be represented on the staff of the new FIOB. For instance, it would be one Zapoteco, one Mixe, one Mixteco, and one Chocholteco. We will propose that, and watch to make sure that candidates really belong to each indigenous group. (C. Sánchez 1994).

Indigenous needs and perspectives have been represented by missionaries in colonial times, as well as by teachers, anthropologists, and government officials. Such mediation or intermediation is seen by leaders as a means of manipulating the indigenous people in pursuit of interests not their own. The idea of setting up indigenous people in ethnically homogeneous organizations can guarantee that they are not infiltrated by mestizos who could take over their leadership. Many express concerns about recovering their own voice ("speaking for oneself," or "speaking with one's own words").

> I don't need somebody to tell me what I must do anymore. Those people, like CROC [Confederación Revolucionaria de Obreros y Campesinos] or CTM [Central de Trabajadores Mexicanos], tricked us. They took everything for themselves—the land plots and gifts, all things. I want to talk directly with the government and with the people or my friends. I think that with my own face and my own head, even though I am an illiterate person, I can do it alone, without those people. . . . I think it works better with my own words. (Santos 1994)

For these reasons, the role of the indigenous leadership is to represent the community's own interests and to mediate between the members of the community and state institutions and places of origin or arrival.

In their life stories, leaders have expressed concerns about the requirements for legitimacy. The bases of legitimacy include such things as bona fide membership in the local community—acquired by having been born and raised in the hometown—mastery of indigenous languages, indigenous physical characteristics, and a way of life marked by responsibility and commitment to community and family. A controlled and accountable accumulation of wealth also lends legitimacy to a leader; wealth must stay within the limits of what the community deems acceptable.

Wealth is becoming an issue within the organizations; gradually, these leaders have created institutional mechanisms to ensure a democratic process for electing representatives and the open rendering of accounts. In a recent conflict among FIOB members, wealth was a central issue. In 2002, at a transnational meeting of FIOB, Arturo Pimentel was expelled for a lack of accounting. This had serious consequences for organizations and, in particular, for their finances. The loss of financial credibility, especially in the United States, prompted changes: a mechanism for supervision of leaders, decentralized decision making, and financial accounting. As Rufino Domínguez states, corruption has become an issue in all social and political organizations in Mexico, not just the indigenous ones.

> Although the FIOB has enjoyed important success, we need to move ahead with much more ambitious projects on both sides of the border. Admittedly, FIOB has not escaped the corruption, authoritarianism, arrogance, and manipulation that we so often criticize. Yet these ills are not inherent to our indigenous culture; they are the product of mestizo political culture. Therefore, it is vitally important to "decolonize" our thoughts and practices—both individually and within our communities, organizations, and municipalities. By doing so, we can demonstrate how to govern with justice, humility, honesty, and accountability and work toward greater transparency. (Domínguez 2004, 79)

The Oaxacan government and federal Mexican institutions stayed out of this controversy. There was a quite different reaction in the United States. Agencies cut financial support and relations with Pimentel almost immediately. It is important to point out that this difference in attitude creates challenges for the transnational agents. Migrants' concerns about the homelands have brought new participation and new decisions, affecting the life of the people who live in those communities. Communication problems within the organizations have prevented a common understanding of the conflict. For example, in the opinion of a San Quintin leader, the Pimentel issue was a problem between Mexican leaders and U.S. indigenous leaders. From his perspective, the U.S. leaders did not realize what happened and how the politics played out in Mexico.

Ethnic Alliances and Transnationalization. One of the most significant changes associated with migration has been the relocation of geographic ethnic boundaries. As was documented in the previous chapter, the new territories of migration create ethnic relations between Mixtecos, Zapotecos, Triquis, Mixes, Nahuas, and Otomíes that were unlikely to have occurred in the places of origin. In the political arena, this ethnic diversity has caused difficulties, in the opinion of the leaders; it has also, however, accelerated the forging of ethnic alliances around the common problems of indigenous migrants. In the transnational arena, alliances between people from ethnic or other categories—such as the Chicanos or the native Indians of the United

States—have established collective experiences and modified the definition of political struggle; thus, terms such as "indigenous migrants" have given way to new categories such as "continental ethnic minorities." Studies of ethnic mobilization among migrants in developed countries detect the emergence of a pan-Indian identity (Kearney 1991; Verdery 1994) similar to the continental indigenous mobilizations in Latin America in the early 1990s (Radcliffe, Laurie, and Andolina 2002).

Looking to the Future:
Indigenous Migrants or Indigenous Residents

One of the most controversial issues in the ethnic identity project is settlement versus return. All of the intellectuals' life stories mention this when they speak of the future of the indigenous migrant communities. It is also a recurrent theme at meetings and conferences; one organization has as its motto "for a return with dignity" (¡Por un retorno digno!). Despite the breadth of the controversy, people feel different degrees of uncertainty about the future, and have different degrees of nostalgia for places of origin. However, on balance they see as positive what has been achieved in the new settlements.

For Juan Lita (1996), the Vamos por la Tierra movement has a historical sense of the struggle for identity, language, territory, traditional bands, and the dance known as Las Chilenas. This is a trend within what Lita calls the migrant movement. This leader sees that indigenous migrants, like others of Mexican origin, are living in territories occupied by the United States; they are an internationalized workforce. Therefore, their future is by no means certain: "Today we're here, tomorrow over there, or wherever NAFTA leads us." There is no way of knowing for sure if one will be able to remain in California; hence the demand for a "return with dignity." For others, like the teacher Gonzalo Montiel Aguirre (1996) and onetime CIOAC activist José Rojas (1996), the only future is as indigenous residents in Baja California or in California.

> I think . . . about the future of we indigenous people. . . . For example, there are indigenous people who say, "We need a return with dignity." I criticize the concern with a return with dignity because it's never going to happen. I've spoken to Mixtecos from Mexicali who have already been living for thirty years in Baja California; I've spoken to Mixtecos from the Colonia Obrera who have already spent thirty years there; I have talked with Mixtecos from Ensenada; I've talked with Mixtecos from the "other side." If this return with dignity is not going to happen, what we ought to do is organize ourselves and present the government with our demands

regarding housing and services. The fact that we are immigrants is irrelevant. Under the edge [the border], they despise us as indigenous migrants, and sure, we are immigrants, but they are too. They don't realize that we migrants are not invading; we are a cheap workforce for big firms and for the big farmers. Therefore, our future, I think, must be in Baja California. We need to keep on fighting for a territory for the migrants. They must forget about being migrants; we're settled migrants now. (Montiel 1996)

The impulse to settle displaces the vital orientation from the places of origin toward new places. This results in a reworking of the emblems of identity such that common origin comes to be symbolized by other cultural elements such as the indigenous language, festivals, and other traditions. The migrant geographic dispersion itself becomes an emblem of identity.

It may well be that what the future holds is the loss of our language as a result of the North American culture; so in that respect the bilingual schools would have an important part to play. . . . We migrants are also in danger if we don't practice our language, if we don't practice our music, our dance. If we are going to have to adapt to another culture . . . well, let's adapt to another culture. Here's what's needed: support from the government itself, support for a teacher of culture or dance, or a teacher in charge of linguistics, or storytelling workshops. Think of someone disseminating our culture from a bilingual radio station; a place where the old people could narrate their experiences to the children. Maybe this could give our children a better future. (Montiel 1996)

This process has consequences for practices such as remittances and threatens economic investment in the hometowns. Not surprisingly, representatives of local administrations seek to promote links to the migrants' places of origin and, at times, to exploit sentiments of nostalgia for the *patria chica*.[9]

Some Observations on the Ethnic Identity Project

On the whole, these intellectuals construct and act in a heterogeneous transnational-political arena where their role seems to be that of fashioning a politico-cultural voice for the migrant organizations. I interpret this as a manifestation of discursive ethnic consciousness. The unified politico-cultural voice cannot be independent of the subjects who construct it in the system of interethnic as well as intraethnic relations. Thus, as a consciousness, this voice is imbued with a tension between a unity and the diversity that it is striving to represent. The emphasis in this chapter has been on unity—as only a first approach to the heterogeneity that emerges from the discourse of the intellectuals and their position in the arena of interethnic, rather than intraethnic, relations. In this sphere, unity is analyzed as a strategic response to the situation of agents in a field of symbolic struggles organized according to allies and adversaries.

In the transnational-political field, according to the intellectuals' narratives, the "us" is construed as "allies" and the "others" as "adversaries." This chapter holds that the definition of "us" and "others" changes depending on the field of conflict—in other words, on the situation. However, in the dynamics of this conflict, as can be seen in the axes defining the ethnic identity project of these organizations, an adversary emerges from the background: the national state. Although the relationship with the national state is experienced through concrete and clearly defined conflicts with state governments and municipal administrations, leadership discourse constructs a broader "adversary" and assigns it a global rationality of control, co-optation, and political domination. These administrations, as sources of conflict, are credited with the power to "divide and rule," exacerbating differences between organizations. This finding concurs with the work carried out by Stavenhagen (1996) regarding the role of the state in a series of ethnic conflicts that have resulted in varying degrees of violence. Williams's (1989) thesis also confirms that cultural differences are made more significant by the actions of national states, with their capacity to create identities as they construct subjects.

Diversity is the other component of the tension within the ethnic identity project. According to Melucci (1999), the principal challenge of social research is to discover how diversity coexists with and survives beneath strategic unity. Such diversity may be maintained by agents adopting different positions about labor relations, regional ethnic relations, and on class, gender, and generational relations. Thus, analysis can be directed solely at the construction of this strategic unity in the field of transnational indigenous struggle, or at reconstructing the differences that nurture this unity and its representation in the ethnic identity project. Given the difficulty of dealing with diversity in all of its complexity, I will focus on gender differences.

One major element lending unity to the ethnic identity project is the maleness of the intellectuals. This is not to imply that they fail to represent women's interests; nevertheless, given the dominance of male leadership in Mexican indigenous communities, it seems important to make sex a line of investigation. The next chapter, therefore, will address the mechanisms of gender subordination operating in the transnational field that might affect the representation of women's interests. In addition, I will analyze women's interests and feminine agency in the transnational field. The next chapter explores women's contribution to the ethnic identity project in the migrant organizations.

6

Public Voices, Private Silences
The Boundaries of Gender and Ethnicity

This chapter explores the dynamics of gender in the ethnic identity project. It sets out to explore simultaneously the mechanisms of subordination and resistance within ethnic belonging and gender. I focus on the differentiation of women's social action spaces during the experience of migration and emphasize women's participation in migrant organizations in the Mexico–U.S. border region. The principal aim is to define the impact of this differentiation on the construction of ethnic consciousness in the transnational organizational field.[1]

Despite the notable visibility of women as activists in organizations on both sides of the border, this visibility diminishes considerably when one looks at the leadership. As was documented in the previous chapter, most of the intellectuals are men. They hold the leadership roles in a majority of ethnic groups in Mexico, including mestizo groups. Nevertheless, given the importance of women in the ethnic identity project, it seems appropriate to inquire into the ways of and mechanisms for representing female voices. I decided to evaluate the experience of migration, social participation, and the constitution of spaces for women's action, as well as women's impact on the construction of ethnic identity.

The chapter looks at the local spaces for female agency resulting from migration to the Mexico–U.S. region and analyzes women's social participation as leaders in Mixtec migrant organizations in the same border region. As was stated in the "Notes on Methodology" in the introduction, a cadre of male and female leaders was interviewed when they became available during the fieldwork. Analyzing the subgroup of female intellectuals provided a way to understand gender relations in the construction of ethnic identity. Located at the crossroads of gender and ethnicity, the life stories of indigenous migrant women at three geographic points of the Mexico—U.S. border are examined in terms of family, labor, and political participation.

Female Migration: Beyond Gender and Ethnic Boundaries

By "boundaries of gender," I mean the normative demarcation of spaces of social action according to the participants' sex. Such spaces can be distinguished empirically as domestic space and nondomestic space; several distinct spaces—labor, community, and politics—are grouped in the nondomestic category. By ethnic boundaries, I refer to spatial limits that are culturally constructed through how the nation-state classifies indigenous and nonindigenous people. These gender and ethnic frontiers form part of the ideology of spaces of action. Thus, highly varied images in Mexican society—the housewife in the home and the man in the street, or the Indian on his land and the mestizo at his desk, or the quiet woman and the illiterate Indian—illustrate not only their specific forms of action but also the social spaces in which they legitimately act.

Among many notable twentieth-century events, two major social phenomena altered gender and ethnic boundaries in Mexico's public and private social order, especially during the last four decades: the massive incorporation of women into the wage-labor force and the massive migration of rural indigenous populations to the nation's cities and large agricultural centers. Both occurred as part of the country's industrialization, and both modified social relations within domestic space, work, and the urban setting.

In the 1970s, Lourdes Arizpe (1975) called attention to the city's new face: indigenous women who came from the state of Mexico to sell fruit or candy on Mexico City's main avenues. Other studies also reported the presence of Indian women in cities such as Guadalajara, Ciudad Juárez (M. Pérez 1990), and Tijuana (Clark 1991). The flow of Indian women extended further, crossing the nation's border. In the academic literature on women's internal and international migration, the diverse hypotheses advanced about the impact of geographic mobility on women's lives focus on either of two principal spaces. One group of hypotheses focuses on changes in women's position within their families; disruptions in family patterns that follow social mobility and economic independence affect women's autonomy in relation to masculine authority (Hondagneu-Sotelo 1994). The second group of hypotheses stresses changes in women's position in gender-stratified systems, both in the society of origin and the society of destination (Grieco and Boyd 1998; Malkin 1997). This approach assumes that gender relations in the two places will differ. These studies, nevertheless, point out that women have difficulty escaping community-based coercion because of migrant networks and the reconstitution of local communities in the places where they relocate. Women quickly assume domestic responsibilities and begin to participate in activities necessary for the reconstitution of family life. Pardo's (1998) work on these topics discusses immigrant women's ability to mobilize within the communitarian sphere related to the social aid programs that the U.S. government develops for and targets at women. Pardo's approach also seems applicable for analyzing the situation of poor immigrant women in Mexican cities.

To this pair of hypotheses should be added a third, which comes from a different line of analysis regarding the construction of feminine identity in frameworks of nationalism and ethnicity, and which can be applied specifically to indigenous women. This approach posits that feminine identities are objectivized in feminine myths and roles as part of the symbolic order that nourishes national or ethnic identity (Gutiérrez 1999; Pettman 1996). In migration—a situation that often threatens ethnic or national identity—the "traditionalism" of women becomes a sort of safeguard for group identity, and features considered traditional are exaggerated. While the first two hypotheses explore changes in women's condition in society and the family, the third situates such changes in the larger context of national or ethnic community.

The study of women's participation in migrant organizations must be situated in women's dual condition as indigenous and migrants. The concepts of family and community are fundamental to understanding the full range of women's forms of participation in, and access to, new spaces of action. Here it may be useful to reflect on the analytical viability of the public-private metaphor. In studies of women's lives or of gender, the domestic sphere is clearly associated with concepts such as home or domesticity or the family unit,[2] while the same is not true for public or nondomestic spheres. In Mexico, well-documented research shows a series of heterogeneous spaces between these two poles—domestic and nondomestic. Community organization, wage labor, and political representation or participation constitute spaces of social action that can be assimilated into both domestic (private) dynamics and nondomestic (public) (Barbieri 1991; Massolo 1994; Tarrés 1989; Tuñón 1992). This is particularly visible in emigrant indigenous towns where participation in community life is intense (Velásquez 2004). Female migration has called into question what Nyberg-Sorensen (1995, 106) refers to as the dualistic myth of feminine immobility and private domestic space versus masculine mobility and international public space.

A conceptualization of women's spaces of action that disrupts this myth has been accompanied by a search for more complex, theoretical models that admit heterogeneity and focus on the notion of social space.[3] In their writing, academics have used cartographic metaphors to facilitate the study of power and the differences between the sexes, whether from the perspective of subordination or of empowerment,[4] but have seldom addressed the intersection of those spaces. Several studies in human geography (Bondi 1993) have observed the ways in which women negotiate their daily lives in spaces such as home and work, or between different social and cultural classes. The study of the transit between spaces can lead, I maintain, to a more complex cartography of the feminine world. A human geography perspective can offer a useful analytic framework for the study of women's migration and the expansion of

their spaces of action when they move out of their place of origin and construct new households, engaging in wage labor and reconstituting community in new locations. Notable cases include farmworkers living in camps or
street vendors living in urban settlements on the Mexican border.

The constant transit between spaces that characterizes the life of women
in large cities or, as in the case studies, migrant women in another country,
makes us question the universality of the public-private metaphor. It may be
more appropriate to reflect on the particularities of the use, appropriation,
and production of spaces by social agents in contemporary societies.[5]

In this chapter, I explore the ideological mechanisms that influence migrant and indigenous women's transit between domestic and public spaces of
action, that is, the spaces of work, community life, and migrant organizations. I consider this ideology to be normative, regulating both the gendered
and ethnic appropriateness of spaces. The state has an important role in
defining this ideology. For example, a large part of state family policy directed
at women reinforces the dichotomy by assigning principal responsibility for
the family to women.[6] At the same time, as part of an ethnic group, these
women are an important focus of cultural policies based on a traditional
feminine ethnic image (Pettman 1996).

Mixtec Migrant Women Crisscrossing Borders

Migration from the towns and villages of the Mixteca region of Oaxaca to the
northern border of Mexico and the southwestern United States brought
changes to women and their families. The departure of pioneering migrants
from the Mixtec hometowns to Veracruz, Morelos, Mexico City, the fields of
the Mexican northwest, and California's southwest modified social reproduction in Mixtec households and affected family and gender relations. Women
had an essential role in implementing survival strategies when pioneering
migrants were absent from the household.

In the 1950s, adolescent Mixtec women began to leave home for employment in domestic service in Mexico City[7] and the cities of Oaxaca, Puebla,
and other urban centers; alternatively, young married women accompanied
their husbands to work in the fields of the northwest. In the early 1990s,
approximately 20 percent of Oaxaqueños deported from the United States to
Mexico were women. That is higher than the percentage of women in the
general deportation of Mexicans (COLEF and COESPO 1995, 126).

Female Mixtec migration in the 1960s and 1970s was associated with
either domestic service in Mexico City or family migration to the agricultural
centers of northern Mexico. Mixtec women in the 1980s participated in the
settlement of migrant communities in urban zones such as Tijuana, Nogales,

Table 6.1 Sex of Indigenous Migrant Population on Northwestern Border of Mexico and in United States

Place	% Men	% Women	Total	N
California	76.4	23.6	100	5,332
Valle de San Quintín camps	55.2	44.8	100	6,042
Valle de San Quintín colonias	51.2	48.8	100	2,142
Tijuana Colonia Obrera	46.0	54.0	100	652

Sources: California: Runsten and Kearney 1994; Valle de San Quintín Camps: PRONJAG 1999; Tijuana Colonia Obrera: COLEF 1989.

and Ensenada, or around the fields of Sonora, Sinaloa, northern Baja California, and La Paz in southern Baja California, and in a lower proportion in California. This settlement brought changes to family, community, and regional life and was particularly evident in California, where, subsequent to the Simpson-Rodino Act (IRCA) of 1986, male migration could occur under new conditions of legal mobility and settlement. The legal situation of family members varied. Women and men did not necessarily obtain resident status at the same time. The Special Agricultural Workers provision of the 1986 IRCA, which allowed for family reunification, was a recurrent reference in migrant narratives. The arrival of women and children was a high point in the memories of many leaders. They recalled with great enthusiasm that the house, at last, became a home.[8] Generally, women took a leading role in the collective strategies for maintaining the family in the places of origin as well as in the places of arrival during male absences, which were sometimes brief and sometimes long. In the place of arrival they became employed as domestic workers, street vendors, or farmworkers. Nevertheless, women did not develop agency in the community sphere until they took up residency on both sides of the Mexico–U.S. border.

Female Participation in Migrant Organizations and the Dynamics of Gender-Ethnic Conflict

In the migrant organizations, gender is a factor in participation. Men dominate the leadership positions, especially within the transnational organizations. Meanwhile, women occupy treasurers' posts and positions as representatives, along with other positions involving responsibility at the local level. Men dominate both leadership posts and membership in the agricultural organizations, while women exercise greater responsibility in the urban organizations, such as residents' and street vendors' associations and labor organizations.

Men and women tell different stories about the experience of migration. Although men's stories of migration, work, and separations include the principal family events—such as marriages, deaths of parents, birth of children, departure with wives from the hometowns or the arrival of wife and children in the places of migration, and separations—they construct their life stories with little attention to what takes place in the spaces of intimate, personal life. The conflict between political life—what they call their "commitments to the people"—and their family lives, as marriage partners and parents, is resolved in their discourse when they evaluate their role as responsible breadwinners. In their stories, men place a negative value on events that bring about the separation of family, affect political duties, and, most damaging of all, cause marital breakdown. However, I found no cases in which men had decided to abandon their participation in organizations for family reasons. In their reconstructions of tensions between organizational and domestic activity (daily life at home, relations with wife and children), male leaders showed differences in the intensity of their political participation, which was based on their rank in the organization.

On the other hand, Mixtec women's stories of migration, work, and political participation show a remarkable flow between various spaces—personal, domestic, work, community, urban, and political life—the latter being constructed as the space of confrontations with government institutions. The events of home life, the children's school, feeding the family, health problems, and raising children are given much attention in women's life stories; these events are often interconnected with women's presence in the world of community and work. Unlike the men, the women do not express an awareness of the national events that frame the indigenous migrant organization movement (that is, the 1968 student movement, the teachers' movements in Oaxaca, the guerrilla movements of the 1970s, and the agricultural workers' union movement also in the 1970s). In their political participation, women are preoccupied with local, community, and family issues and with their ability to raise demands from the space of domestic life to the public sphere; this distinguishes them from the men who have been activists in political parties.[9]

The following examples show the main paths women have followed in migration and social participation:

1. She leaves the hometown as a young married woman to work in the fields in Veracruz, and then moves to Chiapas and Sinaloa, before settling in Tijuana. As she becomes established in Tijuana, she gains organizational experience by participating in the civic-religious system for some twenty years. Family residency triggers active participation in the regularizing of

deeds, obtaining of services, seeking schooling for children, and finally working as a street vendor in Tijuana.

2. As a little girl, she leaves the hometown with her parents to work in the fields of Sinaloa and Baja California. After moving back and forth between the hometown and Baja California several times, she marries. For ten years, she lives with her husband and children in the camps owned by the agricultural boss. In the 1980s, she takes over a plot of land and establishes her home in Maneadero, Baja California. Her political experience comes from participation in the agricultural workers' struggle of the 1970s and 1980s in the San Quintin Valley. She gains recognition as a leader during the regularization of urban landholdings and through membership in an institutionalized organization.

3. As a child, she leaves the hometown with her parents and goes directly to Tijuana. After several years in the city, she migrates with her family to California and works in agriculture. She obtains U.S. residency papers during an amnesty period under the IRCA. Growing up and working in the fields, she manages to study and get to senior high school. She learns English and after several years achieves fluency in English and Mixtec and some knowledge of Spanish. Her political participation centers on the defense of farmworkers against dismissals and mistreatment; she becomes professionally trained as a legal defender of Mixtec migrants in California agriculture.

4. She was born in California but makes frequent visits to the hometown with her parents. After settling with her family in Los Angeles, she works in the service industry—restaurants and domestic employment. She marries in the United States and has children who grow up with English as their primary language and Spanish as a second language. The children do not know Zapotec or Mixtec, the mother's first language. Her interests are in festivals such as the Guelaguetza, which is an annual event, as well as in the hometown committees, particularly in the collection of funds for improving living standards in the village.

Both family and community control the mobility of women in daily life, though the ways vary according to the stage in the women's life cycle. The departure of women from the hometowns does not necessarily break or weaken family and community control; once the process of migration is under way, if the women are single, the family of orientation (brothers and fathers) exercises control over them. In the case of married women, this supervision passes to the hands of the husbands, and in their absence to the mothers-in-law. Once the children are grown, they in turn supervise the geographic mobility of their mothers. Such supervision affects whether women leave, remain, or return to their villages. These women choose their route of migration based on information provided by the migrant agent to whom they are linked, normally a male family member: father, husband, brother. Rarely, a sister or a female cousin plays the role of migration guide. In general, the family, whether by blood or by marriage, exercises control over women during their entire course of migration and settlement.

In women's experience as agents in a political field, the gender subordination in society comes into play. They also suffer from the same ethnic discrimination, exploitation, and vulnerability experienced by male members as migrants or undocumented workers. Gender subordination takes many different forms in family and community life, but is organized via concrete power mechanisms. During my fieldwork, I constantly encountered references to the "permits" that women had to obtain from their husbands or partners before acting. To work outside the home, they required the approval and explicit permission of their husbands. Similarly, they needed an official permit to exercise the right to work. This was even more clearly defined in the case of political participation. Permission was required to attend meetings, to undertake organizational tasks, to take time off from domestic chores, and to extend workdays. At times, requesting permission was little more than an expression of affectionate respect for the authority of the male partner; at other times, it was mere pretext for avoiding community activity. In any case, as an ideological resource accepted by all, permission from the man clearly shows an effective normativity. The subversion of the normative order (that is, attending meetings and so on) might be approved by partners or husbands, but only if women continued to do the domestic work. In other words, permission did not imply a redistribution of tasks within the household; the man was consenting only to his wife's "getting around" outside the home if she did not neglect her female obligations. Invariably, some family figure enforced this normativity; often this person was the husband's mother. The mother-in-law was the one who made sure there was perfect compliance with gender normativity inside the home. Thus, a woman's rebellion involved not only the husband—who could be forgiven on account of "being a man"— but also someone of the same sex, the husband's mother.

The women's responses to these forms of subordination vary enormously, but in general they are very creative. Factors related to the life stage of the women and their families have a considerable influence on their response to control; but such factors are not in themselves the determining ones. What they represent, rather, are very different domestic burdens, particularly related to the ages of the children. These burdens function as both practical and symbolic bonds limiting the movement of women between different action spaces. Given these burdens, it requires considerable effort from women to subvert the social order that limits them to domestic space.

The three examples of women's experiences in the following section illustrate their movement across the action spaces to carry out their political participation and how they handle the "permits" to act that control this movement. Each represents a different form of gender subordination through control of spatial mobility and of women's resistance to it.

In each case a particular local and national context defines the boundaries between the domestic and extra-domestic spaces of the woman's life. The first case is situated in a colonia popular founded by workers in Maneadero, Ensenada, which has the agro-export profile of the San Quintin Valley. The next case takes place in an urban colonia in Tijuana, where Mixtec families live and where women work in the informal sector as street vendors or domestic workers. The third example takes place in the United States, in a small agricultural town in San Diego County. It is important to note that the three cases are part of the settlement that has occurred in the last decades on both sides of the border. Settlement has brought new conditions to the organization process and to the daily life of immigrants.[10]

Life in Agricultural Work in Maneadero:
"With Permission to Go Out"

Juliana Sánchez, thirty-three years old, is originally from San Pedro Chayuco, in the district of Juxtlahuaca. Her father speaks only Mixtec. Her mother was bilingual in Mixtec and Spanish; Juliana learned both languages. Her parents were landless shepherds (known as *volantes*) who subsisted by herding animals on common lands. It was not long before they decided to search for paid work. In 1977, at age fourteen, Juliana left her village, accompanied by her father and brother, for the camps of San Quintin in Baja California. She had been to primary school in her village, but from that time onward she went to the San Quintin agricultural camps during school holidays. The family established a relationship with a particular boss. The next four years passed, "coming and going," until she married a young man from her village. She stopped studying and worked as a farm laborer, as did her husband.

Work in the fields consisted of picking tomatoes, stringing the plants, disbudding (picking off the surplus young buds to prevent them weakening the growth of the plant), defoliating (picking off the in-between leaves to allow the fruit to develop), and weeding between the plants. The couple's first four children were born in the agricultural camps of San Quintin. After nearly ten years of working in the tomato fields, she felt frustrated ("annoyed," as she put it); she wanted to learn something new. When her compadre arrived and told them that he had been working in Maneadero (toward the north of the peninsula and also in the state of Baja California) in the commercial flower fields, they decided to move. In 1991, they arrived in Maneadero and moved into a small wooden house belonging to the boss; gradually, they became the owners of a plot of land in the Cañón Buena Vista, a ravine to the side of the Baja California transpeninsular highway, close to the fields. When the children were small, she carried them on her back throughout the twelve-hour working day (7:00 a.m. to 7:00 p.m.), including transportation time. She had been taking part in the community organizations, and after the birth of her fourth child she gave up agricultural work and had more time to devote to community activities. In 1996 her children were 17, 14, 13, 10, and 6 years old. The family economy was maintained by her husband's work—he was a driver's helper on a tanker truck that sold water and was the property of the Frente Indígena Oaxaqueño Binacional (FIOB). The oldest son, who was also a farmworker, helped to support the family. Juliana had a family history of work: she had always worked in a group with her husband and their children. During their twenty-two years in the San Quintin Valley, the same boss employed Juliana and her husband; this changed recently when the husband began to work on the FIOB water tanker truck. During the interviews, Juliana never mentioned any income from her handicraft work. I discovered her talent for working *chaquira* (small beads) and making necklaces and bracelets. She had learned the craft in San Quintin from some of the Triqui women with whom she shared a hut in one of the agricultural camps. On weekends in Ensenada, she sold necklaces and bracelets. Juliana tells how she had always liked political or community participation.

> Since I was a little girl, I have liked the struggle. . . . I have known Arturo since I was thirteen. One of my brothers used to go everywhere with him and since my days in the village, I have had in my mind to do something too. . . . At that time I wanted to study more, but since my parents hadn't enough money to pay for me to go to school, I had to go to work to be able to finish primary school. . . . After I began leaving the village to live in the agricultural camps, I tried to help my relatives and other people from back home who didn't know Spanish. . . . When there was any official paperwork or claims to be made, they used to explain to me in my dialect and I would do the talking in Spanish. (J. Sánchez 1996)

In 1994, Juliana joined the Movimiento Indígena de Unificación y Lucha Independiente (MIULI), formed by migrant agricultural laborers of Mixtec and Triqui origin in Maneadero. The same year the movement joined the FIOB, which led to expanded political action and included relations with other organizations of urban indigenous migrant settlers in Tijuana and California. In 1996, Juliana was responsible for the Comisión de Mujeres de la Coordinadora Regional de Maneadero, a part of the FIOB. The major obstacle in mobilizing other women to perform organizational work was the "permission to leave the house" issue.

> One important problem is that our husbands don't let us go out. . . . This is a problem that we have to talk about, both among ourselves as the women we are, and with the men as they are . . . we have to help each other so that men understand what we are doing. Just because I'm in the women's group, I can't go and take the women out of the home. If the husband does not agree to the wife's participation, there will be problems between them, to which I am contributing. For this reason, it is necessary to talk to the husbands.

Juliana seems to apply this same logic to herself:

> Well, as I say, if he [the husband] gives me permission, I go, and if he says, "don't go," then even if I want to, I can't go. He's the one in charge. If I get stubborn and go anyway, then I have problems to face afterward: "I told you not to go and you went just the same." . . . When people vote for us [in a meeting or assembly] it is because they [the husbands] are in favor of women's participation. . . . If my husband doesn't permit me to participate, then I cannot be responsible for anything. (J. Sánchez 1996)

Apparently, Juliana proposes to make the "permits" part of the political agenda of the organization and to make the issue public in order to avoid unfortunate repercussions in the private lives of the women. Juliana adds:

> Everybody knows her race. I cannot visit the woman when the husband is not at home, to try to convince her to participate. They might have been living happily together until then, but now they're fighting. . . . The man and the woman have to be united, so that there are no disagreements. (J. Sánchez 1996)

From 1997 to 1999, Juliana had a conflict with a male organization leader. He accused her, without any proof, of stealing money from the organization. He also attacked her standing and prestige among the organization members and residents in the colonia. She remembers how he spread gossip about her sexual behavior; the situation affected her relations with her husband and children. She recalls with sadness that her companions did not raise their voices to support her; therefore she decided to leave the organization. In 2002, Juliana and her husband received credit from the Secretaría de Desarrollo Social (SEDESOL) and began a small food business at their home. She is not involved as an activist in the FIOB any longer. Nevertheless, she participates in some collective activities that provide services to the colony.

In Tijuana: "With Permission to Work in the Streets"

Ofelia is fifty-one years old and arrived in Tijuana in 1975, after passing through Culiacán and Guamúchil (Sinaloa) and Hermosillo (Sonora). She left her hometown, San Francisco Higos, in the district of Silacayoapan, when she was seventeen, in the company of her three children and her husband. After getting married in her village, she undertook various kinds of work to earn money, whether to supplement her husband's earnings or maintain the household when he migrated to the United States, which began as far back as the 1950s under the Bracero Program. In the process of migrating through the agricultural camps of the northwest, Ofelia worked in the fields as a laborer while also selling fruit or other food; on the migratory trail another five children were born. She arrived in Tijuana accompanied by her husband and eight children. They were among the first to arrive in the Colonia Obrera in Tijuana, which was one of the first Mixtec settlements to be regularized by the local government during the 1980s.

Providing the colonia with a minimum of urban services, along with a children's nursery and bilingual school, kept the Mixtec migrants busy. During the same decade, the Simpson-Rodino Act was approved in the United States, stabilizing the border crossing by men (and some women) who had families in Tijuana. Also at this time, the Mixtec women opened a working space for themselves in the informal economy, similar to that found throughout Latin America. Ofelia and other women went into the streets, particularly on Avenida Revolución, to sell bracelets to tourists. After years of struggle for this urban space, a series of Mixtec informal vendors' organizations formed. In 1994 alone, four such organizations were registered in the tourist zone of Tijuana. Ofelia was one of the main actors in the use of the urban arena as a space for employment and political visibility. After several confrontations with other vendors and with the local authorities under both PRI and PAN administrations, Ofelia became the only woman among Mixtec leaders involved in street vending. Many tasks normally dealt with in the home now took place on the street: the supervision of small children, preparation of food, and interaction with the family. This shift enabled women to resolve the conflict between domestic and family duties and the demands of work along with political and labor organization activities. Ofelia's case shows how leaving home for the city streets was resolved through negotiation with her husband and older sons. The nature of street vending allowed her to carry out many domestic tasks in the street. However, in other cases, negotiations were not always possible without conflict, as her history as a leader documents. Ofelia intervened in many cases of domestic violence sparked by the disobedience of women who went out to sell without their husbands' permission.

All of the women I interviewed had asked for permission to go and work in the street. If they wanted to attend assemblies or special committees, they also had to have their husband's explicit permission. Curiously, in parallel with the "permit" given by the husbands, the municipal authority allowed street vending only to those who had been issued permits.[11]

In Ofelia's narrative about being a street vendor, she devotes particular attention to government permits. Unlike some of the male leaders of vendors, who claimed the right to occupy spaces for selling without municipal permission, she never opposed the requirement for street vending permits. Her triumph, which is a source of great pride, involved discovering the bureaucratic requirements and mechanisms for obtaining the permits. Such permits are given by the municipal authorities and involve payment of an annual fee and registration on a list that includes specification of the types of merchandise to be sold, the physical space, and hours of business. Ofelia did not know the permit application procedures, but once she learned, everything became easier.

> For eight years, I was in the CROC [Confederación Revolucionaria de Obreros y Campesinos]. When I talked to Federico Valdez, municipal mayor of Tijuana, he said, "Look my daughter, tomorrow come to the Municipal Hall, and we are going to talk. I will help you." . . . I went to the appointment and he said, "We are going to give you permits, and we are going to work together." At that moment, I realized what the permits were. I thought that if I wanted to go to sell in the street, nobody had the right to disturb me. I was not stealing anything or killing anyone. Well, I told him: "The government must give me a permit on paper, and that will be enough!" (Santos 1994)

By the early 1990s, Ofelia was a public figure whom the governmental authorities would call on to negotiate the use of the tourist spaces in the city center. Other indigenous vendors would also come to her to describe their problems or request her help in obtaining a selling space.

Early in 1994, the Frente Mixteco-Zapoteco Binacional, as it was then called, became aware of the importance of affiliating the organized indigenous street vendors. A series of meetings took place between the Front's leaders and the street vendors led by Ofelia. At the constitutive assembly that same year (when the joint Frente Mixteco-Zapoteco Binacional changed its name to Frente Indígena Oaxaqueño Binacional), the street vendors' association was incorporated in the Front, and Ofelia took the post of women's action coordinator. After she made several attempts to coordinate concrete actions, the participation of women as members of the Front was annulled and the female vendors left that organization.

One day, a leader of Maneadero came to ask me for space for some vendor women from Ensenada. They wanted to sell in Santa Cecilia Plaza. I was upset with that man because each of these spaces had been won with our struggle. Nobody helped me get permits or bailed me out of jail when we fought with the *carabineros* [other vendors]. That man told me: You must do it because we are in the same organization, and we are indigenous. But I think that man was looking to fight against the government, to oppose it. I don't want to fight against the government. I am looking for advice on how to resolve our problems for our families, our sons and daughters. I prefer to work personally with my own words, with friends of mine, without lies. (Santos 1996)

At the beginning of 2003, Ofelia was still working as a street vendor and was leading the same organization. She was living alone in Tijuana—her family had moved to California. This change in family residence is the result of the new U.S. immigration border policies. Although the new laws have made crossing the border difficult, Ofelia's husband returns each weekend and helps her with the business.

Growing Up and Living in California:
"Without Permission to Cross the Border"

Eloísa Romero is twenty-three years old, and she was born in San Miguel Aguacate, in the district of Juxtlahuaca (the Oaxacan Mixteca). Her mother arrived in Tijuana from the hometown in the 1970s, together with her seven children and Eloísa's father. During their time in Tijuana, the parents separated; the father returned to the hometown, and the mother crossed over to the United States accompanied by a female cousin. Meanwhile, the children remained in Tijuana in the care of their grandmother. Eloísa remembers that they lived in the shantytown known as Cartolandia—a zone of ramshackle buildings very close to the city center. A bridge crossed over the street where they lived and the passing "gringos" would toss coins to them. After Cartolandia flooded, they went to live in Colonia Obrera. Eloísa's mother continued to work in the fields in California as an undocumented laborer. Eloísa and two of the other children used to sell chewing gum on Avenida Revolución or beg for money; their days were spent in the streets among the cars and buses. When they failed to sell anything, they begged. When they saw that women with babies received more money, they wrapped a doll in a shawl. Of course, the "gringos" realized it was only a doll and just laughed. They spent two years like that, while their mother sent them money from California.

In 1979, when she was eight years old, Eloísa's mother came back and took them all to California. In the United States, Eloísa and her brothers and sister went to school. She remembers that at first it was difficult; she used to say to herself: "What am I doing here with these gringos? At times, I didn't understand either Spanish or English. I was ashamed to say I didn't understand anything, and so I kept my mouth shut. It was hard because in those days the Chicanos used to say, 'Go back home, wetback.' They didn't like us; who knows why" (Romero 1994).

With the 1986 amnesty law, Eloísa's mother and all the brothers and sisters were able to obtain residents' permits. Eloísa tells how she managed to get by at school without understanding anything. In high school, her tutors told her what subjects to take in order to pass, but she didn't understand why or what the syllabus contained.

In her opinion, there was a basic difference between the population of Mexican origin and the Chicanos who had been in the United States longer:

> Chicanos have been unable to benefit from the United States because, although there is the opportunity to study, the young people don't want to study. They feel frustrated with discrimination at school, and they withdraw from the struggle, leaving the classrooms open for the gringos. We are different; I want to study, and if I have the chance and the right to do so, I will! Maybe it's that the Chicanos are already children of people with jobs who have achieved a certain level in society and have learned to survive with the least effort. The indigenous peasants, on the other hand, want their children to live better than they do. They know how hard it is to work in the fields, and so they send their children to school. . . . For example, cutting the grapes—when I lived there, cutting began in August. It is the dirtiest kind of work: you work eight hours a day in the dust, putting grapes in boxes of sand. You end up with your shoes full of sand. When you have your period or period pains, there's nothing you can do; you just have to put up with it. I worked with my brothers and sisters in the fields too. (Romero 1994)

After struggling in defense of "peasants'" rights in the United States, Eloísa began to stand out. She had studied up to senior high school, attaining a mastery of English and Mixtec and, with less fluency, Spanish. Her work experience ranged from farmwork to being a typist in a bank; during this time she was an active participant in the defense of farmworkers' rights in the Bakersfield, California, area. In 1994, Eloísa was one of three women who formed the Coordinadora de Acción Femenil of the FIOB. By that year she was engaged to be married to a young man born in the Mixteca who began objecting to her political activities. After the wedding in 1995, her participation in the Front diminished. When she became pregnant, Eloísa withdrew completely from the organization's activities.

Her political commitment changed slowly over time. Motherhood limited her participation, but as the children grew up she returned to some community activism.

In each of these extremely schematized conditions, domestic and extra-domestic spaces were differentiated in response to several factors: the ethnic condition of these migrants in the society of reception, the type of work they engaged in, and the kind of residence lived in. There was another barrier to their participation in organizations. All of them talked about needing their husband's approval, but they also cited conflicts with male leaders. This last conflict was not a decisive factor at the beginning of participation but affected their long-term participation in the organization.

Female Participation and the Ethnic Project

Women's participation and their permitted spaces are perceived ambiguously within the indigenous migrant organizations. In the interviews, the male leaders mentioned the "absence of participation by the women" as a problem for the organizations and the "problem that those who participate either have to attend to their homes, or they get married and have children." When pressed on the matter, and asked "Is it women's business, anyway?" the male leaders blamed "macho husbands who don't give their wives permission to participate." Similarly, the women mentioned husbands not permitting them to act outside the home as an obstacle to their participation in the organizations.

In my interpretation, if women need permission from their husbands to act outside the home, it is because the social order differentiates social action spaces according to sex. There is no escaping the fact that different action spaces are associated with gender identities. Female members of hometown and street vendors' associations, and even male leaders, expressed concern about the permission issue. Not all the leaders questioned the legitimacy of male authority, but there is agreement that husbands should be encouraged to give permission to the women to act outside the domestic space: specifically at work and in the organizations.

The leaders or representatives have starting promoting women's participation in the organizations. At meetings and other events, I have been struck by the constant calls from the leaders to their paisanos to allow the women to participate in the organizations. As the organizations have increasingly become formalized, migrant leadership has also become a more legitimate source of authority. The leaders' urgings for women's participation have received attention from the men, at least according to the women interviewed. I found that a common task of the leaders was to mediate family problems having to do with the husband's reluctance to let his wife leave the house. Sometimes activists had to deal with problems of domestic violence related to the husband's consumption of alcohol. Women's participation can also be seen as a way of bringing private matters into the political arena and of claiming agency for women, empowering them in different spaces while keeping them subject to a social order that legitimizes masculine authority. As Juliana points out, persuading the men to commit themselves publicly (within the organizations) to let their women participate—in other words, to leave the confines of the home—does not imply that the women are excused from their domestic responsibilities. In general, collective discussion of women's participation in the organizations comprises two concerns. The first is the matter of permission: while the male leaders talk about machismo as an abstract problem within migrant families, women refer to machismo in concrete terms relating to their family life, including children. The second concern is domestic violence. The politicization of this matter has involved different agents: on the one hand, influenced by women's rights groups, especially in the United States, women activists have participated in and sponsored meetings where domestic violence was addressed. On the other hand, the male leaders approach domestic violence as a criminal act. Numerous court proceedings involving domestic violence have been instituted in the United States, and organizations have had to deal with the imprisonment of Mixtec and Triqui men for domestic violence. An interviewee points out the difficulty of "making [the men] understand that they are in a different country and that they can't do that sort of thing." Within organizations, the issue of violence against women and children appears at the same time as the issue of male imprisonment. In their accounts, women identify machismo and violence as interrelated negative elements of ethnic identity. Gutmann (1996, 237), studying the working class in Mexico City, found that male abuse against women is a primary element of machismo. As many Mexican writers have pointed out, the macho Mexican is part of the national identity. Among elderly people in Oaxacan towns, machismo is a positive element of male identity. I observed machismo to mean a strong sense of masculine pride and an exhilarating sense of power. Thus, the participation of women in organizational activities can threaten male control of female behavior.

Holding discussions of machismo and permits represents a shift in organizations, as can be seen in the next examples.

On September 2, 1994, the Women's Meeting of the Frente Mixteco-Zapoteco Binacional was held in Tijuana, just before the constitution of the

FIOB. Representatives from Tijuana, Maneadero, Oaxaca, and California took part in the meeting. The primary issues were street selling and day workers in agriculture, as well as participation in the organizations. In both cases, there was repeated mention of problems with obtaining husbands' "permits."

> We as Mexicans have many problems here in Baja California and need to struggle a lot . . . but the bad thing is that the husbands don't give permission. My husband says that I'm crazy, and that is why I want to be outside on the street. I once left my husband on his own for eleven days. Women are not doing anything wrong; we're busy in the struggle, we're searching for the way forward, to see how we're going to get together so that the government takes us into account. For that reason I say to my husband, "Don't imagine I'm going to go out to do anything bad. I am just going to carry on the struggle."[12]

Another meeting took place in Fresno on May 19, 1996. It was the Conferencia de Mujeres Indígenas Migrantes–FIOB (FIOB Indigenous Migrant Women's Conference), and was supported by Fresno State University and financed by the Abya Yala Fund. The subjects dealt with at the conference were domestic violence in the family; alcoholism in the indigenous migrant community; AIDS as a binational problem; and how to organize to deal with these problems. The meeting included childcare and meals.

On February 16 and 17, 2001, a workshop was held on the subject of "Indigenous Women Collaborating and Transforming Lives for the Well-being of Their Families" in Bakersfield, California. It was sponsored jointly by the Farmworker Women's Leadership Network and the FIOB. The central concerns were labor rights, domestic violence, traditions and culture, diabetes, breast cancer, housing, and barriers to civic participation. This workshop was the product of alliances that the FIOB developed during the second half of the 1990s with other Mexican women's organizations and involved female farmworkers in the United States.

The issue of domestic violence was on the agenda at the three meetings, along with other problems affecting the lives of migrant women and their families. In their life stories, many women spoke of being beaten by their husbands as something "natural" and just part of female life. It seems to me that male "permits" and domestic violence form part of the same ideology of gender that subordinates women to masculine authority, making this subordination appear natural. Two frameworks for legitimization of this male authority can be identified: the family and the community. In conditions of migration, if for any reason the control of the family becomes relaxed, that of the community appears. Organizations do not escape the ideology of male authority; they can become a space for controlling female behavior. Family ideology, for instance, puts the primary role of women in the domestic space and is part of the discourse of ethnic identity.

For this reason, discussions of male "permits" and domestic violence within the organizations and among the intellectuals question the "us" that the leadership discourse constructs. Gender relations are a common topic in the narratives of men and women and must be seen as part of the ethnic identity project. That is, machismo, violence toward women and children, and alcoholism are regarded as negative emblems of ethnic identity.

The significance of gender alliances deserves some attention. People took different positions on gender alliances between indigenous and mestizo women, sometimes regarding them with suspicion. Discussions continued through alliances with the Farmworker Women's Leadership Network, the California Endowment, Oxfam America, and female scholars. Residents in the United States met with migrants from Asia—Hmong women. In 1999, Mixtec and Hmong women met in the Central Valley to tell their stories of migration and residency.[13] Similar cultural encounters have not occurred among male leaders, particularly regarding the experience of integration into U.S. society. Intercultural meetings and alliances occur more frequently among female activists of these organizations.

Horizons of Discussion and Some Final Reflections

The following paragraphs offer some conclusions about the problematic aspects of the dynamics of gender referred to in the introduction to this chapter—the mechanisms of subordination and resistance. The first refers to the culture-bound rules that limit women to the domestic sphere. The traditional domestic ideal of women seems to be current among the indigenous migrant communities, permeating the normativity of social relations within communities. What is not so clear is the precise meaning of "domestic" in the indigenous migrant world. While maternity and conjugality are clearly defining elements of women's action spaces, women's participation in activities that generate income was also important, as were their community activities. The latter two aspects seem to form part of the obligations and responsibilities of women: the generation of income for family survival and the collective participation in the survival of the community. Their inclusion may be related to the dynamics and concept of the home in rural indigenous communities, where there are not the same boundaries between domestic and the extra-domestic spaces as there are in the urban communities. In the former, the entire family participates in farming activities and, at the same time, in an intense community life through a system of social organization.

As other scholars have pointed out (Lister 1993; Stephen 1991), this case shows that "the domestic" is not a universal concept, but rather is specified in ethnic and class terms and is extremely sensitive to local conditions. Therefore, ethnic and class conditions are insufficient to define "the domestic," since elements of another order come into play: regional labor markets, degrees of urbanization at a particular location, state policies, and systems of ethnic relations.

The second problematic aspect involves the mechanisms of resistance of women aimed at subverting a social order that limits their capacity for agency. Women, in the midst of a history of poverty and suffering, are proud of their capacity for struggle, having "forged ahead" against the odds. This struggle shows their capacity to move across different spaces: from their hometowns to the cities; from their villages to another country; from their houses to the streets; from their own fields to the vast spaces of agriculture. Research supports the following thesis: while it is true that the ideology of sex limits women to the domestic sphere, they daily subvert the restraining forces while apparently remaining within the traditional framework of the indigenous community. The indigenous migrant organizations function as the space where the social order fragmented by migration is reestablished. The community frames women's actions with an eye to maintaining respect for family norms.

The differentiation of spaces of social action is delimited not only by the gender ideology but by Mexican ethnic ideology, which excludes the indigenous peoples from certain public spaces. The social order relegates different social categories to specific spheres of action. The differentiation of social spaces becomes part of the ethnic and gender systems of a specific society. It explains why in each society female stereotypes make sense in the ethnic or national ideologies. Thus, movement between the domestic and nondomestic spaces can be seen as a subversion of the ethnic order, since it breaks the containment of certain ethnic categories within particular action spaces. At what point can it be said that crossing the public-domestic boundary is empowering to women? Indigenous women are not a homogeneous category, as the three cases above have shown. Nevertheless, all of them have been working since childhood, which is all too common of poor women around the world. The idea of women going out to work as a way to empowerment has been questioned enough in the feminist literature. In general, poor women take on more responsibilities in public spaces as an extension of their responsibilities to the family. Nevertheless, the political sphere can open new horizons to women. Even against their husbands' wills, and despite the reproaches of their children and their neighbors' gossip, women take part in the activities of migrant organizations. I can say that organizations of female vendors subvert the domestic/public dichotomy by bringing the domestic into the public and vice versa. Nevertheless, domestic issues just become part of the organization's agenda until the female voices point out those issues as community or family problems. The criticism and revision of ethnic identity taking place within the indigenous migrant organizations is affecting gender relations; in this process, women's voices have played an important role. The revision of "Mixtec being" reaches into the family and to the Mixtec couple through the issues of "permits," the multiple burdens of work for women, and domestic violence. These issues are recognized by the members of organizations as negative signs or emblems of ethnicity. Conflicts arise from the different approaches to politics by indigenous intellectuals of both sexes. These differences reach into the family, the community, and the political space of the organizations.

7
Mixtec Transnational Identity

Toward the end of the 1960s, Fredrik Barth revolutionized the field of ethnicity studies with a seminal thesis: ethnicity is a way of organizing cultural differences. For this reason, cultural contents are important to the extent that they acquire significance in a concrete situation as ethnic boundaries. Guided by this hypothesis, the present study has focused on the construction of ethnic boundaries by indigenous migrants on the Mexico–U.S. border. The following pages synthesize my main findings.

The constructivist approach of this study has both virtues and limitations, which I have treated as a research challenge. I do think, however, that the approach has enabled me to address the structure-agency dichotomy that, as Barth himself has recognized in recent theoretical formulations (1994), demands attention from scholars of ethnicity. By bringing together two processes—the constitution of social agents and the construction of identity boundaries—the dynamics of ethnicity in Mixtec migrant organizations on the Mexico–U.S. border can be appreciated.

The idea that ethnicity is a product of social action deessentializes ethnicity. The ethnic subject emerges as an active being engaged in its own identity and capable of reviewing its own history and reconstituting itself through social action. This conceptual shift is the result of vigorous reflection on two late-twentieth-century phenomena: international migrations and ethnic mobilizations.

In response to international migrations, ethnic groups have transformed their local and regional boundaries by transcending the territorial limits of national states. The transformation involves an inescapable phenomenon: the dispersion of members of ethnic communities challenges territoriality as the natural basis of ethnicity. The transformation also triggers a series of mechanisms for maintaining the identity of belonging and rearticulating a fragmented community. The physical distancing of members from the home community led scholars, in the 1960s, to view the weaknesses of ethnic communities, along with the increasing individualization of their members, as inevitable. According to this assumption, the assimilation of migrants into the new societies was only a matter of time. However, research accumulated on the subject during the 1990s—to which the present study is a contribution—shows that change does not always follow the predicted course. Instead, a recommitment to community belonging has taken place. The assumption of linear social change—which, until the late 1980s, had made a substantial number of studies on migrant identity unsustainable—also makes the paradigm of modernization equally unsustainable. Without new conceptual tools, the study of postmigrant ethnicity is unable to meet an epistemological challenge that Žižek (1998) identified as key: how community belonging is reconstituted in the era of globalization. To answer this question, I have undertaken a study and analysis of the mechanisms and agents in the reconstitution of community.

In this approach, migrants are seen as having recovered their ethnic condition and, simultaneously, their role as agents in the construction of a sense of community belonging. This conclusion is supported not only by the empirical findings of this study but also by literature addressing the constitution of national and ethnic communities in other parts of the world. I chose as the study's central axis the constitution of ethnic agents in migration and—as a logical consequence—the ethnic community that such agents construct in the transnational political space. The agents were identified empirically—on a collective level—as migrant organizations, and—on an individual level—as the intellectuals associated with these organizations. If the constructivist orientation of the present study defines humans as active beings, with a capacity for steering their own course, the concept of structuration enables me to account for social integration processes of long duration. These processes structure agents' options to be both constitutive of and constituted by the society in which they live. The processes are also subject to structural forces such as the logic of capital and the policies of the nation-state.

The New Contexts for the Transnational Community

Globalization fragments populations because it does not incorporate everyone in the same manner. The freedom with which an executive travels differs from the freedom of an undocumented worker. As Zygmunt Bauman (1999, 28) points out, although the processes of globalization increase freedom of movement for some, for many they are a cruel fate, full of limitations and suffering. For example, Mixtec migrants in Mexico and the United States enter an agricultural or informal labor market that functions according to the logic of accumulation: the utilization of a workforce that is flexible because it is cheap and vulnerable. Transnational logics tie migrants to local conditions that are subject to a nation-state's policies of social and geographic mobility. Thus, their condition as workers without rights (to the degree that, as foreigners or aliens, they do not have local or national citizenship) accompanies the migrants as they enter the flow of workers participating in a transnational market that demands a flexible labor force.

Globalization does not erase the social differences within a nation-state.

In fact, through transnationalization such differences appear to deepen. In the case of Mixtec transnationalization, a set of attributes and social relations, with meaning within one national ethnic system, places Mixtecos in a similar hierarchy within a different ethnic system. Capital draws migrants to a different state system but places them in a similar position of subordination and exploitation. The powers of capital and the state operate according to contradictory logics, but the final outcome benefits capital by making indigenous immigrants more vulnerable, more willing to accept the worst working conditions.

Paradoxically, the more permeable and ambiguous the economic borders, the more the political borders harden, seeking to become impermeable to the flow of workers. This contradiction is a defining trait of the Mexico–U.S. border area. Economic integration coexists with a human displacement that results in suffering and risk for the thousands of people who cross or attempt to cross the border surreptitiously. Globalization for those populations means participating in a primarily agricultural labor market that demands flexibility. It demands it not only individually but collectively, of the kin group, since it requires the creation of family-based living strategies that combine seasonal migration with settlement in distant places and multisectoral work in Mexico and in the United States.

Organizing the Dispersed Community

Vulnerability sums up the broad spectrum of problems and concerns that stimulate the emergence of migrant organizations. The appearance of organizations indicates how migrants create and develop collective action—strategically arranged—when their life conditions are altered by departure from their hometowns. The geographic dispersal of members of the local community brings with it difficulties in communication and in collective action. To organize successfully around an issue in the town of San Miguel Tlacotepec or Nieves Ixpantepec from some point on the Mexican border, or from within the United States, requires modes of communication that minimize geographic distance. Although one would assume this dispersal to be a disadvantage for organized action, it turns out to be, in the end, one of its greatest advantages. Geographic mobility makes it possible to identify new issues and generate new resources that respond to multiple localities simultaneously, even across national borders. As the chronology of organizational development shows (see chapter 3), in the course of migration new organizational contacts are established with individuals from distinct social categories, who become allies in specific struggles. With new urban experiences and new occupations, members of the working class organize and take action around the issues of salary and labor conditions.

On this point, one must highlight the importance of the migrants' communal tradition of organizing. The reproduction of traditional indigenous forms of association was fundamental to the development of the first hometown and savings associations. However, they are transformed into more complex organizational forms (in ethnic and spatial terms) thanks to the encounter between traditional ways of doing politics and other ways learned at the migration destination. The more complex forms of organization that emerge in the colonias populares (squatter settlements), or even in the migrants' work as agricultural laborers, makes successful action possible in these new contexts. Kinship and community loyalties or endogamous celebratory, communicative, and conjugal cultural practices are useful to the survival of the ethnic group, but the group must also have the capacity to learn new forms of organizing, decision making, conflict resolution, and community representation. Ultimately, what counts is the capacity for transformation in the migratory experience; it occurs by creating new issues and resources and updating old ones.

The transformation of community relationships into political resources is related to the theoretical supposition that politicized networks and informal groups are antecedents to the emergence of organizations. Political action is channeled through family and community links, creating cohesion and conflict among members of the migrant network. Kinship and local ties may have already situated a person vis-à-vis a conflict within the organization. Nevertheless, my study found that politicization of the networks is not a necessary precursor to the emergence of the organizations. Instead, it may be a product of the creation of the organization itself. That is, collective actions can be organized from within small groups of activists, or at times even at the personal initiative of a leader. Such efforts rely on basic forms of cohesion (family and community), resulting in the politicization of the kinship and community networks. The role of these individual agents, who in this book I have called intellectuals (in the sense of a Gramscian organic intellectual), is to create emblems of identity that define political loyalties. I will return to this point after explaining the importance of the relationships between organizations and local and federal governments beyond the homeland.

The Challenge of Transnational Organizations

The new context in which the ethnic community is reproduced comprises more than just the local conditions at the migration destination. The dual orientation of first-generation migrants keeps their concerns about their places of origin alive. Their connection to the social and political systems of the sending communities depends on the resources and issues of the organizations in the places of destination. In the case of the FIOB or the ACBJ, it has been shown in the present study how the migrants maintained a relationship with the political system in their hometowns, whether through direct participation in community decision making, by making investments, or by assisting with specific projects. They have even participated by running candidates for electoral seats, such as on the municipal council. But it must be emphasized that the organized migrants' willingness to maintain the connection with that system occurred before the government institutions themselves (on the local, regional, or national level) encouraged political linkage, which led to economic commitments between the organizations and the migrant communities.

The evolution of migrant organizations documented in this study not only reflects a maturation of organizational forms but also the transformation of political conditions in Mexico for migrants to the United States and for the indigenous Mexicans. The Mixtec and Oaxacan migration to the Mexico–U.S. border has begun to bear fruit for the places of origin. That has awakened political and economic interest in the participation of the indigenous migrants in the communities of origin. The government's promotion of extraterritorial and transnational migrant organizations gives these organizations new opportunities for negotiating with the state. The Mexican voter living abroad who favors President Fox's agenda has political strength, which prompts organizations to boast of the economic value of remittances and of the electoral potential of these voters.

During the 1990s, migrant organizations institutionalized in a way that combined the needs of the places of origin with those of the places of arrival. There were two major indicators of this change.

The first of these was a broadening of relations with government administrations: with local and state governments (as Oaxacan migrants) and with the federal government (as undocumented indigenous migrants or residents abroad); this was especially noticeable at presidential elections or when government policies regarding migrants abroad were being defined. In addition, organizations established relations with U.S. federal and state administrations. Relations with different government agencies are themselves a source of cultural differentiation; while local government bodies define migrants as Tlacotepenses, Macuiltianguenses, or Sabineños, the state government defines them as Mixtecos, Zapotecos, or Triquis and, therefore, as Oaxaqueños. But, while the Mexican government's migration policies define them as Mexicans abroad, U.S. federal and state migration policies define them as immigrants, undocumented migrants, and Mexican indigenous. These heteroascriptions, along with the flow of capital, provide the material conditions for the construction of the indigenous migrant subject. At present, relations with state governments are among the most important sources of conflict—not only between organizations and governments but between the migrant organizations themselves.

The second indicator is the forming of interethnic alliances between Mixtecos, Zapotecos, and Triquis. This process has unfolded in the context of indigenous resistance throughout the American continents, triggered by the quincentennial commemoration of the Spanish discovery and conquest of the Americas. The alliances have been based on origin within the politico-administrative confines of the state of Oaxaca, on a common history stretching back beyond the Spanish Conquest, on speaking a pre-Hispanic language, and on being international migrants. In the Frente Indígena Oaxaqueño Binacional (FIOB), for instance, the boundary between Mixtecos and Zapotecos becomes less sharp in view of a shared identity as Oaxacan indigenous people. The step toward claiming identity as indigenous Mexicans seems to have been influenced by the Latin American indigenous movement of the seventies. The breakthrough in Mexico was the appearance of the Ejército Zapatista de Liberación Nacional (EZLN, Zapatista Army of National Liberation) in 1994. While an indigenous identity was already recognized, the boundaries of this identity were constructed in relation to the mestizo as cacique, trader, landowner, and government authority. In the FIOB framework, the boundaries of indigenous identity are marked by relations with the state of Oaxaca and the Mexican national state and, at the same time, through a community conceived as sharing a pre-Hispanic historical origin.

Finally, irrespective of the level of institutionalization, it seems to be a constant that organizations pass through stages in which they largely lack a grassroots movement. Leaders can occupy spaces or forums of ongoing protest, or engage from time to time in concrete actions inspired by communities in the hometowns or on the border. But the only stable membership is that based on belonging to a home community. Beyond that, joining one or another organization tends to be a response to a situation, to concrete demands pertaining to the community more than to the organization itself. Thus, organizations function as executive committees of leaders attending to the needs of the community in the places of origin or arrival and mobilizing resources in regional, state, or national political fields.

Politico-Cultural Representation of the Transnational Indigenous Community

Following the postulates of social action theory, the present study has documented the key role of the leaders for collective action among migrants. In cultural terms, they build a group when they speak in the name of the group.

Paradoxically, both group and representatives are constituted in the very act of representation (Bourdieu 1982, 154).

As has already been mentioned, indigenous representation is one of the most controversial subjects in Mexico. Even after listening to the personal histories of activists, it was not always clear to me how those leaders came to occupy positions of authority. Activism and some linguistic or educational skills are common characteristics among leaders. Sometimes leaders emerge as part of an election process within small groups; at other times they emerge through self-election and the decision to start a new group. An informal source of legitimacy also exists: recognition by the community. This implies that the leaders and their families have been good citizens in terms of commitment to the community.

Therefore, the emergence of intellectuals as representatives generally involves an individual rising to visibility or protagonism, in Gramscian terms. The leaders' life stories continually revealed similar experiences, revolving around conflict in the following areas: hometown community life, linguistic relations, government, political parties and traditional authorities, and labor relations.

As Thompson (1994) points out, conflict is experienced not only personally and biographically but collectively and socially—hence the importance of the collective memory of family and community conflicts. All the leaders recognize hometown experiences as sources of their political activism. They recall conflicts over land, usury, and control of administrative positions, as well as reprisals and humiliation for using the indigenous language. Their sense of history comes not only from their contemporaries but from their forebears (Schutz 1967). A generational conflict coincides with that described by Le Bot (1997) in writing about the Zapatista movement in Chiapas. I refer to the conflict with the indigenous gerontocracy—which many leaders describe with a sadness—and the influence this had on the leaders' growth as migrants and activists. This conflict involved a critique of the political behavior of the traditional communal authorities. These principales recognized no other way of doing politics than through the traditional assemblies and hierarchies. Le Bot (1997) points out that this generational conflict is one of the most important causes of divisions among the indigenous community. Seen from the vantage point of migration on the Mexico–U.S. border, the indigenous community seems to have undergone change, incorporating new forms of doing politics. For this very reason I doubt that such a generational conflict would undermine it.

But though the experience of conflict, in its various above-mentioned forms, was a necessary condition, it was by no means sufficient to ensure the emergence of migrant intellectuals. Their life trajectories show that certain precipitating conditions are needed, such as the individual's joining a political network and contact with political agents as role models at an early stage in life. Family and community life in the hometowns or places of destination constitutes a kind of ethno-political niche. Activism in leftist groups or political parties in Juxtlahuaca towns during the seventies was an important background for migrant activists. San Miguel Tlacotepec, San Miguel Cuevas, and San Juan Mixtepec, all of them in Juxtlahuaca district, are the places of origin of some of the intellectuals in the strongest transnational organizations in Mexico and the United States: the FIOB, COCIO, and ACBJ.

While these intellectuals regard themselves as organically linked to their home and migration communities, they are differentiated by their relatively high level of education and by their bilingualism (in Spanish and an indigenous language) and occasional trilingualism (Spanish, English, and an indigenous language). These characteristics confirm the findings of other studies of the intelligentsia, elite, or intellectuals in Latin America, Asia, and Africa (Anderson 1993; Brass 1991; Gellner 1991; Shils 1972). Such characteristics have facilitated the intellectuals' access to information (based on their education), capacity for mediation (thanks to their fluency in more than one language), and greater capacity for geographic mobility and independence from their families (thanks to being born male). There is, however, another, more subjective element to be analyzed in the life stories: the leaders' sense of vocation toward, of responsibility for, other members of the community.

This leadership vocation has two sources: the family and the community. The dynamics of the family involve assignment of responsibilities and constant recognition of achievement. The civic-religious and traditional authority systems in the communities demand of all members continual participation. Under these circumstances a leader—sometimes the person least expected—may emerge. This means that any migrant is a potential candidate to occupy a post in a cofradía, or a mayordomía, or some other representative position in the community.

What I am attempting to clarify is that the vocation of these leaders is formed in the family and the community, arising as a responsibility and an obligation and only later becoming a privilege. Without this historical perspective it would be difficult to explain the emergence of leaders in the migrant context and their role as mediators or brokers between dispersed communities and the national state. As some specialists have pointed out (Bonfil 1995a,b; Warman and Argueta 1993), a characteristic feature of present-day Mexican "indigenism" is that its spokespersons are intellectuals from the indigenous communities. This is a significant shift in politico-cultural representation and in ethnic consciousness. The possibility of constituting oneself as an ethnic agent "in one's own words," as the leaders would say, indicates the capacity for self-definition in a field of ethnic relations in transnational contexts.

The Ethnic Identity Project beyond the National Borders

Scholars agree from a variety of theoretical viewpoints that the role of intellectuals includes the construction of myths and traditions, the legitimization of authority, and the creation of symbols. As Gramsci (1998) puts it, their function is situated in the superstructure, in the field of ideology. In the case of migrant communities, distance from the places of origin determines the role of the intellectuals; I understand this role as being to construct a narrative of an ethnic community that is dispersed across various territories.

This group of intellectuals acts in a transnational political field, heterogeneous in issues and resources, forging a strategic political unity out of its different voices. In the consolidation of that unity, allies and adversaries are situated in an ethnic narrative that distinguishes the boundaries between "us" and "them" in the political field.

In examining the ethnic narrative constructed in the transnational field of Mixtec migrant organizations, the present work has followed Alberoni (1984) in observing a distinction between the ethical dimension and the political one. The former refers to the indigenous being as a person within a system of social relations and in a structure of opportunities; the political dimension refers to the attempt to gain control of the structures of domination (family, school, authority, and state). The contents of the ethical facet are analyzed, in accordance with the constructivist approach to ethnicity, as positive or negative emblems of ethnicity, while the political dimension is studied as a set of strategic elements in a political struggle.

My findings on the ethical and political dimensions of the ethnic project enable me to reformulate Barth's proposition (1969) regarding the mechanisms and agents that become significant in the construction of ethnic boundaries. An important mechanism is primordialization of the origin, around which various cultural contents are organized as emblems of identity, transformed into the driving forces of a struggle for conservation. Roosens (1994) seems to be correct in identifying the relationship with the place of origin as precisely what distinguishes ethnicity in the historical sense, rendering Barthian situationalism insufficient. Along with this primordialization of the origin, destigmatization of identity is set in motion, involving the rejection of other cultural contents perceived as negative attributes of identity; these then become the driving force of a struggle for change. Hence, historically constructed ethnic boundaries are questioned and oscillate ambiguously between tradition and change. In examining the role of agents in the construction of the emblems that define ethnicity, the present study sees indigenous migrant intellectuals as agents of ethnic identity and the state as a fundamental interlocutor in the political arena. This finding coincides with the remarks of Williams (1989) and Verdery (1994) on the centrality of the national state in the constitution of social—and particularly ethnic—identities. From such a point of view, the state constitutes the subjects in its dominion through government policies. In this way Mexican nationalism, as an instrument of cultural homogenization through the state, "constructed" indigenous peoples as subjects of domination and subordination. The construct is still in evidence; even beyond national borders such state policies continue to affect the material and symbolic conditions of the life of the indigenous subject. Thus the situation concept, initially formulated by Barth (1969), must consider— as he himself and other authors recognized later (Barth 1994; Roosens 1994)—other longer-term processes of social integration, such as articulations of capital and the policies of national states. In each moment of the migrants' lives, capital and policies constrain opportunities for action.

How can indigenous beings escape this situation? They must transform themselves from subjects of identity to agents of identity. An analysis of leaders' discourses revealed a process of primordialization and destigmatization that seems to produce a complex ethnic identity. Today's more complex tools of social analysis reveal how domination and resistance operate simultaneously. A comprehensive study has the challenge of recognizing the subject's claims of a heterogeneous ethnic identity.

Female Representation in the Ethnic Project

The subject of politico-cultural representation leads to investigating gender relations. The construction of ethnic differences is intersected by gender and generational relations, which have scarcely been dealt with in the literature on ethnicity and nationalism. I looked at the impact of female voices on the ethnic project; and this led me to substantiate the way in which gender shapes the ethnic project formulated by the intellectuals in the political field of the organizations.

This study has noted how male authority permeates domestic and public spaces, including the migrant organizations. In the organizations studied, male authority was not questioned. However, there are attempts to make men understand the importance of female participation. The organizations become, simultaneously, a new space in which women's behavior is controlled and a space in which the control mechanisms are questioned. These organizational spaces are open to discussion of certain mechanisms for controlling women, such as the "permits," as well as other matters such as alcoholism, excessive work burdens, and domestic violence. Although alcoholism and domestic violence have been treated as private matters for discussion within the family-community-pueblo of migrants, specific strategies have been developed to combat them. Such matters now appear on the political agendas of the organizations and are seen as negative emblems originating in ethnic and class subordination. The bringing of these issues into the open has not been simply a result of female participation in the organizations. Meetings with women of other national and ethnic groups helped to move the process along. Alliances with feminist activists and female scholars have particularly contributed to the political rise of female activists in those organizations. Settlement in the United States introduced a new legal framework, where some issues, such as domestic violence, are not only a private matter but subject to public and judicial scrutiny. The organizations are thus obliged to open the discussion beyond the confines of the family and express the issues as a problem of the indigenous community in the United States. This new legal framework has helped to increase the attention given to women's voices within the organizations. It has enabled the ethnic community to be nourished by the ethics and politics of Mixtec women. They, like other women mobilized in the United States (Hardy-Fanta 1993), show a considerable capacity to connect the private with the public world by carrying demands from domestic life into the space of the organizations.

Beyond the National State?

The image of indigenous communities, fragmented and dispersed beyond national frontiers, has tempted some analysts to prophesy a weakening of the national state's control over them. To this situation should be added the effects of economic globalization. The role of the national state in international migration varies according to whether the focus is on the Mexican or U.S. government. Other possible factors are the historical period in relations between the two countries (Durand 1994) and the institutional level of the politico-administrative bodies one is considering. The experience of Mixtec migration indicates an intense relationship between the migrant communities and the administrative authorities in their places of origin, in a context of developing relations with authorities of greater politico-administrative scope, such as the state government of Oaxaca. This observation leads me to one last aspect, which deserves attention in conceptual terms and concerns the political dimension of ethnicity.

The political dimension of what I have called the ethnic identity project brings us face-to-face with the question: What is the purpose of the identity strategies we have been examining? According to Le Bot (1997, 99), present-day indigenous movements in Latin America are characterized by the search for recognition of their differences rather than the attainment of power. This thesis seems to shed light on the ethnic identity project of the indigenous organizations in the Mexico–U.S. border region. If I had to provide an overall description of the ethnic identity project of these indigenous migrants, I might compare it to other mobilizations that have sprung up across the world and been described as the politics of recognition of ethnic difference. However, at least in terms of organizational discourse and action, ethnic reformulation does not appear to rule out an increase of the ethnic group's power via the occupation of posts and decision-making spaces within the framework of the national state. To the question of who represents whom, we can add another: Who decides for whom? Decision making brings us into an eminently political field, being a central matter in the new definition of indigenous migrants confronting, on the one hand, their condition as indigenous Mexicans in the Mexican state and, on the other, their condition as Mexican indigenous migrants in the U.S. state.

The territorial indigenous community in Mexico is defined historically by its relationship with the many governments that have held power since the colonial period. The indigenous policies of these governments, along with Mexican history, created an infantilized subject and led to the indigenous being treated as second-class citizens. It is not surprising that in their struggles indigenous peoples have viewed these successive government administrations—colonial, post-independence, and finally the revolutionary state—as opponents. Is it possible for a relationship established over a period of five centuries to be altered by migration? While this question might well guide future research, it is also one that the intellectuals of the migrant and resident indigenous transnational communities are asking themselves. One leader told me that while he lived in his hometown he had never spoken to the mayor; they did speak when the mayor visited California. Such excursions by governors and mayors in search of funds for the hometowns—appealing to migrants' sense of responsibility to their communities of origin—seem an effort to extend their control. In this new situation of dispersion and community fragmentation, the organizations appear to have become mediators between the municipal and state governments of the places of origin and the immigrant communities on the border. The organizations compete not only for resources but for recognition as intermediaries between governments and migrant communities. Migrant relations with local and regional governments have deepened with economic investments by the migrants via their hometown associations or other organizations. The economic value and social impact of these investment projects has only recently received the attention of scholars of international migration. Organizations use such investments to gain greater leverage in negotiations with local and state governments. This economic capital is transformed into political capital when migrants demand political representation of indigenous migrants in their local and regional governments. Participation in the structures of traditional authority and in municipal governments has not ceased with migration; in fact, it is one of the commitments that has become formalized in the migrant organizations.

Another facet of the political aspect of the ethnic identity project concerns relations with the Mexican state; here, the founding of ethnic and pan-ethnic organizations, and even more importantly, transnational ones, has brought about change. Relations with the Oaxaca state government did not bear fruit until the ethnic committees, interethnic and transnational fronts, associations, or coalitions had been set up.

Now, with decades of experience in labor and residential organizations in this border region, migrant populations have generated interest in the new places of settlement. They have presented an agenda, which includes schooling for children, health services, housing, and immigration reform, to local governments on the Mexican side of the border and to the U.S. government. In the United States, these migrants have become residents who encounter very different political practices from those in the places of origin. As migrants become acclimatized to the new political culture, new leaders are emerging who still regard themselves as indigenous Mexicans.

The political experience that the leaders gained in their indigenous communities is one thing that distinguishes Mixtec organizations most clearly from other Mexican migrant organizations (from Zacatecas or Michoacán, for instance), or from organizations of Mexican Americans and the Chicanos in the United States. During my research, I found that the organizations condense a history of community participation going back to modern Mexican state. For centuries, towns and villages of the Mixteca have maintained an intense community political life. This is particularly true of the places of origin of many of the intellectuals interviewed for this study: municipalities in the district of Juxtlahuaca. Migration to the United States has added to the already rich history of activism of those interviewees in their hometowns; recognizing this is fundamental to understanding the migrants' present political activism.

Still, the experience of migration has had a profound politicizing effect. Joining those nuclei of activists or leaders with political experience from the hometowns are those who emerged during the process of migration or in the places of arrival. Inter-pueblo and interethnic political influence is one of the greatest innovations arising from Oaxacan migration in the border region. This study documents the ethnic alliances between Mixtecos, Zapotecos, and Triquis; the latter group's capacity for politicization is one of the least documented, and, given the history of interfamily and intercommunity violence of its towns and villages of origin, it offers an important vein for research. The Triquis in Baja California and California have not reproduced the patterns of violence from their places of origin. The emergence of community organizations and the struggle for agricultural workers' rights may have contributed to interethnic understanding. Interethnic influence in organizations is currently affecting the reconstruction of ethnic identity. It is worth noting the case of the Zapotec Guelaguetza, a festival that—through the initiative of Mixtec activists who undertook to recover it as their own—is being reproduced in modified form as the Mixtec Guelaguetza. It is one concrete example of ethnic revitalization from the political field of the organizations.

Because of recent tendencies in U.S. migration policy, migrant organizations have been called on to play a still more decisive role. Operation Gatekeeper and the Illegal Immigration Reform and Immigrant Responsibility Act of 1996 reflect the U.S. government's position on migration throughout the 1990s and into the new century. If Operation Gatekeeper did not have the expected effects in diminishing the flow of undocumented migrants at the California border, it did increase the risk of crossing and aggravate the anti-immigrant climate that since the late 1980s has dominated the southwestern border of the United States.

On the other hand, the Illegal Immigration Reform and Immigrant Responsibility Act seems to have had other consequences. While the quality of life of undocumented immigrants and residents declines, the costs of migration tend to rise, both in terms of risk and in economic outlay; hence the increasing importance of institutions like the networks and agents such as the migrant organizations. Until 2000, in view of the difficulty of legalizing residency or border-crossing for purposes of work in the United States, there was an increase in the circularity of migration and reduction in the process of residency. At the same time, U.S. laws may encourage settlement on the Mexican side of the border, pushing to Mexican soil the reproduction costs of indigenous labor. The terrorist attacks of September 11, 2002, and Mexico's diplomatic position on the U.S. invasion of Iraq, chilled the incipient negotiations on a new migration treaty between Mexico and the United States. Border controls under the new U.S. security and anti-terror policies forced many Mexican commuters who lacked legal documents or whose families had mixed documentation to move to U.S. soil permanently. Even legal commuters found it harder to cross because of exhaustive inspections at border checkpoints. This encouraged people to move to the "other side" in order to avoid the long waits at the border.

Mexican–U.S. negotiations on migration topics shrank to discussions of the means for deporting undocumented migrants. The government's direct relationship with Mexican-origin immigrants in the United States has revolved around two central topics: remittances and voting from abroad. The Mexican government has its eye on the short- and medium-term rewards of strengthening connections with migrant populations from Mexico. The vigor of this relationship has frightened analysts like Samuel Huntington (2004), who sees it as one of the most notable differences between Mexican migration and other historical migrations to the United States. The geographic contiguity of Mexico and the United States and the historical continuity of the social ties presage strong conflicts between the countries and a process of social and cultural integration that follows the logic of human relations. In this scenario, migrant organizations seem to have a fertile field on which to propagate their demands and resources, and primarily the conditions for transforming the image of the indigenous subject that gives them their identity.

Some Conceptual and Methodological Remarks

Based on my specific findings, I will offer some general conceptual hypotheses about the makeup of the ethnic agents associated with migration in transnational frameworks.

a. The agent is not created with a single stroke and forever. Instead, it is the temporal expression of a strategically organized action. The identity of that agent as a projection is what lets us trace it, even in a set of sporadic actions and in the very act of thinking about organizing.

b. The migratory experience and strategic actions constantly modify the borders of self-definition in a dual play of hetero-ascription and self-description where the political utility of the discourse of identity remains a central element for realizing objectives.

c. The transnational condition of the agent consists of the strategic capacity to combine multiple issues and resources associated with distinct national territorialities while also achieving a future position in a geography broader than that of the place and nation of origin.

d. The nation-state has a particularly important role in the formation of those agents when their field of action goes beyond the local to a transnational field. Residing in another nation's territory creates a form of resistance to the policies of the nation-state of origin. The traditional logic of negotiation becomes unbalanced. Beyond the national territory, other opportunities are available as resources of negotiation.

e. The transnational ethnic agent can be defined by its capacity to promote collective action in a dual system of national-ethnic relations, to confront multiple political "others," and to redefine the category of "us" as indigenous and the "otherness" that has defined "us" historically—in this case study, the mestizo.

Finally, a conclusion of a methodological nature: In the formation of the agent, successful strategic actions are as important as the reflection on that success. Thus, understanding the meaning of the strategic action not only implies analyzing how to get "others" to change their action in the intended direction but also how that success results in reproducing the identity of the agent in ethnic and class relations. That second aspect of the formation of the agent functions in the symbolic struggle to define power hierarchies and their ideological production. These two analytical levels make it possible to observe the structuring of the transnational social field in different arenas. At the first level, it is important to observe the practices that maintain migrant networks and settlement at the migratory destinations as part of the structural foundations that enable an agent to emerge under migratory conditions. In the second, narrative reconstructions of migration and the organization let us know what the migrants think about the meaning of their actions and elucidate the powers that, from their perspective, organize social relations. This reconstruction is a politicized version of the migration, as it is also a history of indigenous migration to the Mexico–U.S. border. In that sense, to tell the story itself is part of the struggle for recognition and part of the formation of ethnic agents.

Notes

Introduction

1. I use the term *political* to refer to an issue that leads to a change in the relationship between the individual and state institutions.

2. The subject of ethnicity has its counterpart in race, which focused on the "color problem."

3. Bourdieu's (1990, 53) concept of habitus is another approach to the duality of structure. See also Sztompka's (1994) introduction to the many concepts that have emerged for dealing with the duality of agency and structure.

4. Farfán (1999, 37) identifies Ulrich Beck, Niklas Luhmann, and Anthony Giddens with the reflexive sociology approach.

5. Constructivist contributions to ethnicity include Barth 1994; Cohen 1969; Vermeulen and Govers 1994a; Govers and Vermeulen 1997; Bartolomé 1997; and Stavenhagen 1996.

6. According to Giddens (1995), agency is the transforming social action through which the actors reach their interests; it is the joining of action and power.

7. Some other sources complemented my research: *Diagnóstico de las condiciones de vida y trabajo de los jornaleros agrícolas del Valle de San Quintin, BC* (PRONASOL 1991); "Encuesta a migrantes mixtecos en Tijuana y el Valle de San Quintin" (COLEF 1991); "Encuesta representativa a hogares mixtecos sobre estrategias de sobrevivencia y migración femenina" (COLEF 1989); and "Survey of Oaxacan Village Networks in California Agriculture" (Runsten and Kearney 1994). For a detailed description of the methodology of the study, see Velasco 1999. Many findings were updated during a 2001–2 period of fieldwork in San Miguel Tlacotepec, Oaxaca, in the San Quintin Valley, and in Lamont, California, and with the "Encuesta sociodemográfica y de migración en la region de San Quintin, BC, 2003" and "Encuesta a jornaleros agrícolas migrates, 2003" (CONEPO and COLEF 2003, 2004).

Chapter 1. Migrant Organizations

1. I have in mind Besserer 1996; Glick-Schiller, Basch, and Blanc-Szanton 1992a; Glick-Schiller, Basch, and Blanc-Szanton 1992b; Goldring 1992; Kearney 1996; Massey et al. 1987; Rivera-Salgado 1999; Roosens 1994; Rouse 1989; and Smith 1995.

2. This literature includes Besserer 1996; Glick-Schiller, Basch, and Blanc-Szanton 1992a; Goldring 1992; Kearney 1995, 1996; Massey et al. 1987; Pries 1998; Rouse 1989; Smith 1995; and Smith and Guarnizo 1998.

3. I refer to literature produced in U.S. universities. British scholars, who study the formation of transnational communities in the political, industrial, state, and consumption spheres, seem to have a broader perspective on the concept. (See the Program of Studies of Transnational Communities of the University of Oxford, founded in 1994, and Vertovec 1999.)

4. Giddens (1995, 51–55) distinguishes between resources of authority and allocative

resources. The first involves control over persons, the second control over objects and material phenomena. A clearer distinction, it seems to me, is that of Sewell (1992, 9), who distinguishes between human and nonhuman resources.

5. This position comes closer to that of Norbert Elias (1982) than that of Foucault (1992). While both understand power as a relationship, for Elías the framework of options is always more ample; thus he is able to speak of a "changing power equilibrium."

6. In the present work, agency is to be understood as transforming or reflexive social action.

7. In Mexico, indigenous thought can be traced to the sixteenth century. Through the centuries, it became institutionalized in modern state policies concerning indigenous peoples. The concept of ethnicity was nurtured by this indigenist tradition, as well as by several European and American approaches. In the United States only migrants have ethnicity, whereas in Mexico only indigenous peoples were considered ethnic groups or had ethnic identity. In Mexico, theories of "the ethnic groups" or ethnicity were based on the study of indigenous populations.

8. The Norwegian Fredrick Barth (1969) broke with the dominant "primordialist" or "culturalist" approach, which defined ethnicity, or ethnic groups, on the basis of a set of cultural attributes, such as language, customs, dress, food or culinary traditions, religious practices, and so on (Epstein 1978; Isaacs 1975), that support a primordial feeling of belonging to a collectivity (Geertz 1963; Shils 1957). From this perspective a primordial form of ethnicity persists through generations in a variety of social forms (Bromley 1974). In Barth's view (1969) ethnicity was a way of organizing cultural differences, starting from the assumption that such differences are constructed in accordance with a particular situation and with the meaning they endow.

9. The instrumentalist approach of Abner Cohen (1969) postulates that ethnicity should be regarded as an economic and political affair and not simply as a form of mutual aid among migrants in their struggle for survival in a complex urban society. From this perspective, retribalization (or ethnic reconstitution) is a process by which one ethnic group manipulates certain customs, values, myths, symbols, and ceremonies with the aim of articulating an informal political organization. Cohen's instrumentalist approach is behind the proposals of Glazer and Moynihan (1975) or Sollors (1989) to observe international migration and study the role of elites or ethnic leaders in the construction of nationalism.

10. An important antecedent to the studies of migrant associations is one that focuses on Mexican urban-rural migration—Hirabayashi's 1993 *Cultural Capital: Mountain Zapotec Migrant Associations in Mexico City.*

11. In the present work, the term "migrant organizations" is preferred over "migrant associations," because of its greater inclusiveness. The word *association* embraces hometowns and other forms of unity based on a common identity linked to place of origin; whereas *organization* refers more widely to labor, residential, and cultural organizations as well as hometown associations.

12. As Giddens states (1995), while it is true that every social action has a historical dimension, this does not always come about intentionally, since, in general, society is the unplanned result of social action.

13. The term *reticulum,* used by Michael Kearney (1996, 126) to study identities, is a metaphor of the biological concept: "one of the branched anastomosing reticuloendo-

thelial cells that form an intricate interstitial network ramifying through other tissues and organs."

14. Bartolomé (1997, 169) distinguishes between the traditional leaders and the cultural brokers in the Oaxacan context. In his view the former do not have the power (or authority) to represent the community. They have the capacity to talk like oracles; therefore, they have the power of the word.

15. Bonfil (1995b, 122–124) recognizes diverse leaderships in the indigenous community: traditional, local, and militant intellectuals. The last category arose during the migration process to the cities and immersion in the non-Indian world.

16. The role that indigenous intellectuals play in the national project seems to be a new area of research (Bonfil 1995b; Gutiérrez 1999; Mallon 1995; Warman and Argueta 1993). The concept of the organic intellectual supposes that the representative is the bearer of a historical vision in conflict with the hegemonic order (Gramsci 1998).

17. See Weiss (1992) for a comprehensive revision of the representation concept.

Chapter 2. Mixtec Migration and National Frontiers

1. I support Alcalá and Reyes's division (1994, 10).

2. Lineage was grounded in family ties, since alliances between kingdoms or people were also cemented by kinship connections or marital alliances (Romero-Frizzi 1988).

3. According to Castro (1993, 125–126), cited by Florescano (1998, 233), "in Spain and its colonies, society, law, and the state did not recognize individuals as such, but rather as members of a class or stratum, a group or a corporation."

4. In the early eighteenth century, patron saints were the legal owners of the livestock of almost all indigenous people. The transference from civil corporations to religious ones seems to have occurred in response to functional substitution in the indigenous economy. According to Pastor (1987, 247), this was a way of evading payment of taxes to Spanish officials, who continually abused the communities.

5. The incorporation of a saint appears to have been a way for indigenous people to restructure their collective production support through a mutual aid institution endorsed by the church (Dahlgren 1990, 211; Pastor 1987, 32–33).

6. The process of privatization is one important difference that, according to Pastor (1987, 262), distinguishes the Mixteca from the Zapoteca region in cultural terms. According to Romero-Frizzi (1990, 324–327), the process was more a de facto transformation than one owing to a change in the legal regime. Frizzi points out that during the seventeenth century haciendas emerged as a more complex property than estancias. They were called *haciendas volantes* in the Mixteca region and were run by nomadic ranchers who rented land from indigenous people. In the transition from the sixteenth to seventeenth century, the ownership of land was the principal reason for conflict between indigenous groups and both caciques and Spaniards (Romero-Frizzi 1988, 154–174).

7. The importance of land and territory to indigenous identity is related to the worldview of the ancient indigenous peoples (Carmagnani 1993, 43–50; Pastor 1987, 122, 147).

8. As mentioned in note 6, the hacienda institution did not dominate Oaxaca, with the exception of Valles Centrales. Nevertheless, a hacienda volante was a particular institution that flourished in the Mixteca region in the eighteenth century. It involved raising

young cattle on land that was rented or purchased, sometimes in illegal transactions (Reina 1988, 194–195; Romero-Frizzi 1988, 160–161).

9. Compared with 30 percent in the Isthmus or 18 percent in the Sierra Norte (Piñón 1988, 314).

10. Until 1994, 20 hectares was the amount of land going to each beneficiary in ejidos. Ejidos combine communal ownership with individual use.

11. During the 1960s, the Mixteca region had the highest migration factor in the country, which was reflected in a population increase of only 8.6 percent, in comparison with 36 percent for the country (Sanders 1975).

12. These case studies of an anthropological and sociological nature were conducted in Oaxacan villages such as San Juan Mixtepec (Besserer 1988; Guidi 1988) and San Martín Peras, in the district of Juxtlahuaca (A. Flores 2000), in San Jerónimo del Progreso, and in the district of Silacayoapan (Kearney and Stuart 1981). There are several studies of Oaxacan immigrants on the northwestern border, such as Tijuana (Clark 1991; Velasco 1991, 1995a,b), and the San Quintin Valley in Baja California (Garduño, García, and Morán 1989; Velasco 1992; Zabin 1992). On the U.S. side, scholars have focused on Oaxacan immigrants in the agricultural sector of California and Oregon (Besserer 1997; Corbett 1992; Kearney 1988, 1994; Krissman 1994a,b; Rivera-Salgado 1999; Stephen 1999; Zabin 1993).

13. The name "braceros" was used colloquially for migrants who worked under the Labor Importation Program of 1942–64 (the so-called Bracero Program). However, this was in fact the second Bracero Program. In 1917 the United States had signed an agreement with Mexico to recruit a labor force to work during World War I (Durand 1994, 87–94).

14. During the 1990s there was increased deportation of Oaxacan migrants in the San Diego–Tijuana area. In 1991 6.2 percent of the deported population was from Oaxaca, and in 1999 10 percent of the deported population in the San Diego–Tijuana area was from Oaxaca (COLEF and COESPO 1995; STPS et al. 2001).

15. A colonia popular is usually created without official approval as subdivisions of house lots obtained through squatter invasions and is generally developed at the cost and initiative of those taking up residence.

16. According to Ofelia Santos and other informants, in 1986 several labor brokers arrived in Tijuana offering papers to those willing to work in the California fields.

17. According to Alegría (1990, 15), in 1990 transmigration along the border was 8 percent, contributing between 14 and 20 percent of the wage income to the largest frontier cities.

18. According to Krissman (1994a, 132), in the 1960s, wages in agriculture fell 10 percent in California, while inflation grew by 4 percent. According to Stephen (2002, 108), the hourly wages of farmworkers fell from $6.89 in 1989 to $6.18 in 1998.

19. A traila is a mobile home on a wooden foundation.

20. Ruiz (2002, 11) reports that, under the Bracero Program, Mexico and the United States signed an agreement to deduct 10 percent of the workers' salaries, which was to be deposited in the Fondo de Ahorro Campesino. Between 1999 and 2002, the Oaxacan state government's migrant service office received a total of 839 complaints regarding the deducted savings of bracero workers.

21. On "Operation Gatekeeper," see the INS 1998 report (INS 2004).

Chapter 3. Crossing the Border

1. The chronology was established by studying the constitutive documents of the organizations, along with minutes of meetings and assemblies, and reviewing twenty-four life stories of leaders and representatives of migrant organizations. During 2000–2001, I carried out seven more interviews with activists or grassroots leaders in California and San Miguel Tlacotepec, Juxtlahuaca, Oaxaca. I took those into account when I updated this study.

2. According to Miguel Bartolomé (1997, 46–47), "most areas of Mexico [marked by] interethnic relations still retain the barbarous colonial epithets designating the Indians as 'people of custom,' as opposed to 'people of reason,' i.e., Whites and Mestizos."

3. This credit relationship was established in the seventeenth century between Mixtecos and Spaniards or Creoles, and it continues today (Burgos 1998, 22; Martínez and Luna 1960, 275, cited in Diskin 1990; Romero-Frizzi 1990, 444).

4. Lomnitz-Adler (1995, 42) presents findings about the power of the secretary in the municipal councils in the state of Morelos; their power is a reward for literacy and mastery of written Spanish.

5. Since 1995, the "customs and uses" system has been a legal method of electing municipal authorities in the state of Oaxaca.

6. In 1981, Veracruz was still the third most important destination for migration from the Oaxacan Mixteca, after Mexico City and Oaxaca (Velasco 1986, 110).

7. *La migra* refers to agents of the border patrol of the U.S. Immigration and Naturalization Service (INS).

8. For an account of the historical context, see Meyer (1994, 170).

9. In the case of Chiapas, Yvon Le Bot (1997, 84) defines the male gerontocracy as a vertically hierarchical system of elderly men with authority.

10. The date was confirmed by Velasco 1995a, Besserer 1988, and M. Sánchez 1995.

11. Those interviewed frequently mentioned that they lacked documents to prove their Mexican citizenship.

12. According to Jorge Bustamante (1994, 258), the greatest risk reported by migrants crossing the border was extortion by the police. He also identified Oaxaqueños as the group most subjected to extortion.

13. Coyotes are people who smuggle undocumented migrants across the border.

14. Vans customized to sell prepared foods.

15. In the eighteenth century, the cajas populares were expropriated by the Spanish government, along with the cofradías (Florescano 1998, 314).

16. A member of the Vamos por la Tierra movement. Interviewed in Tijuana, 1996.

17. A leader of the Vamos por la Tierra movement. Interviewed in Tijuana, 1996.

18. The Asociación Cívica Benito Juárez was formed in 1986 in Fresno and Madera, California, to defend human rights and labor and cultural rights.

19. The Organización Regional Oaxaqueña was founded in 1988 in connection with the Guelaguetza Festival in Los Angeles.

20. Rufino Domínguez is founder of the Organización del Pueblo Explotado y Oprimido (OPEO) and the Comité Cívico Popular Mixteco (CCPM). At the time of the

interview (San Joaquin Valley, 1996), he was vice-general coordinator of the Frente Indígena Oaxaqueño Binacional (FIOB); since December 2001, he has been general coordinator.

21. In that decade it was possible to speak of a national indigenous movement in Mexico. Until the 1970s, there was no organization at the national level that acknowledged an indigenous movement comparable to the urban and peasants' movement (Castellanos 1991; Warman and Argueta 1993, 8–9).

22. "Declaración de la Selva Lacandona" (EZLN 1994, 33–35).

23. There were several meetings between scholars, human rights activists, and leaders of grassroots Oaxacan organizations. Two examples are "A Dialogue among Mixtec Leaders, Researchers, and Farm Labor Advocates," conducted on February 15, 1990, by Carol Zabin (Zabin 1992), and "Indigenous Mexican Migrants in the U.S.: Building Bridges between Researchers and Community Leaders" on October 11–12, 2003, organized by Jonathan Fox and Gaspar Rivera in Santa Cruz, California.

24. The FIOB's report and evaluation of activities for the September 1994–March 1996 period (FIOB 1996).

25. Regional delegate of the FIOB, interviewed in Tijuana, 1997.

26. In March 1998, I visited San Miguel Tlacotepec and observed the activities of the Nopal Forrajero Community Committee, which was made up primarily of women. In March 2001, I paid another visit and observed a fall-off in participation on the project committee. Some of the women explained that this was because of their inability to sell the crop, which meant that there was no financial return to the participants.

27. Two cases will serve to illustrate the type of problems that the FIOB dealt with. One was the case of Santiago Ventura, a nineteen-year-old Mixteco who spent three years in prison, accused of a murder he did not commit. He was freed after a defense in which the interpreters network took part in 1997. The other, summarized by the lawyer Claudia Smith, concerned an indigenous Mexican who spent two years in a psychiatric hospital in Oregon after having been diagnosed as a paranoid schizophrenic by authorities who were unable to communicate with him in English or in Spanish (Linares 1997, 8).

28. See the list of interpreters working with the FIOB at http://www.laneta.apc.org/fiob/ours.html.

29. According to Rufino Domínguez (2004, 75), between 1998 and 2001 the Front received approximately $184,700. Most of the money came from the McArthur Foundation. Within Mexico, money came from the Instituto Nacional Indigenista and from the Oaxaca House of Representatives.

30. The actual coordinator of the FIOB criticized the Oaxacan government and Mexican federal institutions, such as the INI, for giving financial and political support to the former coordinator when the corruption problem was a public issue (Domínguez 2004, 74–75).

31. In 2004, the FNIC mobilized a group of people, demanding regularization of colonias in San Quintin Valley and asking for the dismissal of the delegate of the National Commission for Indigenous People's Development (earlier the National Indigenist Institute) in Baja California.

32. For a more detailed description of the FOCOICA, see Rivera-Salgado and Escala (2004).

Chapter 4. Networks and Migrant Organizations

1. The reference is to ravines in the Del Mar area of San Diego County, California.

2. Fawcett (1989) recognizes as "agents" only those actors who possess a certain degree of institutionalization in the framework of production and migratory policy. For me, this outlook unnecessarily excludes other agents who emerge from within the migrant populations and whose resources and interests differ from those considered by Fawcett.

3. In Mixteca in the mid-1980s the economic product of migration was equivalent to the value of agricultural and livestock production (Gobierno del Estado de Oaxaca, Programa de Desarrollo Rural Integral de las Mixtecas de Oaxaca 1984–88).

4. According to the survey carried out in Tijuana and the San Quintin Valley (COLEF 1991), this migrant population has, on average, 4.2 years of education. In 1995, the average number of years of education in the state of Oaxaca was three, compared to a national average of seven (INEGI 2000).

5. The prevalence of written communication was confirmed by Arturo Neri, director of the bilingual radio station La Voz del Valle, in the San Quintin Valley: "I don't know how to describe it, but . . . after calling on the workers in the fields to send in letters . . . the letters started to arrive at an extraordinary rate; we don't have the precise figures, but in one month they reached over 20,000. Of course, the letters have to be 'translated' because they are very badly written, or they get someone to write for them; they also include with them a lot of drawings" (Arturo Neri 1996).

6. The same function is served by the sending of videos from the Ticuanan community in New York to Ticuani in the state of Puebla (R. Smith 1995).

7. The distinction between strong and weak links in migrant networks derives from Wilson (1998).

8. Melucci (1991) states that a configuration of social networks must exist prior to a social movement.

9. In 1999, a department within an agency in the state of Oaxaca was assigned to oversee links with migrant organizations (A. Ruíz 2002).

Chapter 5. Indigenous Intellectuals

1. According to Arditi (1995, 337), conflict is a constitutive element in politics, and political relations are relations of strength and power organized around the friend-enemy dichotomy.

2. It may be that the men interviewed were unwilling to speak frankly on this subject with a woman.

3. In 2000, the average number of years of education in the indigenous population was four compared with a national average of seven (INEGI 2000).

4. Benito García is a pioneer in the farm union struggles of northwestern Mexico; as a Mixtec leader his style of intermediation with governments and growers has been controversial among other leaders and activists of the migrant communities.

5. Savater (1998, 30) has stated that ethics seeks to improve persons, while politics seeks to improve institutions.

6. "Zapatist movement" refers to the uprising of indigenous people in Chiapas—the EZLN insurrection of January 1994.

7. Méndez is referring to organizations in northern San Diego County, specifically the COCIO, which has promoted a strong cultural program.

8. Cadena (1997, 8–9) analyzes how education was an important element to distinguish "whites," "mestizos," and "indios." In Peru, education became a sign of decency, and it was naturalized as part of race—educated people were decent people. Education was a way to become mestizo or white people.

9. *Patria chica* refers to a feeling of belonging to a small locality.

Chapter 6. Public Voices, Private Silences

1. This chapter is modified from the article "Migración, género y etnicidad: Mujeres indígenas en la frontera de California y Baja California" (Velasco 2000).

2. One of the main applications of the public-private metaphor is in the study of women's roles in domestic space (Douglas 1991).

3. As Gupta and Ferguson (1992, 6) have noted, within social theory in the last two decades there has been a growing interest in theorizing space. David Harvey (1989) offers one illustration of the way space is holistically conceived. According to his definition, space is always being produced, appropriated, and controlled by social actors' practice, perception, or imagination. Thus each social actor, through specific social action, establishes the limits and borders of social spaces and moves between those spaces.

4. As Price-Chalita (1994) indicates, feminist writings of the sixties used spatial metaphors to convey the loss or absence of women in certain spaces, emphasizing subordination. New approaches present routes that empower women to speak of the appropriation of spaces or even the revalorizing of spaces that had previously been represented as having negative effects on women (such as domestic space). Thus, the spatial metaphor has been useful in analyzing how the public-private dichotomy affects subordination, as well as for moving beyond that analytic dichotomy in studying how women gain power.

5. Divisions and dichotomies are transcended in women's daily lives. According to Vaiou (1992, 255), in everyday life in large cities neither women nor men identify exclusively with just one part of such a dichotomy.

6. Ruth Lister (1993) documents this paradox in the case of England.

7. In 1981, 38 percent of the migrants leaving the Mixteca region were women; they left mainly for Mexico City to work in domestic service (Velasco 1995a).

8. The feminine nature of the family home is a recurrent theme in the narrations of migrant men.

9. An exception in this regard among those interviewed is Ofelia Santos (in Velasco 1996 she appears under the pseudonym "Felipa Reyes").

10. As table 6.1 indicates, different sources show the presence of women on both sides of the border. The proportion of women is higher in the urban colonias on the Mexican side than in the labor camps and rural areas of California. Surveys carried out in 2002 and 2003 showed similar findings for the San Quintin Valley (53.5 percent males and 46.5 percent females in the camps, and 50.1 percent males and 49.9 percent females in the colonias (CONEPO and COLEF 2003, 2004).

11. In Spanish, the same word (*permiso*) refers both to permission in the general sense

and to permits issued by an official authority; this gives the word a curious ambiguity in this context.

12. Words spoken by a Mixtec woman from Maneadero, Ensenada (transcription of the women's meeting in preparation for the Constitutive Assembly of the FIOB, September 2, 1994).

13. In 2001, the Central Valley meeting was published as a calendar "Immigrant Women Weaving Cultures," with twelve life stories of Mixtec and Hmong women. The Hmong are an ethnic group in China; "Hmong" means "lived above the clouds, who were the first to see the sun rise and the last to watch the sun set." During the early nineteenth century, a small group fled to the countries of Southeast Asia (Vietnam, Laos, and Thailand). Beginning in the 1960s, Hmong from different countries began to arrive in the United States (Martínez 2001).

Bibliography

Primary Sources

Domínguez Santos, Rufino. 1996. Coordinator of FIOB. Interview by author, San Joaquin Valley, CA.

Flores, Everardo [pseudonym]. 1996. Interview by author, Tijuana, BC.

Hernández, Florencio. 2001. President of the Colonia 13 de Mayo in San Quintin Valley. Interview by author, San Quintin Valley, BC.

Hernández, Rafaela [pseudonym]. 1994. Activist for a street vendors' organization. Interview by author, Tijuana, BC.

Iñiguez, Jesús [pseudonym]. 1996. Interview by author, Santa Cruz, California.

Lita, Juan. 1996. Activist for Vamos por la Tierra. Interview by author, Tijuana, BC.

López, Antonio. 1996. OPT activist. Interview by author, San Quintin Valley, BC.

Méndez, Rogelio. 1996. Activist for Vamos por la Tierra. Interview by author, Tijuana, BC.

Méndez, Sergio. 1996. FIOB delegate. Interview by author, Tijuana, BC.

Montiel Aguirre, Gonzalo. 1996. Principal of Valle Verde primary school, Secretaría de Educación de Baja California, and activist for COCOPLA. Interview by author, Tijuana, BC.

Morales, Algimiro. 1996. Member of COCIO. Interview by author, Vista, CA.

Neri, Arturo. 1996. Director of La Voz del Valle, bilingual radio station run by the INI in San Quintin Valley. Interview by author, San Quintin Valley, BC.

Pérez, Tiburcio. 1996. Supervisor in the Dirección General de Educación Indígena, Secretaría de Educación de Baja California. Interview by author, Tijuana, BC.

Pimentel, Arturo. 1994, 1995. Former coordinator of FIOB. Interviews by author, Tijuana, BC, and Mexico City. Actually, he is an FNIC activist.

Quiroz, Olga. 2001. FIOB delegate. Interview by author, San Miguel Tlacotepec, Oax.

Reyes, Antonio. 2001. Síndico suplente to the municipal presidency of San Miguel Tlacotepec, Oax. Interview by author, San Miguel Tlacotepec, Oax.

Rojas, José. 1996. Member of CIOAC. Interview by author, San Quintin Valley, BC.

Romero, Eloísa [pseudonym]. 1994. Interview by author, San Diego, CA.

Salazar, Maura. 2001. Member of the Programa de la Mujer Indígena, Organización en California de Líderes Campesinas. Interview by author, Lamont, CA.

Sánchez, Juliana [pseudonym]. 1996. Member of the MIULI. Interview by author, Maneadero, BC.

Sánchez Liévano, César. 1994. ORO activist. Interview by author, Tijuana, BC.

Santiago, Bernardino Julián. 1996. FIOB activist. Interview by author, Maneadero, BC.

Santos, Ofelia. 1994, 1996. Member of the Unión de Vendedores Ambulantes y Anexos Carlos Salinas de Gortari (UVAM CS). Interview by author, Tijuana, BC.

Secondary Sources

ACCR (Agricultural Commissioners' Crop Report). 2000–2001. Sacramento: California Agricultural Statistics Service.

Aguirre Beltrán, Gonzalo. 1957a. "Los problemas humanos de las Mixtecas." Foreword to *La ciudad mercado (Tlaxiaco)*, by Alejandro Marroquín. Mexico City: Imprenta Universitaria.

———. 1957b. *El proceso de aculturación.* Mexico City: UNAM.

Alarcón, Rafael. 2000. "The development of home town associations in the United States and the use of social remittance in Mexico. Final version." Department of Social Studies, COLEF, Tijuana, BC. Computer printout.

Alberoni, Francesco. 1984. *Movimiento e institución (teoría general).* Madrid: Editorial Nacional.

Alcalá, Elio, and Teófilo Reyes. 1994. *Migrantes mixtecos: El proceso migratorio de la Mixteca Baja.* Mexico City: INAH.

Alegría, Tito. 1990. "Ciudad y transmigración en la frontera de México con Estados Unidos." *Frontera Norte* 2, no. 4 (July–December): 50–93.

Anderson, Benedict. 1993. *Comunidades imaginadas: Reflexiones sobre el origen y la difusión del nacionalismo.* Mexico City: FCE.

Arditi, Benjamín. 1995. "Rastreando lo político." *Revista de Estudios Políticos* 87 (January–March): 333–351.

Arizpe, Lourdes. 1975. *Indígenas en la ciudad de México: El caso de las "Marías."* Mexico City: Secretaría de Educación Pública, SepSetentas.

Baca, Reynaldo, and Dexter Bryan. 1981. "Mexican undocumented workers in the binational community: A research note." *International Migration Review*, 15, no. 4:737–748.

Bachelard, Gaston. 1986. *La intuición del instante.* Mexico City: FCE.

Banks, Marcus. 1996. *Ethnicity: Anthropological constructions.* London: Routledge.

Barbieri, Teresita de. 1991. "Los ámbitos de acción de las mujeres." *Revista Mexicana de Sociología* 1 (January–March): 203–224.

Barrón, Ma. Antonieta. 1997. *Empleo en la agricultura de exportación en Mexico.* Mexico City: Facultad de Economía–UNAM/Juan Pablos.

Barth, Fredrik, ed. 1969. Intro. to *Ethnic groups and boundaries: The social organization of cultural difference.* London: George Allen & Unwin.

———. 1994. "Enduring and emerging issues in the analysis of ethnicity." In Vermeulen and Govers, *The anthropology of ethnicity.*

Bartolomé, Miguel Alberto. 1997. *Gente de costumbre y gente de razón: Las identidades étnicas en Mexico.* Mexico City: Siglo XXI, INI.

Bartolomé, Miguel, and Alicia Barabas. 1996. "La pluralidad desigual en Oaxaca." In *Etnicidad y pluralismo cultural: La dinámica étnica en Oaxaca*, ed. Alicia Barabas and Miguel Bartolomé. Mexico City: CONACULTA.

Basauri, Carlos. 1990. *La población indígena de Mexico.* Vol. 1. Mexico City: INI, CONACULTA.

Bauman, Zygmunt. 1999. *La globalización: Consecuencias humanas.* Buenos Aires: Fondo de Cultura Economica de Argentina.

Baumann, Gerd, and Thijl Sunier. 1995. Intro. to *Postmigration ethnicity: De-essentializing cohesion, commitments and comparison*, ed. Gerd Baumann and Thijl Sunier. Amsterdam: Het Spinhuis.

Bean, Frank, Barry Edmonston, and Jeffrey S. Passel, eds. 1990. *Undocumented migration to the United States: IRCA and the experience of the 1980s.* Santa Monica, CA: RAND Corporation; Washington, DC: Urban Institute Press.

Besserer, Federico. 1988. "NNA CHCA NDAVI: Internacionalización de la fuerza de trabajo y conciencia de clase en la comunidad mixteca migrante de San Juan Mixtepec. Análisis de la historia de vida de Moisés Cruz." Master's thesis, UAM–Iztapalapa.

———. 1996. "Un viaje por las aproximaciones teóricas a las comunidades transnacionales y cuatro tarjetas postales de la Comunidad de San Juan Mixtepec." Zamora, Mich., June 6.

———. 1997. "La transnacionalización de los oaxacalifornianos: La comunidad transnacional y multicéntrica de San Juan Mixtepec." Paper presented at the 19th Coloquio de Antropología e Historia Regionales, Zamora, Mich., October 22–24.

Bondi, Liz. 1993. "Gender and geography: Crossing boundaries." *Progress in Human Geography* 17, no. 2:241–246.

Bonfil, Guillermo, comp. 1981. *Utopía y revolución: El pensamiento político contemporáneo de los indios en América Latina.* Mexico City: Editorial Nueva Imagen.

———. 1995a. "La dirigencia de los movimientos indios frente al racismo." In *Obras escogidas de Guillermo Bonfil,* vol. 4. Mexico City: INI, INAH, CONACULTA, Fideicomiso Fondo Nacional de Fomento Ejidal–SRA, CIESAS.

———. 1995b. "El pensamiento político indio: Proyecto de civilización y demandas inmediatas." In *Obras escogidas de Guillermo Bonfil,* vol. 3. Mexico City: INI, INAH, CONACULTA, Fideicomiso Fondo Nacional de Fomento Ejidal–SRA, CIESAS.

Boruchoff, Judith. 1997. "Equipaje cultural: Objetos, identidad y transnacionalismo en Guerrero y Chicago." Paper presented at the 19th Coloquio de Antropología e Historia Regionales, Zamora, Mich., October 22–24.

Bourdieu, Pierre. 1982. *Ce que parler veut dire.* París: Libraire Artheme Fayard.

———. 1989. "Una antinomia en la noción de protesta colectiva." In Foxley et al., *Democracia, desarrollo y el arte de traspasar fronteras.* Mexico City: FCE.

———. 1990. *The Logic of practice.* Cambridge: Polity Press.

Bourdieu, Pierre, and Loic J. D. Wacquant. 1995. *Respuestas: Por una antropología reflexiva.* Mexico City: Grijalbo.

Brass, Paul. 1991. *Ethnicity and nationalism: Theory and comparison.* London: Sage.

Bringas, Nora. 1991. "Diagnóstico del sector turístico en Tijuana." *Grupos visitantes y actividades turísticas en Tijuana,* ed. Nora Bringas and Jorge Carrillo. Mexico City: El Colegio de la Frontera Norte.

Bringas Rabágo, Nora, ed. 2004. "Turismo fronterizo: Caracterización y posibilidades de desarrollo." Reporte de Investigación. COLEF-CESTUR-SEXTUR, Tijuana, BC.

Bromley, Yulian. 1974. "The term ethnos and its definition." *Soviet ethnology and anthropology today,* ed. Yulian Bromley. The Hague: Mouton.

Browing, Harley, and René Zenteno. 1993. "The diverse nature of the Mexican northern border: The case of urban employment." *Frontera Norte* 5, no. 9:11–32.

Burgos, Elizabeth. 1998. *Me llamo Rigoberta Menchu y así me nació la conciencia.* Mexico City: Siglo XXI.

Bustamante, Jorge. 1994. "La participación ciudadana en el programa paisano y sus derivados." In *Participación ciudadana y control social,* by María Elena Vázquez Nava et al. Mexico City: Miguel Angel Porrúa Ed.

Butterworth, Douglas. 1975. *Tilantongo: Comunidad mixteca en transición.* Mexico City: Instituto Nacional Indigenista.

Cadena, Marisol de la. 1997. *La decencia y el respeto: Raza y etnicidad entre los intelectuales y las mestizas cuzqueñas.* Documento de trabajo, 86. Serie Antropológica. Lima, Peru: Instituto de Estudios Peruanos, Agosto.

Carmagnani, Marcello. 1993. *El regreso de los dioses: El proceso de reconstitución de la identidad étnica en Oaxaca, siglos XVII y XVIII.* Mexico City: FCE.

Caso, Alfonso. 1948. "Definición del indio y lo indio." *América Indígena* 8, no. 4 (October): 239–247.

CASS (California Agricultural Statistics Service). 2002. *Summary of County Agricultural Commissioners' Reports, 2000–2001.* Sacramento, CA. ftp://www.nass.usda.gov/pub/nass/ca/AgComm/200108cavtb00.pdf (accessed March 3, 2005).

Castellanos, Alicia. 1991. "Para una propuesta de autonomía de las regiones étnicas de Mexico." In *Alteridades: Anuario de Antropología*: 139–156.

Castro Gutiérrez, Felipe. 1993. "Revuelta y rebelión en una sociedad colonial: Los movimientos populares de 1767 en Nueva España." PhD diss., Universidad Nacional Autónoma de México.

Clark, Víctor. 1991. "Los mixtecos en la frontera (Tijuana), sus mujeres y el turismo." *Cuadernos de Ciencias Sociales* 4, no. 10:1–52.

Cohen, Abner. 1969. *Custom and politics in urban Africa: A study of Hausa migrants in Yoruba towns.* London: Routledge and K. Paul.

Cohen, Robin. 1997. *Global diasporas: Introduction.* Seattle: University of Washington Press.

COLEF (El Colegio de la Frontera Norte). 1989. "Encuesta representativa a hogares mixtecos sobre estrategias de sobrevivencia y migración femenina." In Laura Velasco, *Migración femenina y sobrevivencia familiar (Un estudio de caso de las mixtecas en Tijuana).* Research report for Programa Interdisciplinario de Estudios de la Mujer. Tijuana, BC: COLMEX.

——. 1991. "Encuesta a migrantes mixtecos en Tijuana y el Valle de San Quintin." In Laura Velasco, "Identidad y migración: El caso de los mixtecos en la frontera noroeste de México." Master's thesis, UNAM, Mexico City.

COLEF and COESPO (El Colegio de la Frontera Norte and Consejo Estatal de Población de Oaxaca). 1995. *La migración nacional e internacional de los oaxaqueños.* Mexico City: COLEF and COESPO.

Commission on Immigration. 1991. *Studies of the Immigration Control Act's impact on Mexico.* N.p.: Commission on Immigration.

CONAPO (Consejo Nacional de Población). 1990. *Información básica sobre migración por entidad federativa.* Mexico City: CONAPO.

CONEPO (Consejo Estatal de Población en Baja California) and COLEF. 2003. "Encuesta sociodemográfica y de migración en la región de San Quintín, B.C." In *Estudio integral de migración en la región de San Quintin, B.C.*, ed. Rodolfo Cruz et al. Tijuana, BC.

——. 2004. "Encuesta a jornaleros agrícolas migrantes." In *Estudio integral de migración en la región de San Quintin, BC*, ed. Rodolfo Cruz. Tijuana, BC.

Contreras, Enrique, María Elena Sánchez, and Miguel Calderón. 1999. "Cooperación rural, uso de remesas y formación de un capital humano en la migración binacional: Ideas para una política social especializada." In *Coloquio Nacional sobre Políticas Públicas de Atención al Migrante* [memoria]. Ciudad de Oaxaca de Juárez: Gobierno Constitucional del Estado de Oaxaca.

Corbett, Jack. 1992. "El contexto de la migración temporal Oaxaca-Oregon: Elementos del mercado de empleo en el Estado Receptor." In *Migración y etnicidad en Oaxaca*, ed. Jack Corbett et al. Nashville, TN: Vanderbilt University.

Dahlgren, Barbro. 1990. *La mixteca: Su cultura e historia prehispánicas.* Mexico City: Universidad Nacional Autónoma de México.

De la Peña, Guillermo. 1994. "Estructura e historia: La viabilidad de los nuevos sujetos." In *Transformaciones sociales y acciones colectivas: América Latina en el contexto internacional de los noventa.* Mexico City: COLMEX, Centro de Estudios Sociológicos.

Diskin, Martín. 1990. "La economía de la comunidad étnica en Oaxaca." In *Etnicidad y pluralismo cultural: La dinámica étnica en Oaxaca*, ed. Alicia Barabas and Miguel Bartolomé. Mexico City: CONACULTA.

Domínguez Santos, Rufino. 2002. "La experiencia del FIOB, crisis interna y futuros retos." Paper presented at the conference Construyendo puentes entre académicos y activistas, Santa Cruz, CA, October 11–12.

———. 2004. "The FIOB experience: Internal crisis and future challenges." In Fox and Rivera-Salgado, *Indigenous Mexican Migrants in the United States.*

Douglas, Mary. 1991. "The idea of a home: A kind of space." *Social Research* 58, no. 1:287–307.

Durand, Jorge. 1994. *Más allá de la línea: Patrones migratorios entre Mexico y Estados Unidos.* Mexico City: CONACULTA.

———. 1999. "Perfil migratorio actual y problemática familiar." In Ward, *Reducing vulnerability.*

Elias, Norbert. 1982. *Sociología fundamental.* Barcelona: Gedisa.

Epstein, Arnold Leonard. 1978. *Ethos and identity: Three studies in ethnicity.* London: Tavistock.

Escalante, Fernando. 1993. *Ciudadanos imaginarios.* Mexico City: COLMEX.

Esparza, Manuel. 1988. "Los proyectos de los liberales en Oaxaca (1856–1910)." In *Historia de la Cuestión Agraria Mexicana: Estado de Oaxaca, I. Prehipánico–1924*, ed. Leticia Reina. Mexico City: Juan Pablos, Gobierno del Estado de Oaxaca, UABJO, CEHAM.

Espinosa, Víctor M. 1999. *The Federation of Michoacán Clubs in Illinois: The Chicago-Michoacán Project Report.* Chicago: Heartland Alliance for Human Needs & Human Rights and the Chicago Community Trust.

EZLN (Ejército Zapatista de Liberación Nacional). 1994. *Documentos y comunicados.* Vol. 1. Mexico City: Era.

Farfán, Rafael. 1999. "Sociología reflexiona/sociedad reflejada: El diagnóstico de la modernidad en Anthony Giddens." In *Una introducción al pensamiento de Anthony Giddens*, ed. Lidia Girola. Mexico City: UAM–Azcapotzalco.

Fawcett, James. 1989. "Networks, linkages, and migration systems." *International Migration Review* 23, no. 3:671–680.

FIOB (Frente Indígena Oaxaqueño Binacional). 1996. Reporte y Evaluación de Actividades. September 1994–March 1996. Computer printout.

———. 2004. Web home page. http://www.laneta.apc.org/fiob/ours.html (accessed September 25, 2004).

Flores, Atilano, Juan José. 2000. *Entre lo propio y lo ajeno: La identidad étnico local de los jornaleros mixtecos.* Mexico City: INI/PNUD.

Florescano, Enrique. 1998. *Etnia, estado y nación: Ensayo sobre las identidades colectivas en Mexico.* Mexico City: Aguilar, Nuevo Siglo.

——. 1999. *Memoria indígena.* Mexico City: Taurus.

Foucault, Michel. 1992. *Microfísica del poder.* Madrid: La Piqueta.

Fox, Jonathan. 2001. "Evaluación de las coaliciones binacionales de la sociedad civil a partir de la experiencia México-Estados Unidos." *Revista Mexicana de Sociología* 5, no. 63 (July–September): 211–68.

Fox, Jonathan, and Gaspar Rivera-Salgado. 2003. Conference "Indigenous Mexican Migrants in the U.S.: Building Bridges between Researchers and Community Leaders." Santa Cruz, CA, October 11–12. http://lals.ucsc.edu/conference/English/programingles.html (accessed September 25, 2004).

——, eds. 2004. *Indigenous Mexican migrants in the United States.* La Jolla, CA: Center for U.S.-Mexican Studies and Center for Comparative Immigration Studies, UCSD.

Foxley, Alejandro, et al., ed. *Democracia, desarrollo y el arte de traspasar fronteras: Ensayos en homenaje a Albert Hirschamn.* Mexico City: FCE.

Friedland, William, Amy Barton, and Robert Thomas. 1981. *Manufacturing green gold: Capital, labor and technology in the lettuce industry.* Cambridge: Cambridge University Press.

Gamio, Manuel. 1948. *Consideraciones sobre el problema indígena.* Mexico City: III.

——. 1975. "Política en general y política de población." In *Antología,* ed. Juan Comas. Mexico City: UNAM.

Garduño, Everardo, Efrain García, and Patricia Morán. 1989. *Mixtecos en Baja California: El caso de San Quintín.* Mexicali, BC: UABC.

Geertz, Clifford. 1963. "The integrative revolution: Primordial sentiments and civil politics in the new states." In *Old societies and new states,* ed. Clifford Geertz. New York: Free Press.

Gellner, Ernest. 1991. *Naciones y nacionalismo.* Mexico City: Alianza Editorial and CONACULTA.

Georges, Eugenia. 1992. "Gender, class, and migration in Dominican Republic: Women experiences in a transnational community." In Glick-Schiller, Basch, and Blanc-Szanton, *Toward a transnational perspective on migration.*

Giddens, Anthony. 1979. *Central problems in social theory: Action, structure, and contradiction in social analysis.* London: Macmillan.

——. 1995. *La constitución de la sociedad: Bases para la teoría de la estructuración.* Buenos Aires: Amorrortu.

Giménez, Gilberto. 1997. "Materiales para una teoría de las identidades sociales." *Frontera Norte* 9, no. 18:9–28.

Glazer, Nathan, and Daniel Patrick Moynihan. 1963. *Beyond the melting pot: The Negroes, Puerto Ricans, Jews, Italians, and Irish of New York City.* Cambridge: MIT Press.

——. 1975. *Ethnicity: Theory and experience.* Cambridge: Harvard University Press.

Glick-Schiller, Nina, Linda Basch, and Cristina Blanc-Szanton. 1992a. "Towards a definition of transnationalism: Introductory remarks and research questions." In Glick Schiller, Basch, and Blanc-Szanton, *Toward a transnational perspective on migration.*

Glick-Schiller, Nina, Linda Basch, and Cristina Blanc-Szanton, eds. 1992b. *Toward a transnational perspective on migration: Race, class, ethnicity and nationalism reconsidered.* New York: New York Academy of Sciences.

Gobierno del Estado de Oaxaca. 1984–88. "Programa de desarrollo rural integral de las Mixtecas de Oaxaca, Mexico." Oaxaca, Mexico.

Goldring, Luin. 1992. "La migración Mexico–Estados Unidos y la transnacionalización del espacio político y social: Perspectivas desde el Mexico rural." *Estudios Sociológicos* 10, no. 29:315–340.

———. 1997. "El estado mexicano y las organizaciones transmigrantes: ¿Reconfigurando la nación, ciudadanía y relaciones entre estado y sociedad civil?" Paper presented at the 19th Coloquio de Antropología e Historia Regionales, Zamora, Mich., October 22–24.

González, Soledad, et al., eds. *Mujeres, migración y maquila en la frontera norte.* Mexico City: COLEF and COLMEX.

Goss, Jon, and Bruce Lindquist. 1995. "Conceptualizing international labor migration: A structuration perspective." *International Migration Review* 39, no. 2:317–351.

Govers, Cora, and Hans Vermeulen, eds. 1997. *The politics of ethnic consciousness.* Houndmills, Basingstoke, Hampshire: Macmillan Press.

Gramsci, Antonio. 1998. "The intellectuals." In *Selections from the Prison Notebooks*, by Gramsci, 3–14. London: Lawrence and Wishart.

Grieco, Elizabeth, and Monica Boyd. 1998. *Women and migration: Incorporating gender into international migration theory.* Center for the Study of Population, Florida State University. Computer printout.

Guidi, Martha. 1988. "Estigma o prestigio: La tradición de migrar en San Juan Mixtepec." Master's thesis, Escuela Nacional de Antropología e Historia, Mexico.

Gupta, Akhil, and Ferguson, James. 1992. "Beyond culture: Space, identity, and the politics of difference." *Cultural Anthropology* 7, no. 1 (February): 6–23.

Gurak, Douglas, and Fe Caces. 1992. "Migration networks and the shaping of migration system." In *International migration system: A global approach*, ed. Mary M. Kritz, Lin Lean Lim, and Hania Zlotnik. Oxford: Claredon Press.

Gutiérrez, Natividad. 1999. "Theories of nationalism revisited." In *Nationalist myths and ethnic identities: Indigenous intellectuals and the Mexican state*, by Gutiérrez. Lincoln: University of Nebraska Press.

Gutmann, Matthew C. 1996. *The meanings of macho: Being a man in Mexico City.* Berkley and Los Angeles: University of California Press.

Hardy-Fanta, Carol. 1993. *Latina politics, Latino politics: Gender, cultures, and political participation in Boston.* Philadelphia: Temple University Press.

Harvey, David. 1989. *The condition of postmodernity: An inquiry into the origins of cultural change.* Oxford: Blackwell.

Hassig, Ross. 1994. *Mexico and the Spanish Conquest.* London: Longman.

Heller, Agnes. 1998. "Self representation and the representation of the other." In *Blurred boundaries: Migration, ethnicity, citizenship*, ed. Rainer Bauböck and John Rundell. Aldershot, Hampshire, UK: Ashgate.

Hirabayashi, Lane Ryo. 1985. "Formación de asociaciones de pueblos de migrantes a Mexico: Mixtecos y zapotecos." *América Indígena* 14, no. 3:579–598.

———. 1993. *Cultural capital: Mountain Zapotec migrant associations in Mexico City.* Tucson: University of Arizona Press.

Hobsbawm, Eric, and Terence Ranger. 1983. *The invention of tradition.* New York: Cambridge University Press.

Hondagneu-Sotelo, Pierrette. 1994. *Gendered transitions: Mexican experience of immigration.* Berkeley and Los Angeles: University of California Press.

Hugo, Graeme. 1981. "Village-community ties, village norms, and ethnic and social networks: A review of evidence from the Third World." In *Migration decision making: Multidisciplinary approaches to microlevel studies in developed and developing countries,* ed. Gordon F. De Jong and Robert W. Gardner. New York: Pergamon Press.

Huntington, Samuel. 2004. "The Hispanic challenge." *Foreign Policy,* March–April 2004. http://www.foreignpolicy.com/story/cms.php?story_id=2495 (accessed July 30, 2004).

INEGI (Instituto Nacional de Estadística, Geografía e Informática). 2000. *Censo general de población y vivienda.* Mexico City: INEGI.

INI (Instituto Nacional Indigenista). 1989. *Módulo operativo del Instituto Nacional Indigenista.* Valle de San Quintín, BC: INI.

——. 1993. *Migración indígena y economía informal: Comercio ambulante en Baja California, Mexico.* Mexico City: Subdirección de Investigación, Delegación Estatal de Baja California.

INI-IBAI (Investigación Básica para la Acción Indígena). 1990. *Cuadernos de Demografía Indígena: Baja California, Sonora, Chihuahua, Coahuila, Nuevo León y Tamaulipas.* Mexico City: INI-IBAI.

INS (Immigration and Naturalization Service). 2004. "Operation Gatekeeper," 1998 report. http://www.ins.usdoj.gov/graphics/publicaffair/opgatefs.ht.1998 (accessed September 25, 2004).

Isaacs, Harold. 1975. *Idols of the tribe.* New York: Harper & Row.

Jenkins, Shirley. 1988. *Ethnic associations and the welfare state.* New York: Columbia University Press.

Kearney, Michael. 1986. "Integration of the Mixteca and the western U.S.–Mexico region via migratory wage labor." In *Regional impacts of U.S.–Mexican relations,* ed. Ina Rosenthal-Urey. La Jolla, CA: Center for U.S.–Mexican Studies, University of California, San Diego.

——. 1988. "Mixtec political consciousness: From passive to active resistance." In *Rural revolt in Mexico and U.S. intervention,* ed. Daniel Nugent. La Jolla, CA: Center for U.S.–Mexican Studies, University of California, San Diego.

——. 1991. "Borders and boundaries of state and self at the end of empire." *Journal of Historical Sociology* 4, no. 1:53–74.

——. 1994. "Desde el indigenismo a los derechos humanos: Etnicidad y política más allá de la mixteca." *Nueva Antropología* 46:49–67.

——. 1995. "The effects of transnational culture, economy, and migration on Mixtec identity in Oaxacalifornia." In *The bubbling cauldron: Race, ethnicity, and the urban crisis, ed.* Michael Smith Peter and Joe R. Feagin. Minneapolis: University of Minnesota Press.

——. 1996. *Reconceptualizing the peasantry: Anthropology in global perspective.* Boulder, CO: Westview Press.

Kearney, Michael, and Carol Nangengast. 1989. "Anthropological perspectives on transnational communities in rural California," Working Group on Farm Labor and Rural Poverty, Working Paper #3. Davis, CA: California Institute for Rural Studies.

Kearney, Michael, and James Stuart. 1981. "Causes and effects of agricultural labor migration from the Mixteca of Oaxaca to California." Research Report Series, no. 28. La Jolla, CA: Center for U.S.–Mexican Studies, University of California, San Diego.

Krissman, Fred. 1994a. "Comparing the impacts upon Mexican binational migrants of incorporation into network-based institutions in California." Paper presented at the Latin American Studies Association's 18th International Congress, Atlanta, March 11.

———. 1994b. "The transnationalization of the North American FVH agricultural sector: Mechanization or 'mexicanization' of production?" Paper presented at the Latin American Studies Associations 18th International Congress, Atlanta, March 12.

———. 1995. "Farm labor contractors: The process of new immigrant labor from Mexico and Californian agribusiness." *Agriculture and Human Values* 12, no. 4:18–46.

———. 1996. "Caught between borders: The living and working conditions for farm workers in San Diego County." Paper presented at the conference "Immigration and the Changing Face of Rural California," Riverside, CA, April 17.

Le Bot, Yvon. 1997. *Subcomandante Marcos: El sueño zapatista.* Mexico City: Plaza and Janés.

Lejeune, Catherine. 1990. "El concepto de la frontera dentro de una perspectiva comparativa: Unos cuantos comentarios sobre el caso de Estados Unidos, Mexico y Europa." In *Culturas hispanas de los Estados Unidos de América,* ed. María Jesús Buxó Rey and Tomás Calvo Buezas. Madrid: Ediciones de Cultura Hispánica.

Lestage, Francoise. 1998. "Los indígenas mixtecos en la frontera norte (1977–1996)." *Notas* 4:18–27.

Linares, Jesé. 1997. "Voces precolombinas en la corte." *La Opinión* (Los Angeles), March 14, p. 8.

Lipiansky, Edmond Marc. 1992. *Identité et communication.* Paris: Presses Universitaries de France.

Lister, Ruth. 1993. "Tracing the contours of women's citizenship." *Policy and Politics* 21, no. 1:3–16.

Lomnitz, Larissa de. 1976. "An ecological model for migration studies." *Rice University Studies* 62, no. 3:131–146.

Lomnitz-Adler, Claudio. 1995. *Las salidas del laberinto.* Mexico City: Joaquín Mortiz.

Lowell, B. Lindsay, and Rodolfo O. de la Garza. 2000. "The developmental role of remittances in U.S. Latino communities and in Latin American countries: A final project report." Washington, DC: Inter-American Dialogue. Computer printout.

Malkin, Victoria. 1997. "Reproduction of gender relations in the Mexican community of New Rochelle, N.Y." Paper presented at the 19th Coloquio de Antropología e Historia Regionales, Zamora, Mich., October 22–24.

Mallon, Florencia E. 1995. *Peasant and nation: The making of postcolonial Mexico and Peru.* Berkeley and Los Angeles: University of California Press.

Manrique, Leonardo. 1994. *La población indígena mexicana.* Mexico City: INEGI, INAH, IIS-UNAM.

Marcus, George. 1995. "Ethnography in/of the world system: The emergence of multi-sited ethnography." *Annual Review Anthropological* 24:95–117, 106–111.

Martin, Philip, and Edward Taylor. 1995. "Immigration and the changing face of rural California." Summary report of the conference Immigration and the Changing Face of Rural California," Asilomar, June 12–14. http://www.farmfoundation.org/martin/asilomar.pdf.

——. 2000. "For California farmworkers, future holds little prospect for change." *California Agriculture*, January–February, 19–25.

Martínez, Jorge, and Gustavo M. de Luna Méndez. 1960. *Efectos sociales de la Reforma Agraria en el ejido de Guelavía, Estado de Oaxaca.* Mexico City: UNAM, IIS.

Martínez Nateras, Myrna, ed. 2001. "Immigrant women weaving cultures" (2001 calendar). Central Valley, CA: Pan Valley Institute of the American Friends Service Committee.

Massey, Douglas. 1990. "Social structure, household strategies, and the cumulative causation of migration." *Population Index* 56:3–26.

Massey, Douglas, et al. 1987. *Return to Aztlan: The social process of international migration from western Mexico.* Berkeley and Los Angeles: University of California Press.

Massolo, Alejandra. 1994. "Política y mujeres: Una peculiar relación." In *Los medios y los modos: Participación política y acción colectiva de las mujeres,* ed. Alejandra Massolo. Mexico City: El Colegio de México.

Melucci, Alberto. 1991. "La acción colectiva como construcción social." *Estudios Sociológicos* 9, no. 26:357–364.

——. 1992. "Frontier land: Collective action between actors and systems." In *Studying collective action,* ed. Mario Diani and Ron Eyerman. London: Sage.

——. 1999. *Acción colectiva, vida cotidiana y democracia.* Mexico City: COLMEX.

Meyer, Lorenzo. 1994. "El último decenio: Años de crisis, años de oportunidad." In *Historia Mínima de Mexico,* ed. Daniel Cosío Villegas et al. Mexico City: COLMEX.

Mines, Richard. 1981. *Developing a community tradition of migration: A field study in rural Zacatecas, Mexico, and in California settlement areas.* San Diego: California Program in United States–Mexican Studies.

Monaghan, John. 1995. *The convenants with earth and rain: Exchange, sacrifice, and revelation in Mixtec society.* Norman: University of Oklahoma Press.

Morrison, Andrew, and Carol Zabin. 1994. "Two-step Mexican migration to the United States: The role of Mexican export agriculture." Research report. Miami: North-South Center of the University of Miami.

Mummert, Gail, ed. 1999. *Fronteras fragmentadas.* Mexico City: COLMICH.

Nolasco, Margarita. 1979. *Aspectos sociales de la migración en Mexico.* Vol. II. Mexico City: SEP-INAH.

Nyberg-Sorensen, Ninna. 1995. "Roots, routes and transnational attractions: Dominican migration, gender, and cultural change." In *Ethnicity, gender, and the subversion of nationalism,* ed. Fiona Wilson and Bodil Folke Frederiksen. London: Frank Cass.

Orellana, Carlos. 1973. "Mixtec migrants in Mexico City: A case study of urbanization." *Human Organization* 32, no. 3 (Fall): 273–283.

Palerm, Juan Vicente. 2000a. "Farmworkers putting down roots in Central Valley communities." *California Agriculture*, January–February, 33–34.

——. 2000b. "Los nuevos californianos rurales." *Memoria* 141 (November): 1–5. http://www.memoria.com.mx/141/Palerm/ (accessed April 4, 2004).

Pardo, Mary S. 1998. *Mexican American women activists: Identity and resistance in two Los Angeles communities.* Philadelphia: Temple University Press.

Pastor, Rodolfo. 1987. *Campesinos y reformas: La mixteca, 1700–1856.* Mexico City: COLMEX.

Pérez, Maya Lorena. 1990. "Ser mazahua en Ciudad Juárez." *México Indígena* no. 4 (January): 15–22.

Pettman, Jan. 1996. "Second class citizens? Nationalism, identity, and difference in Australia." In *Gender, politics, and citizenship in the 1990s,* ed. Barbara Sullivan and Gillian Whitehouse, 2–24. Sydney: University of New South Wales Press.

Piñón Jiménez, Gonzalo. 1988. "Crisis agraria y movimiento campesino (1956–1986)." In *Historia de la cuestión agraria mexicana: Estado de Oaxaca,* ed. Leticia Reina. Vol. 2, 1925–1986. Mexico City: Juan Pablos, Gobierno del Estado de Oaxaca, UABJO, CEHAM.

PIRCS-UABCS-SEDESOL. 1998. *Diagnóstico sobre los jornaleros agrícolas en Baja California Sur.* La Paz: Programa de Investigación Rural en Ciencias Sociales, Instituto Nacional Indigenista, Universidad Autónoma de Baja California Sur.

Pizzorno, Alessandro. 1989. "Algunas otras clases de otredad: Una crítica de las teorías de la 'elección racional.'" In Foxley et al., *Democracia, desarrollo y el arte de traspasar fronteras.*

Poirer, Jean, et al. 1983. *Les récits de vie: Théorie et pratique.* Paris: Press Universitaires de France.

Portes, Alejandro. 1998. "Globalization from below: The rise of transnational communities." Transnational Communities Program working paper. http://www.transcomm .ox.ac.uk/working%20papers/portes.pdf.

Pozas, Ricardo. 1971. *Los indios y las clases sociales en Mexico.* Mexico City: Siglo XXI.

Price-Chalita, Patricia. 1994. "Spatial metaphor and the politics of empowerment: Mapping a place for feminism and postmodernism in Geography?" *Antipode* 26, no. 3:236–254.

Pries, Ludger. 1998. "Las migraciones laborales internacionales y el surgimiento de espacios sociales transnacionales." *Sociología del Trabajo* 33 (Spring): 103–129.

PRONASOL (Programa Nacional de Solidaridad). 1991. Encuesta PRONSJAG. *Diagnóstico de las condiciones de vida y trabajo de los jornaleros agrícolas del Valle de San Quintín, BC.* San Quintin, BC: PRONSJAG.

PRONJAG (Programa Nacional de Jornaleros Agrícolas). 1999. "Panorámica general de la problemática de los jornaleros agrícolas en el Valle de San Quintín, Baja California. Reporte de trabajo." Ensenada, BC. April.

Radcliffe, Sarah, Nina Laurie, and Robert Andolina. 2002. *Indigenous people and political transnationalism: Globalization from below meets globalization from above?* Transnational Communities working paper. http://www.transcomm.ox.ac.uk/working%20 papers/WPTC-02-05%20Radcliffe.pdf.

Ravicz, Robert. 1965. *Organización social de los mixtecos.* Mexico City: Instituto Nacional Indigenista.

Reina, Leticia. 1988. "De las Reformas Borbonicas a las Leyes de Reforma." In *Historia de la Cuestión Agraria Mexicana: Estado de Oaxaca, ed. Leticia Reina.* Vol. 1, *Prehipánico–1924.* Mexico City: Juan Pablos, Gobierno del Estado de Oaxaca, UABJO, CEHAM.

Rex, John. 1991. "Ethnic identity and ethnic mobilisation in Britain." Research Monograph No. 5. Center for Research in Ethnic Relations, University of Warwick, Coventry.

Rex, John, and David Mason, eds. 1986. *Theories of race and ethnic relations.* Cambridge: Cambridge University Press.

Ritzer, George, and Pamela Gindoff. 1994. "Agency-structure, micro-macro, individualism-holism-relationism: A metatheoretical explanation of theoretical convergence between the United States and Europe." In Sztompka, *Agency and structure.*

Rivera-Salgado, Gaspar. 1999. "Migration and political activism: Mexican transnational indigenous communities in a comparative perspective." PhD diss., University of California, Santa Cruz.

Rivera-Salgado, Gaspar, and Luis Escala Rabadán. 2004. "Collective identity and organizational strategies of indigenous and mestizo Mexican migrants." In Fox and Rivera-Salgado, *Indigenous Mexican migrants in the United States.*

Roberts, Bryan. 1974. "The interrelationships of city and provinces in Peru and Guatemala." *Latin American Urban Research* 4:475–491.

Romero-Frizzi, María de los Angeles. 1988. "Época: Colonias (1519–1785)." In *Historia de la Cuestión Agraria Mexicana: Estado de Oaxaca,* ed. Leticia Reina. Vol. 1, *Prehipánico-1924.* Mexico City: Juan Pablos, Gobierno del Estado de Oaxaca, UABJO, CEHAM.

———. 1990. *Economía y vida de los españoles en la Mixteca Alta: 1519–1720.* Mexico City: INAH, Gobierno del Estado de Oaxaca.

———. 1996. *Historia de los pueblos indígenas de Mexico: El sol y la cruz: Los pueblos indios de Oaxaca colonial.* Mexico City: CIESAS–INI.

Roosens, Eugeen. 1994. "The primordial nature of origins in migrant ethnicity." In Vermeulen and Govers, *The anthropology of ethnicity.*

Rouse, Roger. 1989. "Mexican migration to the United States: Family relations in the development of a transnational migrant circuit." PhD diss., Stanford University.

———. 1992. "Making sense of settlement: Class transformation, cultural struggle, and transnationalism among Mexican migrants in the United States." In Glick Schiller, Basch, and Blanc-Szanton, *Toward a transnational perspective on migration.*

Ruiz García, Aída. 2002. *Migración oaxaqueña: Una aproximación a la realidad.* Oaxaca City: CEAMO, Gobierno del Estado de Oaxaca.

Ruiz Marrujo, Olivia. 1995. "A Tijuana: Las visitas transfronterizas como estrategias femeninas de reproducción social." In Gonzalez, *Mujeres, migración y maquila en la frontera norte.*

Runsten, David, and Michael Kearney. 1994. "A survey of Oaxacan village networks in California agriculture." Davis, CA: California Institute for Rural Studies.

Sack, Robert. 1988. "El lugar y su relación con los recientes debates interdisciplinarios." *Documents d'Analisi Geografica* 12:224–241.

SAGARPA Programa Agrícola. 1992–93, 1995–96, 2003–4. Elaborated by COLEF-CONACYT, "Migración, trabajo agrícola y etnicidad," 2003–6 project.

Sánchez, Martha Judith. 1995. "Comunidades sin límites territoriales: Estudio sobre la reproducción de la identidad étnica de migrantes zapotecas asentados en el área metropolitana de la ciudad de Mexico." PhD diss., COLMEX.

Sánchez Muñohierro, Lourdes. 1994. *Jornaleros indígenas en el noroeste de México.* Mexico City: PRONJAG, SEDESOL.

Sanders, Thomas. 1975. "Migration from the Mixteca Alta." *North America Series* 3, no. 5 (August).

Savater, Fernando. 1998. *Etica, política, ciudadanía.* Mexico City: Editorial Grijalbo, Raya en el Agua and Causa Ciudadana.

Schutz, Alfred. 1967. *Fenomenología del mundo social.* Buenos Aires: Paidós.

Sewell, William. 1992. "A theory of structure: Duality, agency, and transformation." *American Journal of Sociology* 90, no. 1 (July): 1–29.

Shils, Edward. 1957. "Primordial, personal, sacred, and civil ties." *British Journal of Sociology* 8:130–145.

———. 1972. *The intellectuals and the powers and other essays.* Chicago: University of Chicago Press.

Smith, Michael P., and Luis Guarnizo, eds. 1998. *Transnationalism from below.* New Brunswick, NJ: Transaction.

Smith, Robert. 1995. "Los ausentes siempre presentes: The imagining, making, and politics of a transnational migrant community between Ticuani, Puebla, Mexico, and New York City." PhD diss., Columbia University.

Sollors, Werner, ed. 1989. Introduction. *The invention of ethnicity,* by Sollors. Cambridge: Oxford University Press.

Speck, Ross, and Carolyn Attneave. 1990. *Redes familiares.* Buenos Aires: Amorrortu.

SRE (Secretaría de Relaciones Exteriores). 1998. *Gaceta* 6, no. 41 (January): 1–16.

Stavenhagen, Rodolfo. 1968. *Clases, colonialismo y aculturación: Ensayo sobre un sistema de relaciones interétnicas en Mesoamérica.* Seminario de Integración Social Guatemalteca, Working Paper No. 19. Guatemala: Ministerio de Educación.

———. 1989. *Problemas étnicos y campesinos.* Mexico: INI, CONACULTA.

———. 1996. *Ethnic conflicts and the nation-state.* London: Macmillan Press, United Nation Research Institute for Social Development.

Stephen, Lynn. 1991. *Zapotec women.* Austin: University of Texas Press.

———. 1999. "Divided and united transnational indigenous families: Oaxacans on the border and in the northwest of the United States." In Ward, *Reducing vulnerability.*

———. 2002. "Globalización, el estado y la creación de trabajadores agrícolas mixtecos en Oregon." *Relaciones* 23, no. 90 (Spring): 80–114.

STPS (Secretaria del Trabajo y Previsión Social) et al. 2001. *Encuesta sobre migración en la frontera norte de Mexico 1998–1999.* Mexico City: STPS.

Sztompka, Piotr, ed. 1994. *Agency and structure: Reorienting social theory.* London: Gordon and Breach.

Tarrés, María Luisa. 1989. "Más allá de lo público y lo privado: Reflexiones sobre la participación social y política de las mujeres de clase media en Ciudad Satélite." In *Trabajo, poder y sexualidad,* ed. Orlandina de Oliveira. Mexico City: COLMEX, Programa Interdisciplinario de Estudios de la Mujer.

Thompson, E. P. 1994. *Historia social y antropología.* Mexico City: Instituto Mora.

Touraine, Alain. 1985. "An introduction to the study of social movements." *Social Research* 52, no. 4 (Winter): 749–787.

———. 1995. *Producción de la sociedad.* Mexico: UNAM–IFAL.

Tuñón, Pablos Esperanza. 1992. "Women's struggles for empowerment in México: Accomplishments, problems, and challenges." In *Women transforming politics: Worldwide strategies for empowerment,* ed. Jill Bystydzienski. Bloomington: Indiana University Press.

Vaiou, Dina. 1992. "Gender divisions in urban space: Beyond the rigidity of dualist classifications." *Antipode* 24, no. 4:247–262.

Valdés, Luz María. 2000. *Población: Reto del tercer milenio: Curso interactivo introductorio a la demografía.* Mexico City: UNAM and Porrúa.

Velasco Ortiz, Laura. 1986. "Los motivos de la mujer migrante de la Mixteca de Oaxaca." BA thesis, UNAM.

——. 1990. "Mixtecos: Una cultura migrante." In *Mexico indígena* 4:46–50.

——. 1991. "Identidad étnica y migración: El caso de los mixtecos en la frontera noroeste de Mexico." Master's thesis, UNAM.

——. 1992. "Notas para estudiar los cambios del comportamiento migratorio de los mixtecos." In Corbett, *Migración y etnicidad en Oaxaca.*

——. 1995a. "Migración femenina y sobrevivencia familiar: Un estudio de caso de los mixtecos en Tijuana." In Gonzalez, *Mujer, migración y maquila en la frontera norte de Mexico.*

——. 1995b. "Entre el jornal y el terruño: Indígenas migrantes en la frontera noroeste de Mexico." *Nueva Antropología* 14, no. 47 (March): 113–130.

——. 1996. "La conquista de la frontera norte: Vendedoras ambulantes indígenas." In *Estudiar a la familia, comprender a la sociedad,* by Laura Velasco, Elena Lazos Chavero, and Lourdes Godínez Guevara. Mexico City: PUEG, DIF, UNICEF, UAM Azcapotzalco.

——. 1999. "Comunidades transnacionales y conciencia étnica: Indígenas migrantes en la frontera México-Estados Unidos." PhD diss., COLMEX.

——. 2000. "Migración, género y etnicidad: Mujeres indígenas en la frontera de California y Baja California." *Revista Mexicana de Sociología* 12, no. 1 (January–March): 145–171.

——. 2002. *El regreso de la comunidad: Migración indígena y agentes étnicos; Los mixtecos en la frontera México–Estados Unidos.* México. El Colegio de México; El Colegio de la Frontera Norte.

Velásquez, María Cristina. 2004. "Migrant communities, gender, and political power in Oaxaca." In Fox and Rivera-Salgado, *Indigenous Mexican migrants in the United States.*

Verdery, Catherine. 1994. "Ethnicity, nationalism, and state-making: Ethnic groups and boundaries: Past and future." In Vermeulen and Govers, *The anthropology of ethnicity.*

Vermeulen, Hans, and Cora Govers. 1994a. Introduction to Vermeulen and Govers, *The anthropology of ethnicity.*

——, eds. 1994b. *The anthropology of ethnicity: Beyond "Ethnic Groups and Boundaries."* Amsterdam: Het Spinhuis.

——. 1997. "From political mobilization to the politics of consciousness." In Govers and Vermeulen, *The politics of ethnic consciousness.*

Vernez, George, and David Ronfeldt. 1991. "The current situation in Mexican immigration." *Science* 251 (March): 1189–1193.

Vertovec, Steven. 1999. "Conceiving and researching transnationalisms." *Ethnic and Racial Studies* 22, no. 2:447–462.

Ward, Peter M., ed. 1999. *Reducing vulnerability among families in the Mexico and U.S. border region.* Final Report on a Series of Research and Policy Workshops, University of Texas System, USA, and Desarrollo Integral de la Familia (DIF) Nacional, Mexico.

Warman, Arturo, and Arturo Argueta, eds. 1993. *Movimientos indígenas contemporáneos en Mexico.* Mexico City: UNAM and Porrúa.

Warman, Arturo, et al. 1970. *De eso que llaman antropología mexicana.* Mexico City: Editorial Nuestro Tiempo.

Weber, Devra. 1994. *Dark sweat, white gold: California farm workers, cotton, and the New Deal.* Berkeley and Los Angeles: University of California Press.

Weiss, Johannes. 1992. "Representative culture and cultural representation." In *Theory of culture*, ed. Richard Münch and Neil J. Smelser, 121–144. Berkeley and Los Angeles: University of California Press.

Whiteford, Linda. 1979. "The borderland as an extended community." In *Migration across frontiers: Mexico and the United States*, ed. Fernando Cámara and Robert V. Kemper. Albany: State University of New York.

Wilson, Tamar Diana. 1998. "Weak ties, strong ties: Network principles in Mexican migration." *Human Organization* 57, no. 4:394–403.

Williams, Brackette. 1989. "A class act: Anthropology and the race to nation across ethnic terrain." *Annual Review of Anthropology* 18:401–444.

Wolf, Eric. 1957. "The closed corporate peasant community in Mesoamerica and Java." *Southwestern Journal of Anthropology* 13 (Spring): 1–18.

Woo, Ofelia. 1995. "Las mujeres mexicanas indocumentadas en la migración internacional y la movilidad transfronteriza." In González et al., *Mujeres, migración y maquila en la frontera norte.*

Zabin, Carol. 1992. "Mixtec migrant farmworkers in California agriculture: A dialogue among Mixtec leaders, researchers, and farm labor advocates." Davis, CA: California Institute for Rural Studies and Center for U.S.–Mexican Studies.

——. 1993. "Labor market interdependence between Mexico and the United States: Wage convergence or new gender and ethnic hierarchies in California and Baja California Agriculture." Computer printout.

Zabin, Carol, and Luis Escala. 2002. "From civic association to political participation: Mexican hometown associations and Mexican immigrant political empowerment in Los Angeles." *Frontera Norte* 14, no. 27 (January–June): 7–42.

Zeitlin, Judith Francis. 1994. "Precolumbian barrio organization in Tehuantepec, México." In *Caciques and their people: A volume in honor of Ronald Spores*, ed. Joyce Marcus and Judith Francis Zeitlin. Anthropological Papers No. 89, Museum of Anthropology, University of Michigan, Ann Arbor.

Zenteno, René. 1993. "El uso del concepto de informalidad en el estudio de las condiciones del empleo urbano: Un ejercicio para la frontera norte y principales áreas metropolitanas de México." *Frontera Norte* 5, no. 9:67–96.

Žižek, Slavoj. 1998. "Multiculturalismo, o la lógica cultural del capitalismo multinacional." In *Estudios culturales: Reflexiones sobre el multiculturalismo*, ed. Fredric Jameson and Slavoj Žižek. Buenos Aires: Paidós.

Index

About the Author

Laura Velasco Ortiz received a Ph.D. in social sciences (sociology) from El Colegio de Mexico (COLMEX) in 1999. Since 1993 she has been professor-researcher in the Cultural Studies Department at El Colegio de la Frontera Norte (COLEF), in Tijuana, Mexico. Since 1999, she has also been a researcher in the Mexican National Researcher's System of CONACYT. She is the recipient of the 1995 Prize for Research on Family and Emergent Social Problems in Mexico. She has been visiting professor in the Gender Program at COLMEX (1993) and in the Department of Sociology of the University of Warwick, England (2001).

She is co-author (with Elena Chavero and Lourdes Godínez Guevara) of *Estudiar a la familia, comprender a la sociedad* (1997); co-editor (with Soledad González, Olivia Ruiz, and Ofelia Woo) of *Mujeres, migración y maquila en la frontera norte* (1996); and author of *El regreso de la communidad: Migración indígena y agentes étnicos; Los mixtecos en la frontera México–Estados Unidos* and some twenty articles in Spanish journals and books.

Her current research interests are ethnicity and migration, gender and ethnicity, ethnic agents, migration and national boundaries, and transnational grassroots organizations and nation-states.